Contemporary issues in health, medicine, and
social policy · *General Editor: John B. McKinlay*

Epidemiology and health policy

Edited by Sol Levine and Abraham M. Lilienfeld

Epidemiology and health policy

Tavistock Publications · New York · London

First published in 1987 by Tavistock
Publications in association with
Methuen, Inc., 29 West 35th Street,
New York, NY 10001

Published in the UK by
Tavistock Publications Ltd
11 New Fetter Lane, London EC4P 4EE

© 1987 Tavistock Publications Ltd

Printed in the United States of
America

*British Library Cataloguing in
Publication Data*
Levine, Sol
Epidemiology and health policy. –
(Contemporary issues in health,
medicine and social policy) – (Social
science paperbacks; no. 343)
1. Public health – Great Britain
2. Medical policy – Great Britain
3. Epidemiology – Great Britain
I. Title   II. Lilienfeld, Abraham M.
III. Series
363'.0941   RA485

ISBN 0–422–78000–6
ISBN 0–422–78010–3 Pbk

*Library of Congress Cataloging in
Publication Data*
Epidemiology and health policy.

(Contemporary issues in health,
medicine, and social policy)
Includes bibliographies and index.
1. Medical policy.
2. Epidemiology – Government
policy.
3. Medical policy – United States.
4. Epidemiology – Government
policy – United States.
I. Levine, Sol, 1922–   .
II. Lilienfeld, Abraham M.
III. Series.   [DNLM:
1. Epidemiology.   2. Health
Policy.   WA 105 E643]
RA394.E64   1986   362.1
86–14446

ISBN 0–422–78000–6
ISBN 0–422–78010–3 (pbk.)

Contents

List of contributors

Editors

Sol Levine PhD is University Professor and Professor of Sociology and Public Health at Boston University. He has served as Chairperson of the Department of Sociology at Boston University and of the Department of Behavioral Sciences at the Johns Hopkins School of Hygiene and Public Health, and as Director of the Social Science Program at the Harvard School of Public Health. Dr Levine is a member of the Institute of Medicine of the National Academy of Sciences and a past chairman of the Medical Sociology Section of the American Sociological Association. He was a member of the Health Services Research Study Section and Chairman of the Study Section of the National Institute of Alcoholism and Alcohol Abuse. Dr Levine has written several books and numerous articles on the social aspects of health. He has done inaugural work on social stress and illness, and on the importance of quality of life in assessing health interventions.

Abraham M. Lilienfeld MD, MPH, was University Distinguished Service Professor of Epidemiology and Acting Chairman of the Department of Behavioral Sciences at the Johns Hopkins University School of Hygiene and Public Health. Earlier, he had served as Chairman of the Department of Epidemiology and of the Department of Chronic Diseases. He held an honorary doctorate from the University of Maryland and was a fellow of the American Public Health Association, which gave him its Bronfman and John Snow awards. Dr Lilienfeld was a former president of the American Epidemiological Society and was elected to the Institute of Medicine of the National Academy of Sciences. In addition, he was a recipient of the Research Career Award of the National Institutes of Health. Through his efforts, chronic disease epidemiology became an important branch of medicine and public health. He also contributed important examinations of cancer, cerebrovascular disease, digestive diseases, and birth defects.

Contributors

Susan P. Baker MPH is Professor of Health Policy and Management at The Johns Hopkins University School of Public Health, with a joint appointment in pediatrics at the Johns Hopkins School of Medicine. An epidemiologist specializing in injury control, she is senior author of *The Injury Fact Book* (Lexington Books 1984) and served as vice-chair of the National Research Council's Committee on Trauma Research. Her teaching, research, and extensive writing have emphasized the need for translating injury data into effective public policy.

Abram S. Benenson is a professor in the San Diego State University Graduate School of Public Health and head of its Division of Epidemiology and Biostatistics. He has been involved in the study of infectious diseases for many years, serving as an army officer as Director of the USA Tropical Research Laboratory in Puerto Rico, as Director of the Division of Immunology and then the Division of Communicable Disease and Immunology of the Walter Reed Army Institute of Research. As a civilian, he has been Director of the Pakistan-SEATO Cholera Research Laboratory in Dacca, East Pakistan,

and later of the Gorgas Memorial Laboratory in Panama, R. de
P. He has held previous faculty positions as Professor of
Preventive Medicine (Epidemiology) at the Jefferson Medical
College, Philadelphia, and as Professor and Chairman of the
Department of Community Medicine, University of Kentucky
Medical College.

Theodore Colton is Professor and Chief, Epidemiology and
Biostatistics Section, Boston University School of Public
Health. He received his doctorate in biostatistics from the
Johns Hopkins School of Hygiene and Public Health and has
held faculty positions at Harvard and Dartmouth Medical
Schools. He is author of the textbook *Statistics in Medicine.*
He has served in numerous capacities as consultant and peer
reviewer for the federal government and, in particular, had a
term of office on the Biometry and Epidemiology Contract
Review Committee of the National Cancer Institute, including
a year as Chair. He is co-editor of the Journal *Statistics in
Medicine,* a member of the editorial board of the *New England
Journal of Medicine* and a statistical consultant to the *Journal
of American Medical Association.* His work and interests in
cancer epidemiology include: population-based tumor registries,
diethystilbestrol (DES) exposure, occupational exposure to
low-level radiation and dioxin (agent organge) exposure.

Erich M. Daub BS, BA, is Research Assistant, Program in Injury
Control, Department of Health Policy and Management, at
the Johns Hopkins University School of Hygiene and Public
Health where he is presently Project Manager for the Maryland
Childhood Injury Study and the Alcohol Related Injury
Surveillance Program. With background training in emergency
medical services, injury epidemiology, and health policy, as
well as professional clinical experience in prehospital and
hospital emergency medical care, he has provided consultation
to national, state, and local health agencies. He is current
research editor for the *Journal of Emergency Medical Services.*

Lenora R. Davis MS is a research associate in the Maternal and
Child Health Department at the Johns Hopkins University
School of Hygiene and Public Health. She has worked for
several years in the field of lactose malabsorption in children.

She has co-authored several original articles in her field. Her current work involves public health nutrition and assisting in the publishing of the *Clinical Nutrition Supplement.*

Jack M. Guralnik MD, PhD, is a Research Fellow in Epidemiology at the National Institute on Aging in the National Institutes of Health. Prior to his training in epidemiology he worked in family practice and public health. His research interests include the epidemiology of chronic disease and the effects of chronic disease on an aging population. His recent work has focused on factors associated with functional level and disability in the elderly.

Ian T. T. Higgins MD, FRCP, is Acting Chief of Epidemiology at the American Health Foundation in New York City and Emeritus Professor of Epidemiology and of Environmental and Industrial Medicine at the University of Michigan School of Public Health. Main interests: chronic respiratory diseases, cancer (focusing in particular on environmental factors), coronary heart disease. Past member of EPA's Clean Air Scientific Advisory Committee, NAS-NRC Medical and Biological Effects of Environmental Pollutants Committee, and Committee on Toxicology.

Ralph W. Hingson is Professor of Socio-medical Sciences and Chief of the Social and Behavioral Sciences Section at the Boston University School of Public Health. He has been Principal Investigator on several major studies in the field of alcoholism and has a strong interest in alcohol treatment programs and the relationship between alcohol consumption and highway accidents. He has served on government study sections, including chairing the NIAAA study section. Dr Hingson was selected by the Junior Chamber of Commerce as one of the most outstanding young men in America.

Gerald L. Klerman MD is Professor of Psychiatry and Associate Chairman for Research in the Department of Psychiatry at Cornell University Medical School and New York Hospital–Payne Whitney Clinic, New York, NY. His main academic interests have been in teaching and research on affective disorders and anxiety disorders and the evaluation of mental health programs. During the Carter administration 1977–80, he served as Administator of the Alcohol, Drug Abuse and Mental Health Administration (ADAMHA) in the Public Health Service, Department of Health and Human Services. His main efforts have been directed towards improving the scientific basis of clinical psychiatry and the implications for social policy.

C. Arden Miller, a pediatrician, is Professor and Chairman, Maternal and Child Health, University of North Carolina School of Public Health. During recent years Dr Miller has focused interest on public policy, advocating improved health services for children, and reporting on personal health services as rendered by community health agencies. He directs the Child Health Outcomes Project which monitors trends in child health, relating them to changes in social policy and financing. During 1974–75 Dr Miller served as President of the American Public Health Association. He has also served as a trustee of the Appalachian regional hospitals, on the board of directors for Planned Parenthood Federation of America, and as Chairman of the Board for the Alan Guttmacher Institute. He was a Markle Scholar in Medical Sciences and was elected in 1980 to membership in the Institute of Medicine, National Academy of Sciences. In 1984 he received the Martha Mae Eliot Award of the American Public Health Association.

David M. Paige MD, MPH, is Professor of Maternal and Child Health at the Johns Hopkins University School of Hygiene and Public Health, and holds a joint appointment in pediatrics at the Johns Hopkins University School of Medicine. He has specialized in maternal, infant, and child nutrition. His research interests have included the nutritional consequences of milk intolerance, diarrheal disease, and the supplementation of pregnant women and school-age children. His programmatic activities have focused on the establishment and oversight of the US Department of Agriculture Supplemental Feeding Program for Women, Infants, and Children (WIC) as well as other domestic and international feeding programs. He has served as a consultant with the US Department of Agriculture's advisory panel to the national WIC evaluation. He is consultant to numerous federal, state, and local agencies responsible for nutrition programs. He is editor of the nutrition textbook *Manual of Clinical Nutrition,* and editor-in-chief of the journal *Clinical Nutrition.*

Marianne N. Prout MD, MPH, is a medical oncologist and former Chief of Medical Oncology at Boston City Hospital who has redirected her career into cancer prevention, obtaining a master's degree in Public Health and receiving a Preventive Oncology Academic Award from the National Cancer Institute. Her teaching focuses on multidisciplinary approaches to cancer prevention. Her research interests include practical interventions to prevent so-called avoidable cancer deaths.

Robert A. Smith PhD is Assistant Professor of Public Health, Social and Behavioral Sciences Section, at Boston University School of Public Health. His research interests are in the area of the epidemiology of injuries and cancer, and the interplay between politics and science in the shaping of public health policy.

S. Leonard Syme is a professor of epidemiology at the University of California, Berkeley. His research has focused on the influence of social and cultural factors in the etiology of disease with special emphasis on coronary heart disease. In recent years, he has also become involved in several community intervention programs to prevent disease and his current work is now increasingly directed towards the development of environmental approaches to disease prevention and health promotion. He recently was co-editor of *Social Support and Health.*

Stephen P. Teret JD, MPH, is Associate Professor of Health Policy and Management at the Johns Hopkins University School of Hygiene and Public Health. He has extensive experience as a trial lawyer and currently teaches in the areas of injury prevention and injury epidemiology. His recent work has focused on the role of litigation in injury prevention, with particular emphasis on air bags, guns, and cigarettes as objects of product liability litigation. He also works in the area of childhood injury prevention and holds a joint faculty appointment in pediatrics at the Johns Hopkins University School of Medicine.

Diana Chapman Walsh PhD is Associate Director of Boston University's Health Policy Institute and Associate Professor of Social and Behavioral Sciences and Health Services at Boston University School of Public Health. She is the principal investigator and project director of a randomized controlled trial of alternative treatments for problem drinkers identified at their place of work. Initiated by the Commonwealth Fund, this eight-year project is now funded also by the National Institute of Alcohol Abuse and Alcoholism. Additionally, she is directing a study of post-hospital convalescence and rate of return to work, and another examining health risks in a large industrial population. Dr Walsh is the author of over fifty journal articles and book chapters, and is the co-editor of the eleven-volume series on *Industry and Health Care*. A four-year study she conducted of physicians in corporations will be published this summer by Yale University Press.

Acknowledgments

We wish to express our thanks to Ms Edna Newmark whose intelligence, diligence, understanding and unusual secretarial skills were applied most fruitfully and helped to make this volume a reality. We also wish to thank Dr Diana Chapman Walsh, a contributor to this volume, for her helpful editorial advice and suggestions.

Preface

A few words should be said about the co-editor, Abraham M. Lilienfeld, who died while this volume was in preparation. He fervently believed that epidemiology should be more prominent in the formulation of health policy. He also argued that implementation is a crucial component of policy and he regretted that well intentioned health policies are often rendered ineffective in the implementation phase. He felt that this volume could fill an important gap in our understanding of the relationship between epidemiology and health policy.

He participated actively, indeed, he characteristically played the leadership role, in delineating the chapters for the volume and in selecting the appropriate authors to prepare the individual chapters. The chapter on cancer was to be written by him but his passing made it necessary for me to select other authors of whom I knew Dr Lilienfeld would have approved. In producing the introductory chapter, I made use of extensive notes I had developed in discussions with him and am confident that he would have concurred with the substance of the chapter.

Anyone who has worked in public health, in general, or epidemiology in particular is aware of Lilienfeld's pioneering and monumental contributions. Those who worked with him were privileged to observe a man of brilliance with relentless dedication to the field. Those who knew him personally were inspired by the depth of his humanity and generosity of spirit.

Sol Levine

Introduction

Sol Levine and
Abraham M. Lilienfeld

This volume is inspired by the conviction that the discipline of epidemiology should be a major pillar in the formulation and implementation of health policy. We hope this volume will serve to deepen our understanding of the interplay between epidemiology and health policy in a number of specific areas, the contribution that epidemiology has made in the past, the roles it plays today, and its prospects for the future. In many respects, the questions we address reside within a larger ancient concern about the role of knowledge as a guide for human action.

To those who are committed to a rational strategy for effecting change and who are sanguine about the influence of science in human affairs, the relationship between epidemiology and health policy may appear to be simple and straightforward. In this view, one might expect that epidemiological knowledge, as all scientific knowledge, accumulates progressively in linear fashion as new findings or increments are added to our store of information. Health policy, in turn, would be expected to accommodate to and incorporate the new accretions of knowledge. Thus, health policy would become increasingly formidable in addressing the health problems of society.

We know, however, that this ideal model does not obtain in the real world. Knowledge often accumulates more willy-nilly than in the linear, progressive fashion of the rational model and, as Kuhn has taught us, old basic tenets, conceptual models, and paradigms often defy the challenge of new findings that contradict but fail to unseat the older causal formulations. Nor does health policy automatically adjust to the changing knowledge base of epidemiology. Indeed, the influence is not always one directional from epidemiological findings to the formulation of health policy. The chapters in this book document frequent instances when changes in health policy occur for reasons quite separate from the acquisition of new knowledge. Particular economic, political or ideological factors may stifle any policy reforms or, when circumstances are propitious, give birth to new specific regulations, laws or policies without any impetus from new epidemiological data. Changes in health policy, in turn, may determine the research priorities and questions that command the attention of epidemiologists. For their part, policy-makers may seek to justify their new policies by making use of established or "rediscovered" epidemiological findings. They may also support funding for studies that are likely to generate data that are relevant for the new health policies.

If we could make use of existing epidemiological knowledge, with all its limitations, the effects on society's health would be enormous. Understanding why health policy has not been sufficiently enlightened or shaped by epidemiology requires us to attend to the problems and deficiencies that may reside in epidemiology and in health policy and in the relationship between the two. In some substantive areas such as mental health, the knowledge base of epidemiology historically has been thin and scanty. In short, there often has been little firm knowledge to transmit to those who forge health policy. Many epidemiological studies are replete with problems of conceptualization, classification, and the correct interpretation of findings; other studies might succeed in producing findings that are significant statistically but which explain relatively little in magnitude of the phenomenon under study; and a good number of studies yield results that are inconsistent or in conflict with one another. To produce findings which may be offered with confidence as a basis for policy formulation may often require study designs that are expensive and of long duration.

Epidemiologists are still struggling to free themselves of the older model of a single etiological agent producing a specific disease to one that encompasses the dynamic influence of social and environmental influences on the distribution of disease in a population. Stallones, for example, has drawn attention to the limitations of mathematical models to capture the subtleties and interaction effects of social and biological factors. He acknowledges that epidemiologists, most of whom are physicians, have become habituated to think in uniform ways that may stifle creativity. Their common training and experience leave them "deeply imprinted and reluctant to accept that most biomedical research is irrelevant to the solution of community health problems" (Stallones 1980: 76). One unfortunate consequence of the medical culture's influence on epidemiology, Stallones observes, is the commitment to a system of disease classification that was generated and utilized mainly by practitioners of clinical medicine and which fails to "take account of the social and environmental causes of disease distribution." Some epidemiologists have given thought to the development of other schemes of classification which are not derived from clinical medicine or from pathology, in which diverse types of diseases may be grouped according to other properties they may have in common. Thus, as Stallones indicates, "we may think, for example, of diseases of industrial societies, diseases that accompany certain kinds of mental or emotional stress, or diseases that follow sensory overload" (Stallones 1980: 77). This type of classification may permit us to take effective preventive interventions even when we know relatively little about the course or progression of specific diseases.

Epidemiologists are mindful of the methodological constraints to their developing a more powerful discipline. Indeed, few fields are as conscientious in their attention to questioning and improving methods of data collection and analysis. The self-critical stance which pervades the discipline is even evident in the frequent efforts to define and delineate the special domain of epidemiology. But if we are to understand the failure of epidemiology to achieve its potential in influencing health policy, we must go beyond the epistemological or technological constraints of the discipline, in search of explanations with political and social foundations.

One such explanation may lie in the professional standing of the field. Ironically, despite its potential to serve as a guide to improve the health of society, epidemiology by a number of indicators has enjoyed relatively low status when compared with clinical medicine as well as with other branches of medical science. This lower status of epidemiology is partly a reflection of the status of the public health profession in general with which epidemiology is associated. The lower position of epidemiology in the prestige hierarchies of medical specialties is reflected, with some glaring exceptions, in the relatively low levels of support provided for epidemiological investigation or for the implementation of epidemiological findings. Our society in general and our medical establishment, in particular, has tended to reward the use of the most "complex" and "sophisticated" skills without regard to how much "good" they do. Despite their enormous implication for health, getting people to stop smoking or to start using seat belts or getting the lead out of paint or the noxious fumes out of a factory – all may appear as unglamorous pursuits compared to transplanting organs or carrying out elaborate surgical procedures.

Thus, while the chapters in this book reveal the untapped potential of epidemiology as a guide to policy, they also document major contributions of epidemiological efforts to the nation's health. Yet the discipline does not enjoy the support of an active constituency as do other scientific or clinical specialties. This is in part because many of the benefits that will accrue from following the recommendations of epidemiologists will take many years to be manifest. Also, epidemiological recommendations often require relinquishing some gratifying experience like smoking, drinking alcohol, or satisfying the palate, with the promise that in the distant future some health benefits may possibly be achieved. With regard to these recommendations, epidemiological prescriptions not only have to contend with the habits and gratifications of individual consumers but equally if not more importantly with the resistance and opposition by powerful commercial interests such as tobacco and alcoholic beverage manufacturers and distributors. These organizations almost inevitably launch information campaigns in an effort to contradict or to mute the findings and recommendations of epidemiologists or to retard remedial actions or regulations which may be warranted.

When epidemiological findings attest to harmful aspects of the occupational environment, they are particularly likely to encounter denials and opposition from company officials. Companies not only wish to avoid the expenditures in time and money entailed in changing the work environment or the production processes which may be required, but they also do not wish to be held responsible for ill health their employees may have suffered. Even when the data are irrefutable, individual industrial firms often are able to delay making changes or complying with government regulations that stipulate specific changes.

When epidemiology and health policy fail to mesh as closely as they should, the problem often resides with those who forge policy. Those who forge health policy generally seem more receptive to epidemiological findings which suggest the need to change individual behavior such as smoking, drinking and excessive eating than those which call for changes in the environment or in the social conditions of the population. Some critics, like Terris, have argued that by focusing on individual behavior society is, in fact, "blaming the victim" and ignoring the degree to which the pressure of daily living and the aggressive advertising campaigns have encouraged individuals to start to smoke and drink and experience ill health in the first place (Terris 1980). Even more, the critics contend, by placing the blame on the individual the society is ignoring the social construction of disease: the importance of social conditions such as those associated with poverty, stress, and hazardous occupational or residential environments.

It is necessary to assume a critical perspective and not to be confined by conventional conceptions of what constitutes health policy. Students who have been following present-day deliberations on health policy must be struck by the almost exclusive emphasis on health services and ways of reducing their costs and the relative absence of epidemiological thought in these deliberations. We have developed a kind of trained incapacity to view health policy as consisting of the programs carried out by health officials; as composed of narrowly defined health inputs, particularly medical services; and we have not been sufficiently cognizant that health policy is also embodied in other less apparent social agenda – in our fiscal, monetary and employment policies – all of which may have demonstrable consequences for the health of the population. The specter of inequality which pervades our society also manifests itself in the health arena. If we could eliminate poverty, we would make a profound contribution to the health of the society.

In drawing attention to the wider scope of health policy, we do not wish to minimize the importance of health services or the concern that resources be deployed more efficiently. Health services remain important even though they may contribute less to mortality and morbidity rates than do social factors, public health measures, and personal behavior. Indeed, there is accumulating evidence that the recent cutbacks in health services for the poor, the old, and the disabled are having deleterious health consequences. Even some who have been avid promoters of cost containment measures are having second thoughts about the extent and direction of the economies that have been instituted and the effects of these measures on the physical health and quality of life of patients. There are indications that epidemiologists and evaluators of health services will make more use of quality of life indicators as dependent variables in their studies.

The authors of the individual chapters in this book are distinguished epidemiologists and public health professionals who are committed to construct more effective health policies that are informed by epidemiology. As editors, we chose not to impose a standard format or uniform mode of organizing and presenting the substance of each chapter. Nor did we confine authors to a single definition of health policy, except in the more general sense. We believe that by providing greater freedom to the authors in approaching their specific subjects, more useful and informative analyses were produced. We have already alluded to some of the general themes which emerge throughout this volume, but each subject also has its own unique aspects and enlightening lessons on the relationship between epidemiology and health policy.

In the chapter on *child health*, C. Arden Miller criticizes the tendency of the United States to allocate inordinate resources for medical care despite epidemiological evidence that the greatest benefits would "derive from emphasis on family planning, nutrition, sanitation, environmental protection, accident prevention, and income supplementation for poor families." Miller points up the deficiencies in our response to the health needs of poor children: income transfer programs such as Aid for Dependent Children and food stamp programs have been frequent candidates for budget cuts, despite the weight of evidence that they contribute to the health of the poor. Miller also regrets that maternal and child health programs reach only a minority of poor children. Studies have demonstrated that when comprehensive health care services are provided they tend to improve the health levels of the population and are successful by a number of other criteria. Although infant mortality rates could be reduced appreciably by participation of high risk women in prenatal care programs, there has been inadequate funding of these programs.

Miller sketches changes in conceptions of health policy from those which provided resources (inputs) in unspecified ways, to those that prescribed the ways in which the resources were to be used (processes) to those that seek to achieve definite objectives (outcomes). He offers a classification of various governmental efforts under these three conceptual rubrics: inputs, process, and outcome. He also discusses some of the methodological problems in studying process and outcomes and challenges epidemiology to use its skills to develop specific outcome measures. Even more, he asks epidemiologists to work on linking specific outcomes for a particular population to antecedent interventions.

The chapter by David M. Paige and Lenora R. Davis on *nutrition* provides further testimony to the complex interplay between epidemiology and health policy and the importance of social and political factors. Granting the inapplicability of simple additive models to capture the complex ways that various forces shape policy, the authors adduce six major components of policy formation: research, contextual economic, political, and ideological factors, constituency actions, governmental, ideas and values, and the media. They demonstrate the role of each of these components by a case description of Special Supplementary Food Programs for lactating women, infants, and children (WIC). Tracing the program through several presidential administrations, they argue that while "epidemiologically based studies formed the backbone of health policy decisions," a variety of individuals, agenda and special interests were at work. There was expected support from anti-poverty advocates, social service providers, school administrators, and a growing constituency in Congress and in public health clinics. But these were also joined by strong agricultural interests seeking outlets for surplus foods as well as by various pharmaceutical firms anticipating new market outlets for their infant formulas.

Another case study is instructive. The authors direct our attention to a major issue in the relationship between epidemiology and health policy: the adequacy of the scientific basis for making recommendations. They report on changes in the formulation of dietary goals for the United States as interest developed in the relationship between nutrition and chronic diseases. Controversy had arisen as to the scientific basis for making a public policy decision that an "epidemic" of chronic degenerative diseases exists and that the modification of diet was recommended to reduce the incidence of degenerative diseases. The authors, then, describe the roles of research in health policy which they categorize as follows: knowledge-building, problem-exploring, policy-forming, and program-directing.

The observations by Paige and Davis about the problems of developing policy recommendations when there is disagreement about the knowledge base is also considered by Syme and Guralnik in their treatment of coronary heart disease (CHD) and health policy. Syme and Guralnik present a lucid assessment of the data on the distribution of CHD in the population as well as an evaluation of the major CHD risk factors. They review some of the studies which have pinpointed the major risk factors – cholesterol, hypertension, and smoking. They also canvas epidemiological studies for other suspected risk factors such as lack of social supports, type A personality, and insufficient exercise.

The authors demonstrate that epidemiological facts do not speak for themselves but are approached differently by people with different priorities and perspectives. Those who formulate policy may differ in their interpretations of evidence, in their preferences for particular types of interventions, and in their notions about whether to intervene on the individual or community level. Even seemingly simple well-based interventions may have unanticipated and undesirable consequences, as in efforts to produce foods in accord with nutrition policy and in the banning of cigarette advertising on television.

Syme and Guralnik point up the important role of physicians in the health policy picture and their tendency to emphasize those risk factors amenable to their technology over risk factors of a psycho-social nature which are beyond the skills of the physician and may require major social changes. The authors provide an insightful critique of the medical model on which most CHD preventive measures have been based. They assess the one-to-one medical model which aims to identify high risk individuals and to treat them by lowering the risk. They then contrast the medical model with the public health model, which provides health education and community organization to an entire community, and with the ecological model which relies upon structural changes in the community or in the environment instead of change in individual behavior. While the medical model has its uses, the evidence clearly suggests the need to make greater use of the public health and ecological models of intervention.

In beginning their analysis of *cancer epidemiology*, Prout, Colton, and Smith stress that cancer is many diseases, that policy construction is difficult because of gaps in knowledge about the precise mechanisms which culminate in clinical cancers, and no single best strategy has been devised to control or prevent the various cancers. Accordingly, the authors suggest three main approaches:

1 a primary prevention approach for cancers which cannot be treated effectively.
2 screening programs for cancers which can be treated effectively if detected early.
3 prompt referral to treatment and rehabilitation facilities for cancers amenable to effective treatment but not to primary prevention or screening.

Protecting employees' exposure to certain known carcinogens, such as asbestos, would decrease cancer mortality. Sharply decreasing or eliminating tobacco use would dramatically reduce mortality from lung cancer. Unfortunately, the specific contributions of suspected risk factors for many other cancers are not clearly established.

Uneven, complex and contradictory policies are manifest at different governmental levels and within different professional groups. The writers urge the development of an effective uniform policy, involving criteria for evaluating evidence of epidemiological and laboratory studies, and differentiating "acceptable" from "unacceptable" risks. Finally, a cancer policy should also provide some yardstick to monitor, control, and prohibit the entrance of new carcinogens into the environment.

A strong case is made by Higgins for the role of epidemiology in developing *occupational health policy*. While some health hazards in the work-place are conspicuously evident to lay people and are even a part of the folklore of employees, other kinds of occupational hazards are more difficult to detect and require the skills of the epidemiologist. Higgins offers an exotic example of epidemiology linking symptoms of tremor, nervousness, and vasomotor instability among some detectives in England to mercury intoxication. The source was traced to a dusting powder that contained mercury and was used in fingerprinting and inadvertently inhaled. Intoxication varied with degree of exposure. A new non-mercury powder was substituted, thereby eliminating the hazard.

The author provides some rich and precise examples of various diseases associated with such occupational hazards as vegetable dusts, asbestos dust, and coal dust and demonstrates how standard epidemiological methods have been used to describe the natural history of the diseases. Several important policy issues are raised, salient among them being the need to maintain excellent records of the health histories of employees. Indeed, taking all steps possible to improve the ability of the epidemiologist to gather data constitutes an important policy recommendation. Epidemiology can contribute to health policy by ascertaining whether appropriate changes in the occupational settings have, in fact, been instituted and whether they have resulted in the desired outcomes.

Anyone who works in the epidemiology of injuries is likely to question the criteria by which we allocate resources in the health field. In their chapter on *injuries*, Baker, Teret, and Daub inform us that although injuries are the leading causes of death from ages one to forty-four and vehicle accidents alone are the biggest killer of those from one to thirty-four, they are given relatively little attention by professionals in health agencies, by the National Institutes of Health, by schools of medicine, and even by schools of public health. Many injury problems fall under the domain of non-health agencies. Support for research on injuries is spotty and uneven and hardly commensurate with the magnitude of the problem.

The authors provide us with an excellent review of injuries caused by vehicular accidents, alcohol, tobacco (e.g. fatal house fires), firearms, and others. They discuss the magnitude of the problem and the distribution of injuries by age, sex, place of residence, etc. They also raise some basic policy propositions (e.g. educational efforts should focus more on influencing the *decision-makers*). The authors recommend against policies requiring individuals to engage in many actions repeatedly in order to avoid injuries; accordingly, they appear committed to the "ecological" approach discussed by Syme and Guralnik. As a public health principle they favor changes in automobile design and the use of air bags, cigarettes that self-extinguish quickly, and the removal of firearms from the home. The authors discuss efforts to translate epidemiological findings into public policy and the economic, legislative, and attitudinal resistance these proposals often engender.

In the opening of his chapter on *infectious diseases*, Benenson reminds us that policy may range from actions taken by the government to those that are embedded in the everyday practices of laymen; that assumptions of causality may be valid or may reflect the mythology of a particular society or historical period. He reviews the barriers encountered in applying epidemiological knowledge in dealing with such diverse infectious diseases as cholera, Reye Syndrome, swine flu and pertussis. While different circumstances obtained for each of the conditions, Benenson's review points up how such factors as economic interest, the role of the media, and fear of litigation can stymie the implementation of health policies in the public interest.

The Reye Syndrome case, for instance, demonstrates the power of private industry to influence the implementation of health policy. Despite epidemiological evidence, the testimony of scientists and the recommendation of such prestigious groups as the Institute of Medicine – all asking for warning labels on aspirin bottles in cases of childhood influenza or chicken pox – the aspirin industry was opposed to labeling as health policy.

While there have been negative experiences, Benenson points to important and even dramatic health policy strides with regard to a number of infectious diseases: smallpox, measles, diphtheria, tuberculosis, typhoid fever, and malaria. Considerable progress has been made and such organizations as the American Public Health Association have played important roles. The author asks for more responsibility by the media and "trite as it may sound, we need people to work for the common good and not be motivated by personal gain." One might add that we should seek appropriate structures and incentives to encourage people to act in the public interest.

In his chapter on psychiatric epidemiology and mental health policy, Klerman provides an insightful and comprehensive treatment of the subject and sketches in considerable detail the history of public policy concerns about mental illness. He also traces the evolution of the psychiatric discipline and the rise of psychiatric epidemiology in the latter part of the nineteenth century. The author identifies improved access to care as the dominant mental health policy in the urban western societies in recent decades, though this policy has been slowed to a considerable extent with the resurgency of the more conservative view of government. Klerman indicates that epidemiological studies have demonstrated high prevalence of mental illness and provided the justification for increased research support to expand scientific knowledge as well as to increase existing mental health manpower and mental health services.

Mental health policy has been powerless to pursue prevention programs because of limits in epidemiological knowledge and also because the massive social reforms which would more dramatically affect mental health are difficult or impossible to organize. Some social and environmental factors have been identified which might in the future be the basis for a more active prevention program: it is known, for example, that unemployment harms the physical and mental health of the poor, especially members of minority groups. Unfortunately, Klerman indicates, mental health professionals have no clear mandate or expertise to influence the enactment of broad social reforms.

Throughout this volume we have observed that health policy may develop a vigorous momentum even when the knowledge base on which it leans is thin or primitive. Once problems are defined in particular ways and suitable conceptual and causal models are constructed, information which emerges tends to be consonant with the prevailing set of assumptions and perspectives. When new information emerges which is not congruent with prevailing outlooks, it tends to be ignored, reinterpreted, suppressed, or, at times, even condemned. These observations obtain especially in the alcohol research field. Walsh and Hingson present a most clarifying and enlightening portrayal of the tenacity with which the disease model has been embraced in the alcoholism arena, the type of research it has generated and the types of interventions which it has fostered. But the authors also present encouraging information about how epidemiological findings slowly but constantly challenge the orthodox disease model of a single progressive and debilitating disease.

Whereas the traditional disease model was committed to a strategy of early detection and treatment, the new epidemiological studies were not confined to patients in treatment but focused on the larger population; not just the sick or "heavy drinkers" but the problems normal people had when they drank. In addition to studying a more heterogeneous population, the new epidemiological studies challenged some of the main foundations on which the disease model rested.

For example, notions that there is an "alcoholic personality," that alcoholism is inexorably progressive or that complete abstinence is the only effective treatment goal – all have been challenged. The perspective of alcoholism as a unitary disorder has been relinquished in favor of one that captures the varied motives and problems different types of people have with drinking. Finally, a public health approach, with its emphasis on social factors and prevention, is making some inroads on the more restrictive disease model. Although the story is not complete, epidemiology has played an important role in the reshaping of alcoholism policy.

As we have seen, in a number of crucial instances epidemiology has in fact succeeded in shaping health policy. It would also be a mistake to overlook or minimize the influence of epidemiological findings because their impacts are not immediate or instantaneous. Epidemiological data that initially fail to elicit the attention of policy-makers may still linger and percolate and may be rediscovered periodically. When circumstances are propitious they may command the attention of policy-makers and be embodied in legislation or administrative action. And the path of influence need not be a simple one from the scientific articles to the policy-maker. Often, the route is more circuitous as findings are diffused to the popular media, the lay public, health activists, and specific interest groups or constituencies, all of whom, in turn, may become vocal and persistent in confronting policy-makers and in urging them to take action. Health policy requires a closer and more deliberately designed relationship with epidemiology. We hope this volume will serve to strengthen the contribution of epidemiology in constructing and implementing health policy.

References

Stallones, Revel A. (1980) To Advance Epidemiology. *Annual Review of Public Health* 1: 69–82.

Terris, Milton (1980) Epidemiology as a Guide to Health Policy. *Annual Review of Public Health* 1: 323–44.

One

Child health

C. Arden Miller

During the war on poverty in the 1960s, Dr Jack Geiger worked in rural Mississippi to establish a neighborhood comprehensive health center. The work was difficult, leading Dr Geiger to observe in later years that anyone who believes this country does not have a health policy ought to try changing it. He might have added that part of our unwritten health policy holds that there shall be no separately identifiable policy on behalf of children.

A concept of policy

For purposes of this presentation health policy is regarded as the aggregate of principles, stated or unstated, that more or less consistently characterize the distribution of resources, services, and political influence that impact on the health of the population of concern, in this instance the nation's children. This view of health policy emphasizes analysis of what we collectively *do* on behalf of improved health, rather than what we *say* we do. The phrasing of legislative acts, court decisions, and political speeches may all embrace pronouncements that carry the ring of policy declarations. For example, the Comprehensive Health Planning and Public Health Service Amendments of 1966 was introduced by the statement, "The Congress declares that fulfillment of our national purpose depends on promoting and assuring the highest level of health attainable for every person, in an environment which contributes positively to healthful individual and family living." That statement reads like policy that disallows social inequities, medical neglects, and preventable hazards of the work-place, highway, school or home. Abundant evidence that the aspiration was not fulfilled may mean that the policy statement continues to be relevant and should more vigorously guide regulatory authority and distributions of relevant goods and services. On the other hand conspicuous gaps between the declared intent and the achievement may in fact suggest that the statement is hollow, not influential, and not an appropriate expression of actual practice or priorities, and hence not a valid expression of operational policy.

The statement in question begins a paragraph that ends with the caveat that the stated purposes are to be served "without interference with existing patterns of private professional practice of medicine, dentistry, and related healing arts." The idealistic purpose is constrained by protection of a special interest. What is the operative policy? It can be determined only by inferences drawn from careful analysis of how our society distributes relevant power (licensure, accreditation entitlements) and resources (grants, reimbursements, eligibilities, benefits, etc.) that are provided by the programs in question. When such careful analysis, covering a span of years and a variety of programs, yields more or less consistent characterizations, they are legitimately designated as operational policy. The careful analysis that yields generalizations that characterize operational health policy requires the use of epidemiologic skills in ways that will be further amplified.

A clear statement of nominal, as opposed to operational, policy appears in the preamble to the School Lunch Program: "It is declared to be the intention of Congress, as a measure of national security, to safeguard the health and well being of the nation's children" (School Lunch Program, US Code 1751,

1946). Analysis of that program's record has led some critics to suggest that the nutritional interests of children were best served when they coincided with the interests of agribusiness, which welcomed an assured outlet for surplus commodities. By the early 1980s national security was no longer defined in ways that emphasized protection of children's health by means of nutritional supplementation. Large sums were allocated for military preparedness; domestic expenditures for children's health services, including school lunch programs, were drastically reduced. Did the policy undergo a change; did the preamble not accurately reflect operational policy at the time it was written; did higher priorities take precedence over a policy that persists but with a reduced claim to resources? Answers to these questions are not self-evident, and enlightenment may only come by study of many programs that entail some of the same concerns.

These few examples illustrate some assumptions about health policy. Among them is the view that some operational patterns are sufficiently durable to serve as characterizations of health policy, admitting that policy is not immutable and can change over time. Prevailing health policy is seen to emerge as a result of negotiations among competing values promoted by competing interest groups. In those negotiations infants, children, and their parents, who are largely young and poor, lack a competitive advantage either in political or economic terms. The interests of maternal and child health require sponsorship by advocates who attempt to act as surrogates in the arenas of negotiation. These dynamics suggest that epidemiologic data are only one of the considerations that influence health policy. Dominant social values and political influence are also critical determinants. Their influence, at least in the short run, may run counter to the available data. For example, the data on reproductive health might suggest a certain direction for policies about abortion and contraception but the prevailing policy may be pushed in quite another way by certain religious and social values. Control of handguns is another issue where data and policy run counter to each other. Among black males between fifteen and twenty-four years of age homicide and suicide are now the leading causes of death. Handguns are a leading instrument of this mortality, yet policy that would control access to them is effectively resisted.

Formulations of policy

Defensible characterizations of operational health policy might
include the following:

1   As a nation we allocate resources as if medical care were
the major determinant of health, contrary to the weight of
epidemiologic evidence (McKeown 1976). Analysis of children's
health suggests that greatest benefits would derive from emphasis
on family planning, nutrition, sanitation, environmental
protection, accident prevention, and income supplementation
for poor families (Keniston 1977; Select Panel 1981). Such
interventions require public supports and regulations that run
counter to some social values that are even more powerful
than concern for children's health. The operative health policy
appears to seek good health by means of medical care, even at
great expense, rather than to engage in painful social reforms
that would probably be more effective in terms of improved
population-based health outcomes.

Two important programs stand out as exceptions to the
policy formulation that emphasizes achieving favorable health
status by means of medical care. Both programs have medical
components and both have been implemented only by the
greatest perseverance of child health advocates. The first
program is Headstart. For preschool poverty level children the
program provides enriched day care including health check-ups
and supervision, nutritional supplementation, and parent
education. Early evaluations of the program found no durable
benefits, but recent studies of early Headstart enrollees, now
graduated from high school, demonstrated for the enrolled
group reduced school dropouts and reduced need for enrollment
in special education programs for handicapped children (Lazar
1980). The findings were used decisively to preserve public
funding for Headstart at a time when it was earmarked for
drastic reductions.

The other exceptional program is WIC (Special Supplemental
Food Program for Women, Infants and Children). The program
is administered through health agencies, usually the clinics of
local health departments, and provides nutritional supplements
for poverty level pregnant women, infants, and children
through five years of age. It is one of the few food supplemen-

tation programs that unambiguously serves the nutritional needs of a high risk population rather than the economic interests of agribusiness. When Congress authorized and made appropriations for WIC the funds were impounded by the Nixon administration and were released only after prolonged delays, terminated by litigation brought by child advocacy groups. The amount of appropriations has never been sufficient to serve more than about a quarter of eligible women and children. The program has been a special target for further funding reductions by the Reagan administration.

Evaluations of benefits from WIC have been encouraging, but they are not yet decisive enough to persuade all skeptics. Better birth weights and weight gains for infants and children, increased head circumference for infants, and reduced rates of iron deficiency anemia are all encouraging findings (Kennedy and Gershoff 1982; Kennedy *et al.* 1982). Participation in WIC provides another benefit by increasing participation in prenatal and well child care (Kotch and Whiteman 1982). Poor pregnant women appear to attend clinics to obtain food and stay to receive appropriate health services.

A strong case can be made for including the nation's family planning program as a third endeavor (significantly, outside the usual medical care system) that impacts favorably on infant and child health (Morris and Vory 1975).

2 The political power that is associated with delivery of medical care is largely entrusted to physician practitioners. At one time a number of states provided that their Boards of Healing Arts, which grant licensure for practicing the healing arts, should be constituted by the state medical society or some component of it. Other states empowered the governor to make appointments to such boards, but constrained his choice by providing that he must appoint from a panel proposed by the medical society, or from physicians already licensed to practice in the state. These state laws have tended to become less restrictive and to increase the participation of other health professionals and the public at large. Even with these changes the influence of the practicing medical profession in authorizing licensure, accreditation, and certification of health service providers is predominant.

This circumstance has prompted some analysts to suggest

that medical practice in this country functions with the economic characteristics of a monopoly that restricts entry of other providers into the market. Those restrictions serve the public interest by restraining quacks and charlatans, but restrictions also pertain to providers who might be advantageous, especially for children's health. In many parts of the country trained nurse midwives and pediatric nurse practitioners are constrained from rendering services, even to demonstrably underserved populations, in spite of abundant evidence on the effectiveness and economy of care rendered by such mid-level practitioners (Select Panel 1981).

3   Health services are predominantly distributed in a private economic market, on a fee for service basis, an emphasis that is both subsidized and protected by government. About 90 per cent of all children have a regular source of medical care, and that source is a privately practicing physician for about 80 per cent of those served. The distribution is different for poverty level children. About 80 per cent have a regular source of care, and that source is a privately practicing physician for only about half of them. Public clinics and emergency departments of hospitals serve the remainder (Kovar 1982; Miller *et al.* 1981). For selected services, such as immunization and family planning, public providers play a much larger role, rendering about two-thirds of the respective services to minors.

Since enactment of Medicaid and Medicare in 1965 the proportion of the total health outlay that is paid by government has progressively increased. Nearly half of the nation's health bill is paid by government, but only about 3 per cent of the expenditures are made for services by the public health agencies (Comprehensive NPHPRS Report 1980). Predictions in 1970 that 90 per cent of the population would be served by 1980 in systems featuring prepayment for services fell far short of the mark. Fee for service payments characterize care for more than 90 per cent of the population (Saward and Fleming 1980).

Children are less well covered by insurance and public payment systems than any other age group, even though a higher proportion of children than any other age group live in poverty level households (Budetti, Butler, and McManus 1982). As a consequence, out of pocket payments for the health care of children are proportionately higher than for other ages. Since 1980, with rising unemployment rates and loss of job-connected family health insurance, coupled with more restrictive eligibility for Medicaid benefits, the proportion of children who are financially unprotected for health services has been rising.

4 Few personal health services are acknowledged to be a direct responsibility of 'government, and since 1980 the exercise of that limited responsibility has been substantially transferred to the state level. Exceptions to this principle are recognized for American Indians, military personnel and to some extent their dependents, high officers of government, and appropriate preventive care for the public at large when threatened by dread epidemics. A misguided but energetic responsibility was recognized to prevent by means of mass immunizations a threatened swine influenza epidemic in 1975. Protection from dread disease is most readily acknowledged with relation to pestilence. Protection from other kinds of epidemics is more problematic. In the mid-1960s a European outbreak of congenital defects was traced to use among pregnant women of a newly developed tranquilizer. At that time the action of our government to limit distribution of the drug was widely applauded. In more recent years the regulatory and protective activity of the Food and Drug Administration (FDA) has been curtailed. Government's inclination to protect the public against the presumed health hazards of industrial toxins (congenital defects, other poor pregnancy outcomes, and possibly malignancy) has been less than vigorous. Whether this circumstance reflects weak data or weak policy is by no means clear. Better policy may well depend in this instance on better data. If efforts to collect the data are dilatory what policy is implied? (See policy proposition number 5.)

Traditionally government has been recognized as a provider of last resort rendering essential personal health services to populations not reached by private and voluntary provider systems. This responsibility has been most extensively exercised for services that are not economically attractive to the private market, or that require complex community services sytems that have not been extensively developed in the private sector, possibly for lack of economic incentive. Examples are programs for crippled children, mentally retarded, chronically ill, or the emotionally disturbed. Public programs have been developed in all these areas.

Poor women and children not reached by private providers for essential preventive and health maintenance services are another group recognized in some measure as a responsibility of government. Beginning in the early 1920s federal government made grants available on a voluntary basis to assist the states with providing essential maternal and child health services (Sheppard-Towner Act). Some states declined the money altogether, beginning a record that has persisted to the present of great variation among the states in the extent of the responsibility they take to protect the health of poor women and children. This variation is sometimes limited by federal oversight. Title X of the Public Health Act, although largely implemented at state levels, continues federal responsibility to assure access of poor women to family planning services.

The Sheppard-Towner Act to provide federal financing for state-based maternal and child health services was allowed to lapse under pressure from the American Medical Association (AMA) which alleged government's encroachment on the rightful province of private medical practice. This claim was not suported by evidence that the private sector either could or would meet the health needs of poor women and children. A stronger provision for maternal and child health was written into the Social Security Act of 1935. That provision makes grants to the states and requires them to develop plans for dependent children providing "assistance at least great enough to provide, when added to the income of the family, a reasonable subsistence compatible with decency and health." That is the famed Aid for Dependent Children (AFDC) entitlement, that has generated in some quarters the denigration of welfare mothers. Other parts of the Social Security Act required appropriate services for pregnant women, for infants and children, and for crippled children.

AFDC represents one of several income transfer programs that benefit poor families. Another is food stamps, scrip that serves as a money substitute for purchase of food. Both programs are frequent targets for budget slashing. In the first two years of the Reagan administration about 365,000 families were removed from welfare roles, and benefits were reduced for another 260,000. The food stamp program was reduced by more than $2 billion, a million recipients were terminated, and others received reduced benefits (Greenstein 1983). These cuts were made in the face of rising unemployment and increase in the proportion of children living in poverty. Disagreements persist on the extent to which these reductions represent the elimination of wasteful public spending, or deprivations to poor people who, as a consequence, suffer increased jeopardy to their health. Fraud has occurred in the income transfer programs but the documented extent of it is small. In this controversy insufficient attention has been given to the fact that the majority of poor people in this country are under twenty-one years of age. More than 50 per cent of the residents of poverty level households are minors, and conversely a higher proportion of children than any other age group live in circumstances of poverty. The evidence is incontrovertible that poverty among children is associated with extensive disease, death, and disability (Keniston and the Carnegie Council on Children 1977). The record is also clear, but not quite so well documented, on the extent to which income transfers contribute to the improved health of poor children. Other industrialized nations have responded to that dilemma on humanitarian if not on epidemiologic grounds. The United States is the only industrialized nation in the western world that does not provide children's allowances, money granted to families without regard to income, for support of the important work of raising children (Haanes-Olsen 1972). Our nation provides income supplementation and other health benefits without regard to economic need only to people over sixty-five years of age.

A few experiments in new kinds of income transfers have been conducted. Their evaluation suffers, as with much social science research, from insufficient control of relevant variables. One of these experiments reported an impressive increase in birth weights among infants born to poor families with income supplementation through a negative income tax (Salkind and Haskins 1982). That finding, if confirmed, could have enormous significance in negotiations over health policy.

The extension and improvement of maternity and child health services authorized by Title V of the Social Security Act have never been sufficient to meet assessed needs. Davis reported that, after forty years of implementing Title V, services had reached as few as 15 per cent of live-born infants (Davis and Schoen 1978). This failure is especially regrettable in view of findings that unacceptably high infant mortality rates could be reduced by increased participation of high risk pregnant women in early and continuous prenatal care (Kessner 1973; Quick, Greenlick, and Roghman 1981). The limitations of Title V can be attributed both to lack of vigorous national guidelines and standards, and to pernicious underfunding.

During the 1960s federal government contracted with many community agencies to render comprehensive health services to islands of underserved populations. Good examples are the Comprehensive Neighborhood Health Centers started by the Office of Economic Opportunity, part of President Johnson's War on Poverty, and the Special Projects of Title V, the Maternal and Infant Care, and Children and Youth Projects. By every measure that has been applied these projects were a conspicuous success. Utilization and quality of services were high (Morehead, Donaldson, and Seravalli 1971; and Sokol *et al.* 1980), health outcomes were favorable (Gordis 1973), and per capita costs, including cost of administration, were low (Sparer and Anderson 1972). The projects shared the same failing of many successful demonstrations: they were not extended to all populations who would benefit from similar interventions. This failing has led to the proposition by some people that government's operational health policy for poor people, especially politically weak women and children, has been to address their health needs only in token ways. Family planning services stand as an exception to this tokenism. Access to appropriate reproductive services is exceedingly high among all socio-economic levels. That success is attributable to a combined governmental and voluntary effort that does not pertain to other services relevant to maternal and infant health.

5   An arena of policy that invites controversy is the extent that the health of a population is an expendable value that is traded off or expropriated for economic advantage (Illich 1976). The history of child labor and the current condition of the health of migrant families support the contention that economic considerations are sometimes given precedence over protection

against hazards to health. About 25 per cent of disease and disability is thought to be job related, with only variable and uncertain monitoring and regulation to reduce risks at the work-place (APHA Chartbook 1975). Environmental protection, once administered and closely identified with public health, has been split away and become closely identified with industrial interests. These circumstances suggest that economic privilege takes precedence over concern for health, but the priorities are blurred. A community that protects the purity of its air and water in the interests of health may drive away industry and promote joblessness, perhaps the most unhealthy circumstance of all for children and families. The problem is not adequately addressed by a patchwork of local policies, and national policies appear more protective of economic interests than of personal health. Note should be taken that infants and pregnant women are especially vulnerable to environmental toxins (Longo 1980).

6   For many decades the dominant operative health policy in this country held that if sufficient resources for health services could be made available for use in unspecified ways, then important health benefits, also unspecified, would ensue. Initiatives were implemented to provide at public expense the facilities for health care (Hill-Burton Act for hospital construction), manpower (various training grants), research and technology (National Institutes of Health), and financing of services (Titles XVIII and XIX of the Social Security Act). A policy of resource development allowed that the public would subsidize development of resources that would be used predominantly as a kind of permanent subsidy to private systems of care. This policy brought many benefits but also some grave disappointments. The cost was exceedingly high, and many people and services continued to be neglected. Important health indicators suggested a lower level of achievement than that of some other nations that spent less money. Attention began to focus on policies that not only provided resources (inputs) but prescribed the ways in which those resources were to be used (processes).

7   A new emphasis in health policy emerged to prominence

during the 1960s. The emphasis featured some control or inducement for the ways in which resources were used. Planning was emphasized in an effort to close gaps, avoid duplications, and bring appropriate levels of service to health-related needs (Regional Medical Programs, Partnership for Health, National Health Planning Resources Development Act, Regionalized Perinatal Care). Inducements were provided to adopt certain procedures, such as prepayment, either to finance medical care (Health Maintenance Organizations) or to limit excess costs (Professional Standards Review Organizations). Efforts were made to correct maldistribution of resources (National Health Service Corps, certificates of need for hospital construction). These examples all relate to process interventions that focused on change in provider systems and in resource allocation.

Another group of process-oriented interventions promoted a specific service or set of services (e.g. screening or primary care) and left considerable flexibility about systems for providing the service. Funds were made available for identifying and treating health problems among poor children (Early and Periodic Screening, Diagnosis, and Treatment (EPSDT)), but the states were allowed wide discretion on how to approach that task. Emphasis on primary care took the form of selectively subsidizing certain processes of education and training in order to encourage potential family or primary care practitioners. The screening programs, even though seldom reaching more than half of eligible children, confirmed a high degree of untreated disease and disability. About half of the children reached by EPSDT were found to have health problems, most often nutritional anemia, dental disease, visual or auditory disorders (EPSDT 1981).

Policy that strove to modify the processes of provider systems or to prescribe the procedures by which newly available resources might be used emphasized certain qualities such as comprehensiveness and availability. Efforts to improve acceptability and integration of services included the requirement that consumers participate in the control of health services or resources (Office of Economic Opportunity, various planning acts). Strategies for promoting such qualities as comprehensiveness were facilitated by targeting resources for populations in defined geographic areas (Office of Economic

Opportunity and Special Projects of Title V of the Social
Security Act).

Many of the process interventions required a degree of
regulation over providers in ways that were strenuously
resisted. The interventions often strove to enhance accountability and productivity where there was the use of public
funds. A few of the process interventions were identified with
explicitly defined health outcomes (immunization programs
with eradication of disease or reduction of morbidity, maternal
and infant care projects with lowered infant mortality rates)
but these were exceptional.

8 Policies that give priority to considerations of health
outcome have vigorously entered the deliberative stage
of policy-making but have moved only guardedly toward
implementation. The Surgeon General's Report on Health
Promotion and Disease Prevention was framed in terms of five
national goals to be achieved by 1990, each expressed in
measurable terms (DHEW 1979). Serious effort to achieve any
of them, such as a national infant mortality rate of 9 per 1,000
live births, could be expected to have profound effects on both
the inputs and processes of health care as well as on many
other social services and supports. A theoretical advantage of
national policy that defines outcomes is the freedom allowed
state and local levels, and a multitude of provider systems, to
develop strategies toward those outcomes, in different ways
according to local needs and circumstances, so long as
acceptable outcomes are achieved.

Policy that is based on efforts to achieve health outcomes
has had only limited application, too meager for adequate
evaluation. An important beginning was made in recent years
by the Office of Maternal and Child Health of the Department
of Health and Human Services (DHHS), which began to require
that states report Title V programs according to progress
toward achieving measurable outcome and process objectives.
Implementation and evaluation of the Improved Pregnancy
Outcome Program relied for a time on use of outcome
objectives. That strategy was reversed with implementation of
block grants after 1981.

One of the obstacles in the way of more rapid development

of health policy based on efforts to achieve health status outcomes is uncertainty about the availability of valid health status indicators. More is available than is widely appreciated. Some years ago Rutstein *et al.* (1976) proposed a scheme for evaluating the quality of medical care. That scheme identified a number of markers or sentinel events that should never happen (e.g. a case of diphtheria) and others that should happen only rarely, such as diagnosis of carcinoma of the cervix in advanced stages. Rutstein's formulation lends itself to adaptation for identifying health outcome measures.

An ambitious effort was made recently to compile process and outcome measures in a work that proposed community-based health status objectives for the nation (DHHS 1980). More than 220 objectives were proposed, grouped into the following fifteen priority areas: high blood pressure control, family planning, pregnancy and infant health, immunization, sexually transmitted diseases, toxic agent control, occupational safety and health, accident prevention and injury control, fluoridation and dental health, surveillance and control of infectious diseases, smoking and health, misuse of alcohol and drugs, physical fitness and exercise, control of stress, and control of violent behavior. A number of different objectives were specified, fifty-six of them as health outcomes, for each of the fifteen areas. The targets, when taken together, were proposed to enable realization of the overall national health goals set down in the Surgeon General's Report (US DHEW 1979). Not all of the objectives enjoy a ring of plausibility; data relevant to some of them would be difficult for some communities to gather, and recent evidence documents the deterioration of some relevant data sources since 1980 (Green, Wilson, and Bauer 1983). The serious pursuit of even a few of the objectives presumably would reorder priorities for resource development, would require the closest collaboration among a number of agencies and provider systems, both public and private, and would clarify the interests that are served by many public expenditures and interventions. Nominal policy, the synoptic expressions that abound in legislative acts, agency guidelines, and other places, might move closer to the accurate expression of operational policy. This clarity would be an advantage for children whose health has suffered greatly from high promises and low levels of endeavor.

A typology for policy, related programs, and data

The above formulations of health policy are supported by selectively marshalled data and anecdote; personal judgments and prejudices are involved. The formulations are not above controversy, leaving ample room for other analysts to arrive at different formulations. Analysis of health policy is sufficiently imprecise to entertain unsupported assertion and speculation. Here is a task for epidemiologists. What in fact are the working policies that influence children's health? Can the skills of epidemiology be used to identify patterns in public programs and resource allocations, in the same way that patterns are found in illness and human behavior? To the extent that identification of such patterns makes explicit the forces that guide social action, in ways that are powerful but not now recognized or acknowledged, then our understandings of public policy have been enlightened.

The following typology of policy and programs is proposed as a scheme for analysis that may help with understanding their relationships with each other, and their interactions with the kinds of data that are collected.

The simplest systems approach for analysis of complex endeavors can be broken into three parts:

INPUTS → PROCESSES → OUTCOMES

That simple model ordinarily is elaborated with various branches and feedbacks; but for the purpose of categorizing health policy according to its major emphasis the components can be kept uncomplicated. This formulation has been developed by others as a way to analyze health service or administrative systems (Donabedian 1966), but it is not ordinarily regarded as a typology for analyzing public policy. Such an approach may help with considerations of the reciprocal interactive relationships between data and policy

Policy formulation number 6 above describes the emphasis on inputs, or resource development. The guiding perspective was strong, while this policy predominated, that more hospitals, more doctors with better training, improved understanding about human biology, more advanced technology, and reduced economic barriers to medical care would all bring substantial benefits. The processes (or services) that would be generated by those resources were for the most part not specified, and the ultimate societal benefits, presumably some anticipated improved health outcomes, were never defined. Policy that stimulated and financed resource development generated data on the availability and distribution of resources. Standards were proposed on the number of hospital beds or practitioner physicians that should serve a population. Various waves of doctor shortage or surfeit were predicted, and appropriate adjustments were made in training programs. Program and data interacted with each other in a reciprocal fashion.

Data also began to promote consideration of changes in policy. A landmark book on "the doctor shortage" proposed the startling concept that availability of doctors was not the critical determinant for good health. The measure of concern should be access to services, which might be rendered by doctors or by a number of other newly emerging practitioners, some of them with training as nurses (Fein 1967). At about the same time Dr Michael DeBakey of Houston led a medical movement that attempted to equalize access to new research findings for the care of heart disease, cancer, and stroke. For this purpose some resources of medical care were proposed to be regionalized, a process of planning with hints of regulation. Other forces were at work for modifying a policy of uncontrolled resource development. The number of secondary and tertiary physicians increased, and those in primary care decreased. The concentration of physicians and most other health resources increased in larger communities, in the wealthier areas, and in the suburbs (Navarro 1974). Such data on the maldistribution of resources stimulated interventions that were intended to close gaps and avoid wasteful duplication in the distribution of related services. These interactions are diagrammed in *Figure 1.1*.

Data on availability and distribution of resources promoted interest in policy that influenced the use, quality, and cost of services that made use of those resources (column II). Most of the specific programs identified in that column have been briefly described in the preceding text. Several points about them should be noted. Few of the interventions were guided by a commitment to achieve specified health outcomes, and, accordingly, they generated little data of that kind. Instead the programs promoted extensive data gathering on service utilization, and to a lesser extent on quality and cost of services.

Further problems were revealed. Utilization data soon demonstrated that poor children, who during the 1960s made many fewer per capita visits to physicians than non-poor children, had closed the gap and were by the end of the 1970s making a comparable number of visits. No claims were made that poor children, who suffer more disease and disability than the non-poor, were yet receiving care sufficient to their needs. What is their need? What is their health status? Those questions prompt attention to column III, health outcomes.

Interest in a policy to achieve specified health outcomes was promoted by other considerations. After a decade of successive programs for health planning, conscientious planners began to ask "plan for what?" What criteria will be used to measure successful planning? New interest in cost benefit analysis raised questions about which benefits should be costed. Finally new national policies featured increased discretion by the states on resource distribution and on determination of program priorities. Is there no national interest in health status that should guide the limits of state discretion? Answers to all these questions promoted interest in a new level of policy concerned with health outcomes and informed by health status measures.

Further interest in health outcome measures was stimulated by policies that minimized government's responsibility to provide resources or to sponsor essential health services. Documentation that resources and utilizations were declining was not useful for promoting new programs and interventions. Such data, instead, suggested that new policies were in fact working. Measuring the effect of those policies required an examination of the health impact of policy changes on vulnerable population groups.

This typology of policy, programs, and data suggests a rigidity that is not entirely justified. Title V of the Social Security Act is an example of a program with many parts, some of which featured research and training (column I of *Figure 1.1*), or demonstration service projects (column II), and others, for a time at least, required justification in terms of improved health outcomes (column III). Still, each of these components of the Act maintained a separate kind of identity, and each came to prominence at a different time when prevailing policy was receptive to a new emphasis.

Figure 1.1 *Interactions of policy, programs and data for child health*

	I input →	II process →	III outcome
dominant policy theme	*resource development*	*planning, regulation, and delivery of services*	*Achieving health status objectives*
illustrative programs	hospital construction (Hill-Burton)	various planning authorities	reduced rates of low birth weight
	manpower (various training grants)	neighborhood health centers	
	research and technology (programs of National Institutes of Health)	immunization program →	elimination or reduction of certain infections smallpox, clinical polio, diphtheria, rubella
		family planning program	
	reimbursements Medicaid (Title XIX) Medicare (Title XVIII) Title V, Social Security Act	special projects of Title V	
		maternal and infant care →	reduced infant mortality
		children and youth	

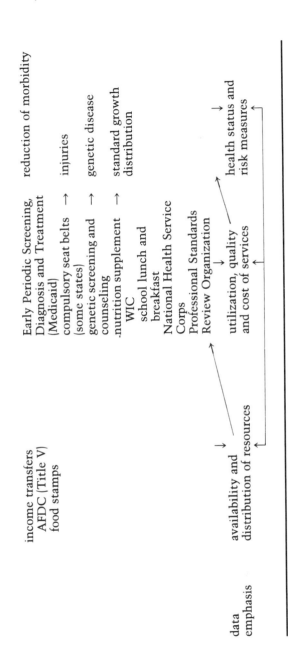

income transfers
AFDC (Title V)
food stamps

Early Periodic Screening, Diagnosis and Treatment (Medicaid)
compulsory seat belts (some states) →
genetic screening and counseling →
nutrition supplement →
WIC
school lunch and breakfast
National Health Service Corps
Professional Standards Review Organization

reduction of morbidity
injuries
genetic disease
standard growth distribution

data emphasis

availability and distribution of resources →

utilization, quality and cost of services

health status and risk measures →

An emphasis on health outcomes

The use of health outcome measures, such as "recovery, restoration of function, and of survival," has been extensively discussed as a device for evaluating the quality of medical care (Donabedian 1966). Serious problems constrain that approach. They include difficulties of definition, especially for functional outcomes as opposed to mortality or morbidity measures, and the long interval required for assessment of some outcomes. The greatest difficulty relates to recognition that many well-defined health outcomes are influenced by factors other than medical care. This circumstance, which limits the utility of outcome measures for the evaluation of medical care, contributes to its value as a measure of the adequacy of social policy. Rutstein *et al.* (1976) illustrate this point with relation to identifying sentinel events, those health outcomes so rare that the occurrence of even one case strongly suggests that public policy or program has gone awry:

> "The chain of responsibility to prevent the occurrence of any unnecessary disease, disability, or untimely death may be long and complex. The failure of any single link may precipitate an unnecessary undesirable health event. Thus, the unnecessary case of diphtheria, measles, or poliomyelitis may be the responsibility of the state legislature that neglected to appropriate the needed funds, the health officer who did not implement the program, the medical society that opposed community clinics, the physician who did not immunize his patient, the religious views of the family, or the mother who didn't bother to take her baby for immunization."
>
> (Rutstein *et al.* 1976, reprinted by permission of the *New England Journal of Medicine*)

Used in this way adverse health outcomes become signals requiring community diagnosis, one of the important missions of public health. That diagnosis requires examination of all possible linkages of outcome with antecedent determinants in order to identify appropriate corrective measures. The aggregate effect of those corrections constitutes a revised and presumably more effective operational health policy.

A reconsideration of health outcomes as a device for

monitoring health policy is prompted in part by the slow emergence of a new way of thinking about health and disease, its causes and cures. Old notions regarded good health as a mystical sublime state, susceptible to disruption by the insult of injury, pest, or toxin (Dubos 1959). The medical perspective held that within poorly defined but dramatically shrinking limits, those disruptions could be corrected by applying the wisdom of biological science. Every disruption, or disease, was thought to have its cause, and every cause its cure, if not presently available then attainable in the future through greater efforts to achieve medical wisdom.

Work on stress, coping, and social support systems fostered a different orientation that required recognition of the multiple causation of disease, and the complex ways of preventing or curing it (Cassell 1974). In the first year after a stressful event, such as death of a spouse or loss of employment, all kinds of diseases (heart disease, diabetes, cancer, stroke) increase dramatically. The risk of serious disease of all kinds is lessened if the stress is mitigated by social support systems such as a loving family, or involvement in a church or social group. The same phenomena pertain to issues of maternal and child health. Among pregnant women whose lives are disrupted by a stressful event, as above, pregnancy outcomes are adversely affected by increased rates of fetal deaths, low birth weight, etc. The adverse effects are mitigated by strong social support systems (Nuckolls, Cassel, and Kaplan 1972). Similar patterns are suggested with relation to child abuse and unemployment. In one report loss of a job did not result in increased child abuse except in single parent families. If day care or an extended family member were present the risk of abuse was substantially reduced even in those high risk households (Kotch and Thomas 1982).

Against these perspectives analysis of child health outcomes becomes a device for emphasizing the aggregate effect of multiple determinants of health, and recognizes that health policy embraces concern for the way our society provides, or neglects to provide, a broad range of supports and services for vulnerable people. Health policy is moved beyond the concerns of medical care. Risk reduction becomes a legitimate component of health policy. Reduced risks may result from participation in such diverse processes as day care, family planning services with counseling for sexually active teenagers, and immunizations for infants and preschool children. Such processes become a legitimate component of favorable health outcomes even though their measures may record processes rather than outcomes in the strictest sense of definition. Sometimes measures of process have greater utility than measures of outcome. For example, a reduction in the number of unwanted teenage pregnancies is a desirable outcome, difficult to measure. Less difficult is the gathering of data on the proportion of sexually active teenagers who participate in family planning services.

Regarding risk reduction as a desirable kind of health outcome requires some trade-offs in priority setting. Participation in day care may reduce some risks, as above, but increase others, such as exposure to certain infections. Hence, priorities may be set one way when planning for certain populations or communities, and ordered another way in clinical management of individual cases.

These formulations identify two additional important tasks for epidemiologic skills in the development of child health policy. The first is definition, if possible fortified by professional consensus, of important health outcome measures. The second and larger task, represented by the bottom line in *Figure 1.1*, requires identifying the linkages on a population specific basis that tie those outcomes to antecedent interventions and supports. A key component of this task is the population base. Effective policy requires that aggregate improvements in health outcomes do not mask neglects and unfavorable outcomes for high risk subgroups. The interventions and supports to effect reduction in infant mortality rate, for example, may be very different for selected age, racial, or socio-economic groups, than for the public at large. It is an epidemiologic problem.

During 1982 a survey was made of non-governmental groups that are engaged in the monitoring of children's health (Schorr, Miller, and Fine 1983). These are groups that are concerned with more than a single locality; they include professional associations, advocacy and policy analysis groups, and university medical center teams. More than twenty-one monitoring projects were identified, gathering data according to forty different indicators of children's health. Outcome measures were a conspicuous part of their measurements. Infant mortality rates for example were used by eight groups, lead toxicity by seven, low birth weight and iron deficiency anemia by six, congenital disorders by five, and child abuse and neglect by five.

The University of North Carolina Health Outcomes Project, beginning in 1982, undertook in consultation among child health experts to develop a list of outcome measures that show promise for gaining wide acceptance (Schorr, Miller, and Fine 1983). A list of measures was compiled according to the following criteria: the measures were widely regarded by experts in the field as reflecting important health or policy concerns; they were understandable and considered significant by the policy-makers who were consulted; data were obtainable with relative ease; evidence was available that the condition measured could be prevented or greatly improved through known and available interventions. Even though various interventions might influence a given outcome, experience was sufficient to confirm that changes in major social or health policies could affect improvements.

For each outcome measure that was selected the following information was compiled: a precise definition of each indicator; a discussion of significant program policy and health implications; data sources, with background information on current findings and trends; risk factors; and US standards and objectives where these have been established. This work was done with a view to making the information available for use by non-medical monitoring groups and by assisting such groups in promptly and easily obtaining the relevant data for a given locality or region. The measures include many that are well known by experts and have already had limited use in the formulation of child health policy, but which might be more influential if presented to the public at large with clear definition and explanation of significance. The following list of proposed health indicators will be refined over time in response to criticism, to experience with use, as well as to new understanding of health needs and of ways for maintaining and promoting health.

Among the health outcome measures identified by the University of North Carolina Health Outcomes Project are the following:

Infant mortality rate

This rate is the number of deaths to infants under one year of age per thousand live births. The infant mortality rate is an important indicator of both the health and welfare of the population. While the rate in the United States has been steadily improving since the beginning of this century, we have not substantially improved our poor standing when compared with other industrialized nations. Great disparities persist in infant mortality rates among population groups within the United States. Gaps between rates for white and non-white populations have failed to narrow substantially over recent decades.

The US infant mortality rate (IMR) of 11.2 deaths per 1,000 live births (which translates into 40,627 deaths) is higher than for seventeen other nations of the world (1983). The United States has maintained a rank of between fourteen and eighteen for the past seventeen years. Black infants born in this country die at almost twice the rate of white infants. In 1979, the infant mortality rate for blacks was 21.8 per 1,000 live births, as compared to a rate of 11.5 for white infants. Even that rate is less favorable than for the leading countries of western Europe. In Sweden a favorable rate is maintained not only for indigenous populations but for immigrant families from southeastern Europe (Smedby and Ericson 1979). The rate for select sub-populations in the United States is greater than the rate in some far less developed nations. In 1980, the rate of infant death in Washington, DC (which is 70 per cent black) was higher than the rates for Jamaica, Cuba, and Costa Rica.

Between 1915 and 1950 there was a steady, dramatic decline in the US infant mortality rate, which is largely attributed to improved sanitation, decreases in infectious diseases, improved maternal and child nutrition, and access to health care. By 1950, our IMR was reduced to 29 per 1,000 live births. After a temporary leveling of infant deaths between 1950 and 1965, the IMR began a second marked descent in the mid-1960s, which continues through the present. This second downward trend has been associated both with an increase in the availability of and access to family planning, prenatal, and other maternal and child health services among underserved populations. The Maternal and Infant Care projects demonstrated that among underserved populations dramatic improvements in infant mortality could be achieved with routine health care services and without changing the educational or socio-economic levels of the families served.

Low birth weight is the most important single factor associated with infant mortality in this country; low birth weight infants account for two-thirds of neonatal deaths and over 50 per cent of all infant mortality in the United States. The remarkable decline in the US infant mortality rate in the past 15–20 years can largely be attributed to a dramatic improvement in the survival of low birth weight infants, brought about through technological advances in high risk maternity and neonatal care. For the future, however, efforts to decrease infant mortality by preventing the occurrence of low birth weight in the first place are likely to have a greater impact on child health outcome than are additional invest-ments in saving babies who are born too soon or too small (Newland 1981). Careful analysis of neonatal mortality in North Carolina indicates that better care for low birth weight babies will not close the gap in survival rates between black and white babies. To achieve that outcome more intensive preventive services are required (David and Siegel 1983).

In 1980 the US DHHS established a national objective for 1990 to achieve an infant mortality rate of no more than 9 deaths per 1,000 live births with no racial or ethnic subgroup of the population to have an infant mortality rate in excess of 12 deaths per 1,000 live births.

Low birth weight infants

Low birth weight infants are those weighing less than 2,500 grams at birth. They fall into two categories: those who are born prematurely, less than thirty-seven weeks in gestation, and those who are full term babies but are small for gestational age. In 1979 almost 7 per cent of all infants born in the United States were classified as low birth weight. The proportion of low birth weight babies born today is only slightly lower than it was thirty years ago. The rate for black populations in this country is substantially greater than for whites and the difference is increasing. International data comparing the United States with nine other industrialized nations indicates that the United States ranks second highest in the proportion of low birth weight infants.

One study involving records in a group of developing countries suggests that high rates of low birth weight can predominantly be accounted for by an increase in babies that are small for gestational age, a circumstance presumed to be most dramatically influenced by environmental factors including maternal nutrition, smoking, alcohol consumption, prenatal care, and maternal age. The relative impact of these determinants is not well understood.

National policy to cope with low birth weight has emphasized a regionalized system of stratified medical care for improving the survival of extreme low birth weight infants. No organized programs have been directed toward preventing low birth weight. In some areas low birth weight babies are transported by helicopter or jet airplane to hospital intensive care units, but funds are not provided to transport poor pregnant women to prenatal clinics, a measure which might reasonably diminish the prospects for giving birth to a baby who would need the helicopter or the intensive care unit.

An objective has been set for the United States urging that by 1990 low birth weight babies should constitute no more than 5 per cent of all live births and that no racial or ethnic group in the population should have a rate that exceeds 9 per cent of live births.

Births to mothers under age fifteen

Biological as well as social and economic health hazards affecting both mother and baby associate with pregnancies in women under fifteen years of age. In 1979 there were 10,700 infants born to mothers under fifteen years of age in this country. A higher proportion of teenagers in the United States become mothers than in any other country in the western world except Poland (McGee 1982). Young black women are almost eight times more likely than young white women to give birth before the age of eighteen. The overall childbearing rate for this group has remained virtually constant for the past decade, approximately 1.2 live births per 1,000 young women under age fifteen. The rate for blacks has decreased slightly and the rate for whites has increased during this interval (Alan Guttmacher Institute 1981).

Infants born to mothers under age fifteen are almost twice as likely to die before they reach their first birthdays, and are more than twice as likely to be of low birth weight, as are infants born to women in their twenties. Later in life, children born to teenage mothers are less likely to adapt well to school, are more likely to score lower on IQ tests, and are at increased risk for repeating at least one grade in school. There is also some evidence that children born to young mothers are at increased risk of mental retardation, congenital defects, and other handicapping conditions such as epilepsy (Baldwin and Cain 1981).

For teenage mothers, early childbearing is associated with an increased risk of toxemia, iron deficiency anemia, and complications associated with premature babies and mortality. Beyond these physical problems, women who gave birth as teenagers are less likely to finish either high school or college than are women who delayed childbearing until at least age twenty. In addition, women who were teenage mothers are more likely to be unemployed, or if employed to hold low-paying jobs. The mean family income of women who gave birth at age nineteen or younger is half that of women who delayed childbearing until age twenty or older (Menken 1981).

Births to women under fifteen years of age are associated with the increase in sexual activity of young teenagers over the past decade. This change is well documented but poorly understood (Zelnik and Kantner 1980). The provocative sexual content of much advertising and entertainment is sometimes held responsible. Other people, without adequate justification, blame easy access to contraception.

The Alan Guttmacher Institute estimates that virtually none of the pregnancies to young women under age fifteen are intended. The first months after initiating intercourse carry the greatest risk of pregnancy for teenagers of all ages. Half of first premarital pregnancies among teenagers occur within the first six months after initiating intercourse, and 20 per cent of pregnancies occur within the first month. The younger the teenager, the less likely she is to use contraception and the more likely she is to become pregnant: teenagers who initiate intercourse prior to age fifteen are twice as likely to become pregnant within the first six months as are teenagers who delay intercourse until age 18–19 (Alan Guttmacher Institute 1981).

Few issues of health policy have aroused more intense controversy than those associated with teenage pregnancy. Access to abortion and contraception, parental involvement, and sex education all arouse intense feelings that are not reduced in all quarters by access to sound data. Data collection and analysis on all these issues is reasonably current except for sex education. Although it is often promoted by conventional wisdom, little is known about its effectiveness.

Immunization Status

This indicator consists of the proportion of two-year-old children in a defined population who are fully immunized against preventable childhood diseases: diphtheria, tetanus, pertussis, measles, mumps, rubella, and poliomyelitis. Strictly speaking immunization status is not a health outcome. However it is so closely and indisputably linked to disease rates that it is included here as a proxy for an outcome measure. Immunization rates of two-year-olds serve the dual purpose of indicating the level of protection of the population against infectious disease and also an indication of the proportion of young children who participate in some form of well child care.

Although most of the vaccines and toxoids for childhood diseases have been available for decades, as recently as 1977 less than two-thirds of US children under age fifteen were fully immunized against measles, mumps, rubella, diphtheria, pertussis, tetanus, and polio. Between 1977 and 1979, the federal government initiated and state and local governments cooperated in a childhood immunization drive which aimed at achieving a 90 per cent immunization rate for the nation's children (targeted age group varied with specific vaccine or toxoid). By fall 1979, through well-orchestrated efforts, this goal was attained for all vaccine and toxoid preventable childhood diseases except mumps. United States Immunization Survey (USIS) data from 1979 to 1981 indicate a general trend toward improved immunization status of children and youths aged 1–19. For all vaccines and toxoids the highest recorded immunization rates were found in the 5 to 6-year-old population (Centers for Disease Control 1982).

In the United States, survey data indicate that non-white children and children whose families are of lower socio-economic status are at increased risk of being unimmunized. In addition, children living in central cities show consistently lower immunization rates when compared to children living in other areas.

In 1980, the DHHS set the following objectives for increasing immunization rates among children: By 1990, at least 90 per cent of all children should have completed their basic immunization series by age two – measles, mumps, rubella, polio, diphtheria, pertussis, and tetanus. (In 1978, completion varied from 50 to 90 per cent.) By 1990, at least 95 per cent of children attending licensed day care facilities and kindergarten through twelfth grade should be fully immunized. Based on data collected during the 1978–79 school year, the immunization level for measles, rubella, polio, and DTP was about 90 per cent for first school entrants overall (US DHHS, 1980).

Participation in early and continuous prenatal care

This measure is proposed to promote risk reduction against maternal mortality and morbidity, low birth weight, and infant mortality. The latter outcome measures are not ordinarily useful for small populations or short time-spans. The effectiveness of prenatal care in reducing risks is not beyond controversy, but the case is reasonably well established for high risk populations, such as minorities, low socio-economic groups, and teenage women (Kessner 1973; Quick, Greenlick, and Roghman 1981). The components that are recommended for inclusion in prenatal care are medical examination with review and oversight; nutrition supplementation; genetic screening at least for selected and older women; counseling against smoking, alcohol consumption, and other substance abuse; restriction on use of medications; counseling and preparation for delivery, and mothercraft; and planning for intrapartum and postpartum care of mother and infant.

Most public health authorities urge a standard that strives for participation of at least 90 per cent of pregnant women in prenatal care beginning in the first trimester. This standard fails appreciably for inner city residents, and for teenagers, many of whom conceal or deny their pregnancies as long as possible. Even among populations for whom participation is high little is known about the rates for inclusion of the various components of care. No reliable data are available on the relative weight that should be assigned those components for achieving favorable outcomes (Sokol *et al.* 1980).

Elevated blood lead levels

Some expert opinion holds that any blood lead level may be adverse. For purposes of screening, the Center for Disease Control has defined an elevated level to be anything in excess of 25 micrograms of lead per tenth of a liter of blood. Children with such levels are thought to require medical supervision to disrupt the exposure to lead and to evaluate for the possibility of adverse mental, behavioral, physical, or biochemical effects. The problem is not a small one; about 4 per cent of preschool children in the United States, 675,000 youngsters, have elevated blood lead levels. Rates are substantially higher for urban, low income, and black children. Among black preschool children from low income families nearly one in five have elevated blood lead levels (Mahaffey *et al.* 1982)

Sources of lead are commonly the painted walls in substandard housing, automobile exhaust, and industrial exposures, but the well-authenticated exposures to these sources account for only a part of the large numbers of children who carry excess amounts of lead in their bodies. A great deal more needs to be known about sources of lead and its significance for children's health. High blood levels are known to associate with poor cognition, behavior disorders, and serious acute episodes of encephalitis with resultant brain damage at times of illness when acidosis mobilizes stored lead out of bones into the blood and soft tissues (Needleman *et al.* 1979). The extent of these associations is not well documented. Much speculation surrounds estimates on the degree to which problems of cognition and behavior disturbance can be attributed to lead poisoning (DHHS 1982).

Population-based growth stunting

If only one measure were available to assess the health of children, their growth rates would be a defensible choice (Hansen, Freeseman, and Evans 1971). With minor exceptions – largely localized tribal groups – the growth of healthy well-nourished children the world over is thought to follow similar patterns and rates of increase. All other things being equal, black children of west African descent may grow a little faster than white children (Owen and Lubin 1973). Population-based growth stunting is defined as a failure to achieve a distribution of height for a given age group that conforms to standards established for a well-nourished healthy population of children. One example of population-based growth stunting would be a population in which 40 per cent of the children fall below the fifteenth percentile on standard growth charts. For a given child, shortness does not suggest poor health, so long as the rate of increase is consistent according to that child's percentile norm. But a group of children that is skewed toward shortness is suspect for stunting, most commonly due to nutritional deficiencies, intestinal infestations, or both.

A major US survey of children's growth was done in 1971, and periodic additional surveys have been done since then (Carter 1974). Populations of children who are poor, minority, or from migrant families show unfavorable growth patterns. Among two-year-old males from low income families, 42 per cent of white and 46 per cent of black children fell below the fifteenth percentile for height. Similar growth retardation was noted among low income families, with 46 per cent of white and 37 per cent of black two-year-olds falling below the fifteenth percentile on standard growth charts (American Academy of Pediatrics 1973).

Iron deficiency anemia

Iron deficiency is a pathologic condition in which there is an abnormally low concentration of hemoglobin, the iron-carrying component of red cells, in the blood. It can be caused by inadequate dietary intake of iron, low iron stores at birth (in the newborn) or blood loss. Elevated blood lead levels may also lead to iron deficiency. Normal hemoglobin and hematocrit levels cover a range that varies with age and gender.

Rates of iron deficiency anemia due to insufficient dietary intake are an indicator of the nutritional status of a population. It is both preventable and treatable, given an adequate diet and/or vitamin supplements. The proportion of pregnant women, infants, children and youth with iron deficiency anemia is thought to reflect the adequacy and availability of food programs, prenatal services, well baby care, and/or general preventive pediatric screening and care within a population (Popkin *et al.* 1981).

Motor vehicle accident fatalities

In the United States, motor vehicle fatalities are the leading cause of death among children and youth aged 1–19. Nearly 14,000 motor vehicle fatalities occur each year in this age group, more than three times the number of deaths from the second leading cause, cancer. Among children under thirteen years old, the highest motor vehicle *passenger* fatality rates occur among infants. The rates are especially high in the first six months of life when they average 9.0 per 100,000 infants as compared to 4.5 for one-year-olds and 3.0 for ages 6–12. The higher motor vehicle passenger fatality rate among infants has been attributed at least in part to the fact that infants are more likely than older children to ride in the front seat, held in an adult's lap, without use of safety restraints. Motor vehicle fatalities account for 20 per cent of all deaths in the 1–14 age group. Between 1968 and 1978, the rate for children under fifteen decreased 12.5 per cent from 10.4 to 9.1 per 100,000 (DHHS 1980).

Children who wear safety restraints, such as special infant or toddler car seats, are 50–70 per cent less likely to be killed in an auto accident than are unrestrained children. (Note: All car safety seats manufactured after 1 January, 1981 must now comply with strict federal safety standards established by the National Highway Traffic Safety Administration.) In Tennessee, the first state to enact legislation requiring use of safety restraints for children under four, the motor vehicle fatality rate for this age group decreased 55 per cent from 1979 (year of enactment) to 1981 (from 7.72 to 3.5 deaths per 100,000) (American Academy of Pediatrics 1981).

A number of environmental and social interventions have been shown to influence clearly and dramatically the motor vehicle fatality rate. A change in the motor vehicle fatality rate is a measure of the adequacy or inadequacy of a broad range of public health interventions; others include requirements that safety restraints be used for auto passengers and helmets for cyclists, changes in legal age for drinking and/or driving, improvements in vehicle and highway safety design, lowering the maximum speed limit, development of alternative bicycle paths, or imposing more stringent penalties on drunk drivers (Select Panel 1981).

Sentinel events (examples)

The following events require careful community diagnosis to determine where failure has occurred in the chain of policy and programmatic responsibility. Effective child health policy regards these as unnecessary events (Rutstein *et al.* 1976).

— Measles, a case or death
— Tetanus, a case or death
— Diphtheria, a case or death
— Tetanus, a case or death
— Congenital rubella syndrome
— Congenital syphilis
— Mental retardation due to untreated phenylketonuria or congenital hypothyroidism
— Vitamin D deficient rickets
— Appendicitis, death
— Death due to infantile diarrhea and associated dehydration

Other conditions that with careful study could provide useful information on health status or outcome for purposes of informing health policy include:

— Home accidents
— Child Abuse
— Suicides
— Homicide
— Abandoned babies

- Runaways
- Failure to thrive
- Multiple foster care placements
- Sexually transmitted diseases
- Handicapping conditions
- Scoliosis
- Learning disabilities and school failure
- Dental disease
- Hearing loss
- Visual problems
- Tuberculosis
- Severe behavioral disturbances
- Mental retardation
- Rh isoimmunization
- Morbidity associated with preventable or controllable environmental factors:

  (a) rodent bites
  (b) pesticide exposure
  (c) exposure to toxic substances
  (d) radiation exposure

- Health conditions associated with health behavior of youths and/or pregnant women:

  (a) smoking
  (b) drug abuse
  (c) alcohol use/misuse
  (d) obesity
  (e) anorexia

All of these conditions would benefit from careful definition, identification of possible data sources, and establishment of associations with their determinants. For purposes of this presentation a full discussion of all relevant child health outcomes is not essential. Analysis of a few of the most important outcome measures is sufficient to illustrate their importance for informing the development of child health policy. Other data, such as availability of resources or utilization, quality and cost of services, have important uses. Such data are abundant but their interpretation is sometimes contradictory when applied to public policy. Recognizing a few exceptions, such data do not provide the logically conclusive insights for advocating effective policy that fulfills explicit goals in terms of children's health. Better understanding of health outcome measures is required for that purpose.

Child health as a social value

The preceding discussion has emphasized three aspects of child health policy that would benefit from a more intense application of epidemiologic skills:

1 Careful analysis of the use of resources and the implementation of programs in order to explicate operative child health policies.
2 Precise definition of health status or health outcome measures for use in monitoring child health policy.
3 Linkage of child health outcomes to a full range of determinants and interventions, enabling better understandings for developing effective health policy on a population specific basis.

The third of these endeavors is by far the most neglected and most difficult. It is also the most controversial. If policy is to be developed that supports interventions of proven linkage to favorable outcomes, then some distortions may occur to some cherished but poorly documented services. These distortions could be harmful for services that might be highly effective, but for which linkage to favorable outcomes is weak only because of limitations of measurement methods. Can education or counseling stand the test that requires demonstrated effectiveness in terms of favorable health outcomes? Will health professionals welcome the de-medicalization of our concepts of health in ways that emphasize precise justification for essential programs and diminish the policy impact of intuition? The use of outcome measures suggests the adoption of outcome standards that allow for methods of accountability and evaluation of provider systems. Will that prospect be welcomed by providers? Answers to all these questions must be hedged in terms of how well the epidemiologic skills can be marshalled to document the relevance of resources and services to specific outcomes. No one knows how precisely that can be done, but the prospects are promising and should not be threatening in the long run. Available data will need to be supplemented by the thoughtful discussion of explicit social values and professional judgments.

The dramatic policy changes of 1980 were put in place, not because the proponents had better data, but because they had a well-structured ideology and political opportunity to implement it. Such policy shifts may well occur again. In these policy swings, children need to be protected against societal neglects, abuses, and oversights. Our prevailing economic and health policies may well continue to be negotiated among competing interest groups, but in that process the well-defined interests of children should be non-negotiable. That priority can be argued on the basis of national security, economy, or compassion. It is best established as a mark of a civilized people. Protecting the interests of children is clearly compatible with a broad range of political and economic styles, as the rest of the world can demonstrate to us.

The children's cause in this country has suffered much from shallow sentiment, from poorly focused good intention, and from diversion of limited resources to special interests. The approaches and techniques of epidemiology are a necessary emphasis for helping to achieve a higher level of collective responsibility for the well-being of children.

References

Alan Guttmacher Institute (1981) *Teenage Pregnancy: The Problem That Hasn't Gone Away*. New York: Alan Guttmacher Institute.
American Academy of Pediatrics (1973) The Ten-State Nutrition Survey – A Pediatric Perspective. Committee Statement. Evanston, Newsletter Supplement, January, 1973.
—— (1981) *A Family Shopping Guide to Infant/Child Automobile Restraints*. Evanston.
APHA Chartbook (1975) *Health and Work in America*. Washington, DC: American Public Health Association.
Baldwin, S. and Cain, V.S. (1981) The Children of Teenage Parents. In Frank F. Furstenberg, Richard Lincoln, and Jane Menken (eds) *Teenage Sexuality, Pregnancy and Childbearing*. Philadelphia: University of Pennsylvania Press, pp. 265–79.

Budetti, P.P., Butler, J., and McManus, P. (1982) *Federal Health Program Reforms: Implications for Child Health Care. Milbank Memorial Fund Quarterly* 60:1, 155–59.

Carter, J. (1974) *The Ten State Nutrition Survey. An Analysis.* Atlanta: Southern Regional Council.

Cassell, J. (1974) Psychosocial Processes and Stress: Theoretical Formulation. *International Journal of Health Services* 4: 471–85.

Centers for Disease Control (1982) Childhood Immunization Initiative, United States – 5-Year Follow-up. *Morbidity and Mortality Weekly Report* 31: 231–32.

Comprehensive NPHPRS Report (1980) *Services, Expenditures and Programs of State and Territorial Health Agencies, 1979.* Washington, DC: Association of State and Territorial Health Officials.

David, R.J. and Siegel, E. (1983) Decline in Neonatal Mortality Rates, 1968–1977: Better Babies or Better Care? *Pediatrics* 71(4): 531–40.

Davis, K. and Schoen, C. (1978) *Health and the War on Poverty: A Ten Year Appraisal.* Washington, DC: Brookings Institute.

DHEW (1979) *Healthy People: The Surgeon General's Report on Health Promotion and Disease Prevention.* Publication No. 79-55071. Washington, DC: US Government Printing Office, pp. 39–47.

DHHS (1980) Public Health Service. *Promoting Health, Preventing Disease: Objectives for the nation.* DHHS Publication No. 017-001-00435-9. Washington, DC: US Government Printing Office, pp. 21–24.

—— Public Health Service, National Center for Health Statistics (1982) Blood Lead Levels for Persons 6 Months to 74 Years of Age: United States, 1976–80. In J.L. Annest *et al.*, *Advance Data from Vital and Health Statistics.* DHHS Publication No. (PHS) 82-1250. Washington, DC: US Government Printing Office.

Donabedian, A. (1966) Evaluating the Quality of Medical Care. *Milbank Memorial Fund Quarterly* 44: 166–206.

Dubos, R. (1959) *Mirage of Health.* Garden City, NY: Doubleday.

EPSDT (1981) *The Possible Dream.* Washington, DC: US DHEW (HCCA, 77-24973).

Fein, R. (1967) *The Doctor Shortage, an Economic Diagnosis.* Washington, DC: Brookings Institute.

Gordis, L. (1973) Effectiveness of Comprehensive Care Programs in Preventing Rheumatic Fever. *New England Journal of Medicine* 289: 331–35.

Green, L.W., Wilson, R.W., and Bauer, K.L.G. (1983) Data Requirement to Measure Progress in the Objectives for the Nation in Health Promotion and Disease Prevention. *American Journal of Public Health* 73: 18.

Greenstein, R. (1983) Center on Budget and Policy Priorities, Washington, cited by Rowan, C.T., *Field Enterprises*, February, 1983.

Haanes-Olsen, L. (1972) Children's Allowances: Their Size and Structure in Five Countries. *Social Security Bulletin*, May 1972: 17–28.

Hansen, J.D.L., Freeseman, A.D., and Evans, D.E. (1971) What Does Nutritional Growth Retardation Imply? *Pediatrics* 47: 299–313.

Illich, I. (1976) *Medical Nemesis*. New York: Random House.

Keniston, K. and the Carnegie Council on Children (1977) *All Our Children. The American Family Under Pressure*. New York: Harcourt, Brace, Jovanovich.

Kennedy, E.T. and Gershoff, S. (1982) Effect of WIC Supplemental Feeding on Hemoglobin and Hematocrit of Prenatal Patients. *Journal of American Dietetic Association* 80: 227–30.

Kennedy, E.T., Gershoff, S., Reed, R., and Austin, J.E. (1982) Evaluation of the Effect of WIC Supplemental Feeding on Birth Weight. *Journal of American Dietetic Association* 80: 220–27.

Kessner, D.M. (1973) *Infant Death: An Analysis by Maternal Risk and Health Care*. Washington, DC: Institute of Medicine, National Academy of Science.

Kotch, J.B. and Thomas, L.P. (1982) *Family and Social Factors Associated with Confirmation of Child Abuse Reports*. Presented at annual meeting APHA, Montreal, Canada, 15 November, 1982.

Kotch, J.B. and Whiteman, D. (1982) Effect of the WIC Programs on Children's Clinic Activity in a Local Health Department. *Medical Care* 20: 691–98.

Kovar, M.E. (1982) Health Status of U.S. Children and Use of Medical Care. *Public Health Reports* 97: 3–15.

Lazar, I. (1980) Social Research and Social Policy – Reflections on Relationships. In R. Haskins and J. Gallagher (eds) *Care and Education of Young Children in America*. Norwood, NJ: Ablex, pp. 59–71.

Longo, L.D. (1980) Environmental Pollution and Pregnancy: Risks and Uncertainties for the Fetus and Infant. *American Journal of Obstetrics and Gynecology* 137: 162–73.

McGee, E.C. (1982) *Too Little, Too Late: Services for Teenage Parents*. New York: Ford Foundation.

McKeown, T. (1976) *The Role of Medicine. Dream, Mirage, or Nemesis?* London: Nuffield Provincial Hospitals Trust.

Mahaffey, K.R., Annest, J.L., and Roberts, J. (1982) National Estimates of Blood Lead Levels: United States, 1976–1980. *New England Journal of Medicine* 307: 573–79.

Menken, J. (1981) The Health and Social Consequences of Teenage

Childbearing. In Frank F. Furstenberg, Richard Lincoln, and Jane Menken, *Teenage Sexuality, Pregnancy and Childbearing*. Philadelphia: University of Pennsylvania Press, pp. 167–83.

Miller, C.A., Moos, M.-K., and Kotch, J.B. (1981) Role of Local Health Departments in the Delivery of Ambulatory Care. *American Journal of Public Health* 71 suppl.: 15–29.

Morehead, M., Donaldson, R.S., and Seravalli, M.R. (1971) Comparison Between OEO Neighborhood Health Centers and Other Health Care Providers of Ratings of the Quality of Health Care. *American Journal of Public Health* 61: 1294–1306.

Morris, N.M. and Vory, J.R. (1975) Shifting Age Parity Distribution in Infant Mortality. *American Journal of Public Health* 65: 359–62.

Navarro, V. (1974) A Critique of the Present and Proposed Strategies for Redistributing Resources in the Health Sector and a Discussion of Alternatives. *Medical Care* 12: 721–42.

Needleman, H.L. and Leviton, A. (1979) Deficits in Psychologic and Classroom Performance of Children with Elevated Dentine Lead Levels. *New England Journal of Medicine* 300: 689–95.

Newland, K. (1981) *Infant Mortality and the Health of Societies*. Worldwatch Paper 46. Worldwatch Institute, Washington, DC, December, 1981.

Nuckolls, K.B., Cassel, J., and Kaplan, B.W. (1972) Psychosocial Assets, Life Crises, and the Prognosis of Pregnancy. *American Journal of Epidemiology* 85: 431–41.

Owen, G.M. and Lubin, A.H. (August 1973) Anthropometric Differences Between Black and White Preschool Children. *American Journal of Diseases of Children* 126: 168–69.

Popkin, B.M., Akin, J., Kaufman, M., and MacDonald, M. (1981) Nutritional Program Options for Maternal and Child Health: A Summary. The Report of the Select Panel for the Promotion of Child Health, vol. IV. *Better Health for Our Children: A National Strategy*. Washington: US Government Printing Office, pp. 87–125.

Quick, J.D., Greenlick, M.R., and Roghman, K.J. (1981) Prenatal Care and Pregnancy Outcome in an HMO and a General Population. *American Journal of Public Health* 71: 381–90.

Rutstein, D.D., Berenberg, W., and Chalmers, T.C. (1976) Measuring the Quality of Medical Care: A Clinical Method. *New England Journal of Medicine* 294: 582–88.

Salkind, N.J. and Haskins, R. (1982) Negative Income Tax. The Impact on Children from Low Income Families. *Journal of Family Issues* 3: 165–80.

Saward, E.W. and Fleming, S. (1980) Health Maintenance Organizations. *Scientific American* 243: 47–53.

Schorr, L.B., Miller, C.A., and Fine, A. (1983) Current Child Health

Monitoring Efforts Using Outcome Measures. Paper presented at Workshop on Indicators for Monitoring Child Health Outcomes, Cambridge, Mass., 23 January, 1983.

Select Panel for the Promotion of Child Health (1981) *Better Health for Our Children: A National Strategy*, Vols. 1, 2, and 3. DHHS, PHS, Publication No. 79-55071. Washington, DC: US Government Printing Office.

Smedby, B. and Ericson, A. (1979) Perinatal Mortality among Children of Immigrant Mothers in Sweden. *Acta Paediatrica Scandinavica Suppl.* 275: 41–6.

Sokol, R.J., Woolf, R.B., and Rosen, M.G. (1980) Risk, Antepartum Care and Outcome: The Impact of a Maternity and Infant Care Project. *American Journal of Obstetrics and Gynecology* 56: 150–56.

Sparer, G. and Anderson, A. (1972) Cost of Services at Neighborhood Health Centers. *New England Journal of Medicine* 286: 3–7.

Zelnik, M. and Kantner, J.F. (1980) Sexual Activity, Contraceptive Use and Pregnancy among Metropolitan-area Teenagers: 1971–1979. *Family Planning Perspectives* 12: 230–37.

Two

Nutrition and health policy

David M. Paige and

Lenora R. Davis

Overview

Nutrition policy involves consideration of health on a broad basis taking into account the entire social, political, and economic fabric of the community, the availability of solid scientific evidence, and the need for modification as conditions change and new information is obtained (Paige and Egan 1985). The National Nutritional Consortium of 1980 arrived at a consensus that the development of nutrition policies should be evolutionary and be based on new scientific information and clinical experience. Nutrition and health policy have occupied the attention of scientists, economists, planners, statesmen, and politicians for a considerable period of time. Volumes of information have been generated over time while many individuals continue to be inappropriately or inadequately fed.

Feeding populations is not a new issue but an old crisis, a matter which has historically been a concern of all governments. It is an old problem that presents its challenge anew in every era. In the late twentieth century, the challenge once again is that of providing food for all amidst crises of energy, population growth, and pollution. In previous times the political, social, and economic problems were different, but the question was the same. Chinese dynasties for example rose and fell strictly by their ability to provide for the distribution of the rice harvest; Henry IV of France pursued a social policy which had as its stated objective that "there be no laborer in his kingdom so poor that he could not have boiled fowl for his Sunday meal." More modern politicians have made similar pronouncements, but in different terms. For example, in 1923 the League of Nations Committee on the Relations of Nutrition to Health, Agriculture, and Economic Policy reported that "the ultimate responsibility for the nutrition and health policy of a nation must rest with that nation's Government." Joseph Goldberg came to the same basic conclusion while studying pellagra in the American South as a member of a government commission. So, both by tradition and the reports of commissions, the responsibility for nutrition is placed squarely on the shoulders of government (Winikoff 1979).

Data requirements

To rationalize nutrition policy and provide the necessary data base for decision-making we require information about the state of health of a population or section thereof, as well as detailed knowledge of the food eaten. The first problem is the definition of optimum health, which is not easy. For example, what are appropriate levels of body weight for different age groups, different sexes, or ethnically different groups of a population (Neuberger 1981)? What is the appropriate weight to height, the proportion of body fat to lean body mass or head circumference in the infant? Triceps and subscapular fat-fold estimates are still being refined and other measures of lean body mass evolving. Are there clearly defined values for hemoglobin levels in man, are there age specific differences, and are they different for the two sexes? Similarly, what is the appropriate cholesterol level? What population specific factors are necessary to consider? Recommended dietary allowances may represent satisfactory estimates of population requirements, but they are however often less than precise. Pragmatic solutions to these questions may be arrived at but the scientific justification for many of the conclusions is often not available (Elwood 1981).

Dietary information

Further, it is difficult to obtain reliable information about individual food consumption patterns over long periods of time. Nevertheless, figures are available of the annual production of food and of imports and exports of a variety of foodstuffs. These figures may provide some information of changes in consumption, but fail to identify how much of the various items actually reaches the table, and how much is wasted, either before or after it is offered to individual members of the household (Elwood 1981).

In addition, no information is provided about individual variation, or variations between different groups. While it is technically feasible to get information about how much an individual actually eats by weighing and accurately recording each food item, this process is costly and replete with its own methodological problems. For example, large-scale assessment is clearly not feasible. Apart from the difficulty of obtaining the necessary cooperation, there is no assurance that those not cooperating are representative of the population of interest. Despite the imprecision of the data some semi-quantitative estimates are available which can be used, and have been used, by those concerned with nutrition policy. This data is useful for planning, agricultural production, food processing, and education. It may also be helpful in identifying certain groups considered to be at nutritional risk.

Additionally, information would be useful in determining how effective dietary advice has been in revising dietary practice. Has, for example, nutrition education influenced the fiber content of the diet, and if so, which segments of the population have altered their practices? Has the proportion of unsaturated fatty acids in the diet been modified? Clearly it is important to health policy that information on these subjects be available. Epidemiologically, monitoring and surveillance of the population may provide this essential data base (Neuberger 1981).

Data synthesis

All too often, nutrition scientists seem unable to correlate
their findings about the state of nutriture of individuals with
socio-economic variables. This inability, coupled with over-
caution in analysis of economic determinants of consumption,
means that advocacy is all too often left to consumer
spokesmen with, frequently, incomplete understanding of
health priorities in human nutrition. The often exaggerated or
inaccurate statements of such spokesmen, instead of prompting
nutrition scientists to seize a more direct educational role,
appear to drive them further away from such a role. For
example, since the 1969 White House Conference on Food,
Nutrition, and Health, federal expenditures on food programs
(food stamps, school lunch and breakfast programs, summer
food programs, community meals and meals-on-wheels for the
elderly and shut-ins, and special programs for pregnant and
nursing women and infants) have risen from $600 million to
over $6 billion without adequate monitoring of their relative
effectiveness.

Ongoing nutritional surveillance of the nation, recommended
by the conference, has not been organized, despite the fact that
in the United States the population has gone through a massive
change in the nature of the food supply, dramatic increases in
the price of many foods, and a deep economic recession. There
have also been changes in welfare and social security legislation,
and in the size of government food programs, all without any
serious effort being made to follow the food intake levels or
other nutritional measures of the various groups in our
population (Dwyer and Mayer 1979).

Nutritional assessment

The nature and scope of nutritional assessment underpins any
nutrition surveillance effort. Assessment of nutritional status
is needed in order to:

1 determine whether poor health results from inadequate or
  inappropriate nutrition;
2 determine the precise nature of the nutritional problem
  underlying such health impairment;

3 provide information on which to base dietary care for health improvement; and
4 evaluate the effectiveness of nutritional interventions that may be undertaken to improve health (Paige and Egan 1985).

Methods of assessment

Methods of nutritional assessment include anthropometry, clinical evaluation, laboratory assessment, and dietary evaluation. Each method has strengths and limitations with no single measure providing a comprehensive index to nutritional health. Anthropometric evaluation provides accurate and reliable measures of body size and proportion that are helpful in detecting nutritional deficiencies or excesses and in delineating normal growth. Anthropometry provides a rapid and quantitative means of nutritional assessment. Nevertheless, it is limited in that it can only identify nutritional abnormalities that have resulted in measurable change. More subtle subclinical changes may not be detected (Trowbridge 1983).

Clinical examination provides an overall index of the nutritional status of the patient. The examination may reveal specific signs of malnutrition when these exist. It is important to note, however, that many early nutritional deficiencies may not yet have reached a clinical threshold and may only be recognized by laboratory evaluation.

The laboratory may be used to identify specific nutrition-related abnormalities such as anemia, iron deficiency, or hypoproteinemia, prior to these conditions being clinically apparent. Nevertheless, biochemical tests are specific for a particular nutrient, so that one must suspect on the basis of clinical assessment that a deficiency may exist in order to employ appropriate biochemical tests. Of course, laboratory results alone may be misleading and thus it is important to review and interpret them in the context of the clinical, anthropometric, and dietary information (Russell and Greenberg 1983; Trowbridge 1983).

Diet evaluation is an important adjunct to anthropometric, clinic, and biochemical assessment. It provides a description of the dietary background that may serve to explain observed clinical or biochemical abnormalities and can suggest appropriate interventions. It is difficult, however, accurately to quantify dietary intake and to infer that dietary patterns obtained by assessment techniques are indicative of long-term dietary habits. Dietary evaluation provides information about dietary habits, patterns, and practices and is not a measure of nutritional status (Trowbridge 1983; Russell and Greenberg 1983; and Kennedy 1983). In addition, data on vital statistics, in particular infant mortality rate, perinatal mortality, and birthweights may augment available information on nutritional status. Such data are of particular value in the context of nutritional assessment in developing countries and in assessing trends over long periods in developed countries (Jelliffe 1966).

Given the broad range of nutritional deficiencies, no single measurement can adequately define nutritional status. The indicators to be used in ascertaining the nutritional determinants of health and diseases within populations must be carefully selected and properly targeted to the objectives. It is important to understand the natural history of nutritional disease and plan assessment accordingly (Béhar 1976; Paige and Egan 1985).

Nutrition monitoring

Nutrition monitoring includes that set of activities which are necessary to provide information about the role and status of factors which bear on the contribution that nutrition makes to the health of populations. The primary nutrition monitoring activities are assessments of nutritional and dietary status through nationwide survey. To date it has hardly fulfilled its potential in serving as a secure basis for the design or implementation of health policy.

A number of reasons are given to support the need for nutrition monitoring of populations in a community which bear directly on public health decisions and nutrition policy. Habicht, Meyers, and Brownie (1982) have cited the following purposes.

1 To identify through screening individuals within the population that may be helped by nutrition programs.
2 To assess the nutritional status of populations and determine the need for programmatic intervention in populations or

appropriately defined subgroups to prevent or reduce specific nutritional deficiencies.

3 To permit the timely identification of a changing, shifting, or a deteriorating nutritional status of the monitored population. This early warning permits modifications or changes in ongoing nutritional programs, including the elimination of old programs which have either succeeded and are no longer necessary or have failed in their objective. It permits the identification of new or continuing deficiencies and permits the targeting of new programmatic efforts.

4 To provide a base for evaluation of a program's effectiveness and efficiency in meeting program objectives, which is necessary to assure wise use of resource.

5 To enable one to make judgments regarding nutritional cause and effect from one location to another.

National nutrition monitoring system

Clearly, epidemiology can serve as a more effective basis for the design and implementation of health policy. In recognizing this fact, the US Congress in 1977 mandated the US Department of Agriculture (USDA) and the DHHS to develop a proposal for a comprehensive nutritional status monitoring system. The proposal, which was submitted in March 1978, had the following goals:

1 To provide the scientific information necessary to maintain and improve the nutritional status of the US population and the nutritional quality of the national food supply.

2 To collect, analyze and disseminate timely data on the nutritional and dietary status of the US population; the nutritional quality of the food supply; and the knowledge, attitudes and practices of the consumer.

3 To identify high-risk populations and geographic pockets of undernutrition as well as shifting patterns of risk in order to facilitate prompt intervention.

4 To develop standardized methods, criteria, policies, and procedures for nutrition monitoring.

5 To evaluate the implications for change in agricultural policy related to food production, processing and distribution.
(Haazland 1980)

The nutrition monitoring responsibilities of the DHHS and USDA complement each other. The DHHS activities generally focus upon health status and the association of health to nutrient intake; the USDA focus is directed at dietary status, the association of diet to socio-economic factors, and assurance that available US food supplies will meet the nutrient needs of the population.

The nutritional monitoring system is a complex assortment of periodically conducted interconnected activities. The activities include:

1 health status measurements
2 food consumption measurements
3 food composition measurements
4 dietary knowledge and attitudes assessments
5 food supply determinations

The basic elements of the federal monitoring system are the National Health and Nutrition Examination Survey (NHANES) and the Nationwide Food Consumption Survey (NFCS) (National Center for Health Statistics 1979; Paige and Egan 1985).

Household food distribution

Additional attention must be given to the systematic study of the household and intrafamily dynamics as they influence and impact the nature, character, and amount of foods consumed. Per Pinstrup-Andersen has warned against the "black box" approach to nutrition programs and policy formulation and evaluation. In this approach the point is made that often all of the multiple issues and processes through which program and policy decisions influence nutritional status are ignored and only the nutritional impact is measured. Rather one should measure key variables as well in determining factors and processes influencing nutritional status. They include:

1 ability of a household to acquire food;
2 household food acquisition behavior;

3 household food allocation behavior which in turn is influenced by:
  (a) perceived food and nutritional need,
  (b) income,
  (c) women's time allocation and constraints,
  (d) food preference,
  (e) cultural factors;
4 intake of nutrients and calories;
5 physiological utilization and activity level

(Pinstrup-Andersen 1983)

Frequently past evaluations have attempted to study the impact on selected indicators of nutritional status. This was done either partially or totally ignoring the intervening and confounding relationships that were responsible for or associated with other factors simultaneously impacting on the program being evaluated. To understand why programs and policies are more or less effective than others requires an understanding of the mechanisms by which their key components link immediate program effects to nutritional impact. One must identify the process components and study their interaction. The evaluation of a particular intervention therefore becomes a question of tracing program effects through specific relevant processes to estimate the impact on each of the relevant components.

Key elements in many, if not all, of the policies and programs are limited in number, yet there is a large number of possible policies, programs, and program combinations. If there is an understanding of how key elements influence nutritional status one may develop more effective policies and programs. This may be accomplished by choosing and combining specific components which are appropriate for the population and its environment.

Variables different from those directly influenced by a given policy must also be identified and measured. This includes the environment in which the program operates, difficult as it is to quantify. In the case of a food price policy or feeding program it is necessary to understand not only the level of nutrient intake but also the influence of sanitary conditions, educational level, economics, and underlying health on the utilization of food. The decision as to which variable to select is an indicator of the degree of penetration of a particular study.

Clearly, the greater the penetration of a particular study the greater the data requirements. An example of a low level of penetration is illustrated by the use of program and policy impact on total food availability. While often misleading and ineffective, this variable is frequently used in assessing food production programs and policies. A greater degree of penetration, albeit limited, is provided by the ability of households with evidence of undernutrition to obtain food. The use of actual household food acquisition patterns as a nutrition indicator is an important improvement insofar as it recognizes household behavior. It is used widely in the assessment of food policy. It is also an indicator of existing malnutrition and its distribution in a population. Estimates of intakes by undernourished and malnourished individuals provide another improvement over household food acquisition data. While sometimes used to study food supplementation programs, these estimates are not used as frequently as estimates of total household food acquisition because of the difficulty in obtaining reliable data.

The activity level of an individual may also be used as an indicator of nutritional effect. This indicator is based on the fact that individuals suffering from inadequate caloric intakes may reduce energy output by lowering their activity levels. This energy conservation may affect the development of children, reduce labor supply, and overall population productivity. Despite the importance of this variable studies have been limited except for a few studies of the impact of food supplementation on labor productivity. The infrequent use of this variable may be in part due to the difficulties in measuring activity levels.

Mortality and morbidity have also been used as indicators of nutritional status. They may have limited usefulness provided that (a) nutrition program impact can be separated from other environmental factors, (b) the study sample is sufficiently large, and/or (c) the rates being studied before program intervention were relatively higher before the program was studied and analyzed. Finally, the clinical and biochemical indicators described earlier may also be utilized as independent or dependent variables (Pinstrup-Andersen 1983).

Despite the data generated by physicians, nutritionists, and economists, they are not likely to solve the problems they must address within the realm of food policy alone. Their disciplines are too narrow and often too parochial to achieve policy objectives. What is necessary lies beyond any and all of these disciplines. It involves policy-planning objectives based on broader considerations than dollars or health. Other considerations based on additional human values and views must be taken into account. To this end policy planning involves a fusion of disciplines, with different objectives and broader intervention strategies (Dwyer and Mayer 1979).

Nutrition policy

It must be realized that policy considerations will only incompletely reflect the scientific data available inasmuch as nutrition policy also reflects the prevailing political and social climate. Further, scientific information, surveillance data, and survey results may be incomplete, ongoing or controversial. Respected investigators not infrequently draw different inferences from similar data sets. The creative tension that results from vigorous scientific debate may often lead to erratic, confused, disjointed, and incoherent nutritional policy. Shifting political considerations coupled with competing economic priorities lead to further inconsistencies in national policy. Commodity support and surplus food distribution may be incompatible with food choice, nutrition education, and the use, for example, of a voucher system or food stamps in the open market-place. Utilization of public health clinics for supplemental food distribution may fail to enroll the hungriest within a community – the migrants, the rural poor with no transportation, the feeble and the elderly.

Clearly one cannot directly connect the results of scientific research to the origins of a particular nutrition policy. Due to the inherent complexity of public policy formation it is difficult to make this sort of connection. Policy formation evolves over time and cannot be attributed to a simple or single event. It involves a large number of decision points involving epidemiologically derived data, scientific testimony, special interest lobbying, a senate vote, a presidential impoundment, or an appellate court ruling (Hayes 1982a: 6–7). Policy formation is therefore not susceptible to easy description by simple additive models. A variety of conditions shape policies. In this dynamic process forces frequently interact in complex ways that are difficult, if not impossible, to disentangle.

Elements of policy formation

Nevertheless one can group the components of the policy formation process into six general categories:

1 Research, including knowledge-building, problem-exploring, policy-forming, and program-directing studies that are introduced into the policy process to support or refute the position of program proponents and/or opponents.
2 Contextual factors, including those social, economic, demographic, political, and ideological factors that shape the overall context of federal decision-making at any given point in time.
3 Constituency activities, including direct and indirect pressure, exerted by both organized and unorganized constituencies outside the federal government.
4 Actors and institutions, including those that participate directly in the federal decision-making process in the legislature, executive, and judicial branches of government.
5 Principles and ideas that shape a participant's vision or policy goal.
6 Media presentations, including television, radio, and the popular print media such as newspapers and magazines (Hayes 1982b: 38).

A case study: WIC

A case study of federal food assistance programs having their origins in the mid-1930s provides the necessary perspective on the evolution of nutrition and health policy. The creation of policy in this area can be traced to Congress passing the Agricultural Adjustment Act which provides for millions of dollars in surplus farm products to be made available to children. This was the forerunner of today's legislation providing for school feeding programs, milk programs, and Special Supplemental Food programs for pregnant and lactating women, infants, and children (WIC). The initial program operated in conjunction with the Work Projects Administration, with the USDA funnelling some surplus food to schools and relief programs. With the wartime disruption of international markets in 1939, the USDA expanded domestic distribution outlets, particularly the School Lunch Program. When the United States entered the war, the food surplus was absorbed by allied and domestic needs. Nevertheless, the USDA continued the lunch program as a wartime exigency. In 1945 the lunch program drew political support not only from farm interests but also from local school districts, PTAs, state school administrators, and health officials. In 1947, Congress made the School Lunch Program permanent.

Until the Great Society programs of the 1960s, Congress enacted only one other food assistance initiative for children: the Special Milk Program. In 1956 a glut of milk increased federal surplus holdings to unmanageable levels. With the support of the USDA and dairy interests, Congress created a milk distribution program for children in schools, summer camps, and other institutions to ease the government's surplus holdings. The Special Milk Program was significant for two reasons. First, the program represented the only postwar effort to provide food assistance to children outside school. Second, every administration since Eisenhower had tried unsuccessfully to curb the program on the grounds of an improved dairy situation or the failure of the program to target aid to needy children.

In 1966, Congress passed the Child Nutrition Act, shifting food assistance resources to children in poor areas, whose nutritional needs were presumably greater. The act was part of a general movement in the mid-1960s away from agriculturally determined food assistance programs and toward programs specifically directed to disadvantaged groups. This movement reflected a growing coalition of school interests and anti-poverty and anti-hunger groups. There was, however, no irreconcilable antagonism between members of Congress representing either farm or anti-hunger groups; indeed, several came to represent both.

Among congressional supporters the idea of targeting food assistance to poor, malnourished children grew in the 1967–68 period. Congressional support increased with growing media exposure to the problem of hunger in the United States.

Attention to economic equality and the civil rights movement prompted an increase in federal food assistance. The Johnson administration responded to these pressures with the Supplemental Food Program. A number of scientific reports have emphasized the vulnerability of the near-term fetus and young infant to nutritional insults. Additional studies suggest long-term developmental sequelae to those pregnant women and young infants inadequately fed. Epidemiologic studies suggest that in addition to stunted growth, cognitive development would be compromised. Based in part on medical research on the effects of inadequate nutrition on fetal and infant development, and in part on the enormous political appeal of feeding infants and pregnant women, the Supplemental Food Program supplied special food packages to provide additional nutrition to this group. The program was modest with a budget of approximately $12 million. This program was quickly engulfed by the Nixon administration's decision to replace all in-kind food assistance with stamps. The administration's decision was predicated on the potential integration of all food assistance programs into a more comprehensive welfare program, the Family Assistance Plan.

To assess the viability of a changeover of the Supplemental Food Program into a voucher program in 1970 the USDA commissioned Dr David Call of Cornell University to assess the viability of creating a voucher program to substitute for the Supplemental Food Program. Call found that targeting particular foods did not significantly increase their nutritional intake inasmuch as the added foods were shared by all members of the family. The failure of this study to show any positive effect and a growing interest in food stamps moved the administration away from targeted food programs. While advocates of the program were able to thwart the suspension of local programs the program remained in political limbo.

In 1972, the Senate Agriculture Committee, through a staff member, James Thornton, was made aware of two local food and medical assistance projects at St Jude's Hospital in Memphis and at Johns Hopkins University. The Johns Hopkins project had evolved from a housing and urban development (HUD) project in Baltimore City which provided iron-fortified infant formula to low income infants residing within their HUD census tracts. With the dissolution of this program a successor project was developed through a consortium of interest between Johns Hopkins University, a citizens' advocacy group, the Maryland Food Committee, and the Preventive Medicine Administration of the State of Maryland. The projects at both sites provided specific nutritional aid and medical care to infants and pregnant women in poor areas.

The projects reported reductions in the levels of iron deficiency anemia among the enrollees. As a result legislation was drafted creating a $20 million federal program in the mold of the Johns Hopkins–St Jude projects. Senator Hubert Humphrey introduced the bill in the Senate. Following a defeat in committee and debate on the floor, the Senate did pass the program as an amendment to the Child Nutrition Act. The House, despite USDA opposition, concurred. President Nixon signed the bill, and the Special Supplemental Food Program for Women, Infants, and Children (WIC) became law in December, 1972.

While the USDA had initially opposed passage of the program, a Senate amendment, included at the request of the department, mandated a complete medical evaluation of the program. It was anticipated that WIC would be found ineffective. The medical and health content of the program provided the rationale for the USDA to try to transfer it to the US Department of Health Education and Welfare (DHEW). Unsuccessful in accomplishing this goal, unclear as to its future course, the USDA was baffled as to the program's design and evaluation.

The USDA was perceived by various advocacy groups as deliberately delaying implementation in order to dismantle the program. Finally, in 1973, after considerable pressure, the Food Research and Action Coalition (FRAC), a public interest law firm, brought suit in federal district court against the USDA to require the department to spend the authorized funds for WIC.

Anticipating litigation when drafting the legislation, Senate staff members had used entitlement language that legally mandated the expenditure of funds. In addition, they had stipulated that WIC draw its support from funds other than the normal appropriations channels in Congress. As a result of these provisions, FRAC successfully obtained a court decision ordering the USDA to spend all the funds authorized for WIC in fiscal 1973. Since the fiscal year had nearly ended, the USDA was compelled to spend $20 million in three months. This order effectively annualized WIC's participation rate at $80 million.

The law and the litigation combined to produce a mechanism by which every delay, intentional or otherwise, or impoundment of WIC funds served only to compress the funds to be spent into a shorter time-span and across a larger number of participants. When WIC's two-year, $40 million authorization expired in 1974, Congress faced a decision concerning a program whose annualized expenditures exceeded $100 million. The following year Congress, amid growing support for the program, passed a child nutrition bill that exceeded administration requests by $1 billion. Included was a $250 million authorization for WIC. Proponents justified this expansion on the grounds of participation rates and evidence of WIC's success drawn from committee testimony and surveys.

Despite the USDA's delaying of WIC's implementation, the Office of Management and Budget (OMB) impounded a quarter of WIC's 1976 funds by spreading the authorization over an additional fiscal quarter. The FRAC again turned to the court and obtained an order compelling the USDA to spend all funds. This had the effect of annualizing WIC to a level of $440 million by the close of fiscal 1978.

Following this final court decision, the WIC evaluation, which was to have determined the fate of WIC, was completed. The WIC evaluation, conducted by Dr Joseph Edozien of the University of North Carolina as principal investigator, was released. Edozien reported that WIC infants evidenced increases in weight, height, head circumference, and mean hemoglobin concentration and that anemia decreased. Despite the evaluation's conclusion, the General Accounting Office (GAO) and several outside reviewers found it fraught with methodological and conceptual problems. GAO went so far as to question whether an evaluation of the type WIC required was even possible. The USDA outside advisory group also raised serious questions as to the conclusions reached in the report.

The Urban Institute study also added to the criticism of the program, demonstrating a series of results corroborating Dr Call's earlier finding of food sharing within the family. Nevertheless WIC programs continued to have an increasing number of supporters. When the GAO reported bad science, WIC's advocates saw only positive findings. What the Urban

Institute regarded as poor targeting, the advocates saw only as increases in clinic visits and a need for further participant education to prevent food sharing. A later evaluation of WIC by the Center for Disease Control reinforced, albeit with severe qualifications, Dr Edozien's conclusions. As a result of their interpretations of these epidemiologically based studies, advocates claimed that WIC was a positive program with demonstrated success; Congress agreed.

The USDA's food assistance program took on a new direction with the Carter administration. The WIC program became the centerpiece for the new administration's nutrition policy. WIC easily rebuffed a muck-raking attack on its efficacy that appeared in the *New Republic* and a futile attempt by HEW to have it transferred into the Bureau of Community Health Services. There was no significant support either for denigrating WIC or for removing it from the USDA once these advocates controlled its administration. Although in positions of authority at the USDA, however, they still had to deal with the OMB.

The USDA's initial proposal for the expansion of WIC called for a $600 million authorization in fiscal 1979. OMB scaled it back to $535.5 million and deleted the entitlement language from the bill. In the Senate, a bill similar to the administration's proposal was introduced but retained the entitlement language and set authorization levels of $550, $800, $900, and $950 million, respectively, for fiscal years 1979 through 1981. The OMB and the congressional budget committees resisted the entitlement language. Advocates managed to convince the committees to make an exception for WIC, due to its previous history of impoundments. OMB opposed the bill and rec- ommended a presidential veto. Pleas from the USDA and a congressional promise to reduce WIC's fiscal 1980 authorization to $750 million persuaded President Carter to sign the bill in the fall of 1978. Earlier efforts to restrain WIC's growth created a context in which congressional proponents and advocates could, even years later, expand the program at a rate unpre- cedented for social programs in the late 1970s (Hayes 1982c: 15–20; Radzikowski and Gale 1984).

In this case study it is clear that epidemiologically based studies formed the backbone of health policy decisions. It is equally clear, however, that the decisions were themselves complex policy issues which involved the interaction and balancing of many interests, agendas, and individuals. The

WIC program had, as an example, the strong endorsement of very powerful agricultural interests searching for new outlets for surplus foods. The needs of hungry children or pregnant women were not the central basis of their support. The strong interest on the part of a number of pharmaceutical houses was essentially the challenge of opening up new and relatively untapped markets in the public health area for infant formula distribution. The interests of a number of university scientists testifying in support of their research findings and the need for national intervention strategies were different. Yet a consortium of interest coalesced around a single nutrition health policy issue. Joined by anti-poverty and anti-hunger groups, as well as school administrators and social service providers, and reinforced by an increasing constituency in Congress and in public health clinics throughout the United States, the underpinning of the WIC program was served.

A case study: dietary goals

A case study of the scientific and policy considerations surrounding the formulation of the dietary goals for the United States is equally instructive. Prior to 1977, most public advice regarding diet planning was based on the "Basic Four Food Groups" published in 1957 by the USDA. Based on the Recommended Dietary Allowances (RDA), the "Basic Four Food Groups" translates needs for calories, protein, minerals, and vitamins into suggested numbers of servings of four categories of related foods (that is, meats and legumes, fruits and vegetables, dairy products, and cereals and breads). The most recent edition of *Food* (USDA 1979) created a fifth group. The grouping of foods into groups made a valuable tool for broad educational programs (McNutt 1980).

During the decade following the introduction of the "Basic Four Food Groups" there was increasing interest in the relationship of nutrition to the chronic degenerative diseases. This relationship was discussed and debated within the scientific and medical literature. A series of American Heart Association (AHA) statements released periodically beginning in 1957 illustrates the progression in their thinking about the diet–heart hypothesis. Their hypothesis ranged from an association of variables to a causal relationship between dietary fat and cholesterol and coronary heart disease (McNutt 1980).

In 1957, Dr Page *et al.* prepared a report to the AHA summarizing the evidence on the relationship between diet and atherosclerosis. The following conclusions were drawn from the available data presented:

1 diet may play an important role in the pathogenesis of atherosclerosis;
2 the fat content and total calories of the diet may be the dominant contributing factors; and
3 the type of fat, or the balance between saturated and unsaturated fats, also may be important (Grundy *et al.* 1982).

In 1961 a report was given to the AHA by an ad hoc committee authorized by the association to examine the possible relation of dietary fat to heart attacks and strokes (American Heart Association 1961; Grundy *et al.* 1982; McNutt 1980). This committee reached the following conclusions:

1 overweight persons should decrease their caloric intake and attempt to achieve their desirable weight;
2 weight reduction should be facilitated by regular, moderate exercise;
3 the composition of the diet should be altered by reducing intakes of total fats, saturated fats and cholesterol, and by increasing polyunsaturated fats;
4 particular attention should be given to dietary alteration by men at increased risk for CHD (e.g. those with a previous atherosclerotic event, a strong family history of CHD, elevated plasma cholesterol or hypertension); and
5 for those at high risk dietary changes should be carried out under medical supervision (Grundy *et al.* 1982).

In 1965, another statement on diet was issued by the AHA. It recommended caloric restriction to achieve desirable weight, substitution of polyunsaturated fats for saturated fats where possible, reduction in cholesterol intake and inclusion of the whole family in dietary changes. This report did not set limits for the different dietary constituents nor specify precise quantities. Three years later a new statement by AHA followed the same general recommendations, but it tried to define more precisely desirable intakes of different nutrients. Eight dietary guidelines were released (AHA 1967; Grundy *et al.* 1982; McNutt 1980). These were:

1 weight reduction to maintenance of ideal body weight;
2 reduce animal fat;
3 intake of fat set at 30–35 per cent of total calories with a distribution of one-third saturates, one-third monounsaturates, and one-third polyunsaturates;
4 a reduction of cholesterol intake to less than 300 mg/day;
5 apply dietary recommendations early in life;
6 maintain the principles of good nutrition with the change in diet;
7 adhere to dietary recommendations; and
8 make sound food habits a family affair.

Two statements have been issued since 1968, one in 1973 by the AHA Committee on Nutrition and the most recent in 1978, also by the AHA Committee on Nutrition. In 1972, the Committee on Foods and Nutrition of the American Medical Association (AMA) and the Food and Nutrition Board (FNB) of the National Academy of Sciences jointly advised physicians to employ dietary fat modification to lower serum lipids in high risk patients and to determine the extent to which such lowering reduced the risk of developing coronary heart disease. In 1977, the Senate Select Committee on Nutrition and Human Needs, chaired by Senator George McGovern, released a staff report entitled *Dietary Goals for the U.S.* This report made very specific, quantitative recommendations about a number of macro-nutrients (including fat, complex carbohydrates, and sugar), cholesterol and salt. Absent were two conventional admonitions: 1 maintenance of ideal body weight and 2 select a variety of foods each day (McNutt 1980). The report was revised in 1978 with the following specific goals:

1 to avoid overweight;
2 to increase consumption of starch by 20 per cent and decrease sugar consumption by 8 per cent and, thereby, to increase carbohydrate consumption by 12 per cent of total caloric intake;
3 to decrease consumption of monounsaturated and saturated fatty acids, and increase consumption of polyunsaturated fatty acids, to provide 10 per cent of each while reducing total fat consumption to 12 per cent of total caloric intake;

4 to reduce cholesterol consumption to 300 mg/day; and
5 to limit salt intake to 5 g/day (Harper 1981).

Congruent with the Senate Select Committee on Nutrition and Human Needs, the AHA in their 1978 statement had continued to recommend that the general public consume a diet containing no more than 30–35 per cent of calories as fat. They further stated that the decrement in saturated fats should be replaced by complex carbohydrates and polyunsaturated fats, but intake of polyunsaturates should not exceed 10 per cent of total calories. Cholesterol was limited to 300 mg/day. Relative low intakes of salt were suggested because evidence existed that suggested current levels of sodium intake may raise blood pressure in many people (Grundy *et al.* 1982).

The controversial nature of the dietary goals approach to disease control became immediately evident. Comments made by many scientists and organizations pointed up a number of oversights in the original edition (AMA 1977; Council for Agricultural Science and Technology 1977; Enloe 1977; Harper 1978; Hegstead 1978; Leville 1977–78; Mayer 1977; Oace and Ullrich 1977; Olson 1978; Senate Select Committee on Nutrition and Human Needs 1977; Simopoulos 1979). The authors of the report did not come to grips with the major questions raised about the appropriateness of the proposals. Underlying the proposals for dietary goals was the assumption that:

1 changes have occurred in the food supply and diet during this century;
2 an "epidemic" of degenerative diseases has occurred in the United States;
3 it was associated with the changes that have occurred in the food supply; and
4 modification to the diet was an effective method for the population at risk of reducing the incidence of chronic degenerative diseases.

Clearly, to determine whether the recommended action is appropriate is to consider the accuracy and reliability of the assumptions. The assumption that there have been changes in the food supply and thus in diets, is corroborated by the USDA data on food utilization. The quantity of calories from fat has increased approximately 12 per cent and the quantity from starches has decreased 12 per cent. Further, chronic degenerative diseases are the major causes of death in the United States and represent major medical problems, especially among the elderly, but the assumption that they are "epidemic" may not be accurate and their relationship to diet requires additional study. Inasmuch as an epidemic is the widespread occurrence of a disease not ordinarily present in a population, this may not be an accurate description. Chronic degenerative diseases have been endemic for centuries and accounted for 18 per cent of all deaths in the United States, even at the turn of the century when most deaths occurred from infectious diseases (Harper 1981).

If an epidemic is not an accurate characterization of the facts, then the implication that health has deteriorated as a result of a changing food supply and consumption patterns and that this has led to an epidemic level of chronic diseases requires further evaluation. Detailed information about the food supply indicates quantities of essential nutrients per capita equal to or exceeding those available earlier in the century. Nutritional deficiency disease is no longer a serious health problem. On the other end of the spectrum morbid obesity is a problem. The nutritional sequelae and health implications of mild to moderate obesity, the most commonly identified nutritional problem in the United States, is being debated.

The basis for dietary goals for the population is predicated on the fact that half the population is at risk of death from heart disease and has one or more risk factors. Thus the population is not to be considered healthy. While it is difficult to define health, those under sixty-five lose between five and six days per year from work, more than half of which are from accidents and acute illness (DHEW 1978). Under forty-five the major cause of death and disability is accidents or other forms of violence. Males who reach age forty-five have a life expectancy of 71–75 years, and females 77–80 years, white and non-white respectively (DHEW 1979). Health status has continued to improve during this century, and life expectancy at each age has increased. The assumption therefore that eating patterns and practices of this century represent "a critical public health concern" must be considered in the context of this fact.

The controversy over the promulgation of dietary goals when properly analyzed is a controversy over the adequacy of the scientific data for going beyond nutritional guidelines for health and recommending modification of diet as a public policy action for reducing the incidence of chronic degenerative diseases. The starting point for a public policy decision of this type should logically be the critical evaluation of the relevant scientific information to ensure that the action will both be appropriate and effective. After establishing this, further decisions as to the use of the information to achieve a policy objective may, at times, involve compromise.

Assessing the reliability of information used as the basis for proposing dietary goals or guidelines is a scientific problem. It can be resolved only through the use of the scientific method. In dealing with complex problems, such as relationships of diet and chronic disease, it may be difficult to design and conduct definitive experiments. New techniques and new information from other disciplines may be needed before this can be accomplished. Handler (1979) has noted that, despite these demands, implementation of public policy may be based on superficial and misleading interpretation of scientific information. The interpretation is often influenced by competing interests and pressure groups. He has emphasized that "the necessity for scientific rigor is even greater when scientific evidence is being offered as the basis for formulation of public policy, than when it is simply expected to find its way in the market place of accepted scientific understanding."

Nevertheless, in making decisions about public policy issues, other factors may be as important, or even more important, than scientific knowledge that clearly supports a specific decision. Political considerations, emotional reactions, pressures from groups who may profit from the policies, moral and ethical beliefs, and a desire to create the appearance of doing something about a difficult problem that is not understood, are just a few of the factors that may enter into public policy decisions. Consensus is commonly accepted as an appropriate method for deciding a public policy issue on which there is divergence of opinion. The FNB has developed a substantial list of needed research to establish dietary guidelines. It would appear much more logical to accumulate the knowledge necessary for establishing policy through research than to institute the policy before the research has been done (Harper 1981).

Role of research

The role of research in health policy can be categorized as knowledge-building (contributing to fundamental understanding of social and behavioral processes), problem-exploring (contributing to the definition of social problems), policy-forming (contributing to the formulation of policies to address specific social problems), and program-directing (contributing to the design and improvement of established programs). Each can have a different kind of influence on policy-making. Knowledge-building and problem-exploring research, for example, is most often influential in defining a problem or providing supporting justification for the initiation of a policy proposal. Policy-forming research is similarly influential at the stage at which a social problem is recognized and alternative policy proposals are under consideration or when a particular policy initiative is being conceived. Program-directing research usually has its greatest impact when specific programs are being designed or refined (Hayes 1982b: 38).

No single type of research appears certain to influence policy. An example of knowledge-building research on brain development and nutrition was extremely influential in the WIC program's initiation, debate, and expansion. There appear to be mediating events in this instance, however. The Johns Hopkins and St Jude's nutrition projects for pregnant women demonstrated to policy-makers how research on neurophysiological development could be employed to deal with a social problem. After WIC's inception this basic research remained a significant justification for the enactment and eventual expansion of the program.

Two examples of program-directing research, the Call study of the pilot voucher program and the USDA's study of the WIC program's delivery costs, had an influence on decision-making. This was used successfully to support opposition to the program's expansion for a period of time. Research can thus affirm or deny the policy initiative and have significant impact on the policy formation process.

On the relation of timing to influence, there are several examples of research having an impact at different points during the policy formation process. The more exploratory the research is, the more far-reaching its potential influence on the policy process. Conversely, the more directed toward specific programs the research is, the less applicable it is to contexts other than the operation and expansion of the particular program or immediate decision. Even if program-directing research is more likely directly to influence policy operation and expansion, it seems less likely to influence decision-making related to the formation of any other policy. The more directly focused a piece of research or analysis is on the operation of a particular program or decision, the more crucial its timing becomes. Hence, the Urban Institute's evaluation of the WIC delivery system had relatively little impact because it was introduced in the policy process after crucial decisions concerning the program's expansion had already been made.

The conflict between research studies related to WIC's program operation and those related to its medical justification illustrates the interaction of research with other components in policy formation. Although opponents of target-specific food assistance in the USDA and OMB did not deny the medical evidence linking proper nutrition to healthy infant development, they pointed to the two evaluations of target-specific delivery systems by Call and the Urban Institute as evidence of programmatic ineffectiveness. They argued that whatever its theoretical merits, food assistance could not be made target-specific. The USDA's determination stemmed from the overall administration policy of replacing all direct food distribution programs with food stamps and, ultimately, a unified, income-based welfare system. Further, the administration sought to eliminate programs with expensive delivery systems. There was a general resistance to take on any new food assistance program. The USDA was fearful of a shift from their traditional role of aiding farmers through price supports and marketing. The research that the USDA considered relevant or influential was a function of the larger policy imperatives.

Proponents of the program were selective in their use of the research data. Results that contradicted their assertions about WIC's efficacy were dismissed. Methodological criticisms were ignored as were other reservations concerning the quality of the evaluative research. In the debate over WIC's effectiveness, the proponents of the program were nevertheless successful. Two important factors were operating in their favor, one scientific and the other ideological: (1) basic research under-pinning the principle that good nutrition is required for optimal human development was unquestioned, and (2) feeding infants who were hungry was an activity that existing social values and sentiments reinforced. Congressional decision-makers had the intuitive sense that an effort of this type was good policy, both politically and morally.

During the program's development, evaluative and epidemi-ologically based research generated ambiguous results, although scientific findings introduced as evidence in the policy debate had affirmed the link between proper nutrition and healthy fetal and infant development. Equally consistent were the evaluations of target-specific food delivery systems: they did not work well. Other complicating factors were the result of two studies which had yielded results indicating that a carefully administered program could produce measurable effects. Yet the Edozien study encountered methodological criticisms, and the other, the Center for Disease Control study, qualified its conclusions to the point of precluding any program-wide extrapolations. Research and evaluation was relevant to policy formation only insofar as selected results were useful to proponents or opponents in advancing their causes (Hayes 1982: 83).

Difficulties exist in the interpretation of research data and its use in promulgating dietary goals. Animal studies provide interesting but limited assistance in interpreting the potential effectiveness of dietary goals (Kritchevsky 1979).

Species-specific differences, coupled with the ability sharply to manipulate components of the diet, make extrapolation difficult. In addition, the difficulty of assessing diet alone as an independent variable may be appreciated when one learns that as many as thirty-seven variables may be considered, on the basis of statistical correlations, to be associated with an increased risk of heart disease (Ernst and Levy 1980). Increased risk is associated with the male sex, smoking cigarettes, hypertension, elevated blood cholesterol, and diabetes. Lesser risk factors include physical inactivity, susceptibility to stress, certain dietary patterns, and overweight (Kannell 1978). It is clear that a large number of individual traits and environmental variables may be associated with the risk of degenerative diseases.

Epidemiology and nutrition policy

Epidemiology has not as yet fulfilled its potential in serving as a secure basis for the design and implementation of nutrition and health policy. Necessary changes predicated on a national scientific basis can only come about through the design, application, and utilization of epidemiologically based studies. This includes nutritional assessment of the population, nutrition monitoring, surveillance, national surveys of health and nutritional status, and food consumption surveys. Information gathered on an ongoing as well as intermittent basis will serve to describe the population, identify deficiencies, the level of risk, if any, and the subgroups of the population requiring intervention. Complementing this body of data will be scientific reports of dietary and nutritional needs as developed through experimental and applied study. Finally, a coherent national policy of dietary goals and objectives predicated on scientifically derived information will serve to provide the social, economic, and political context by which to attack this multifaceted set of issues.

References

American Council of Food and Nutrition and the Food and Nutrition Board (1972) National Research Council/National Academy of Sciences. *Journal of the American Medical Association* 222: 1647.

American Heart Association (1961) Ad Hoc Committee on Dietary Fat and Atherosclerosis. *Circulation* 23: 133–35.

—— Committee on Nutrition (1965) *Diet and Heart Disease*, pp. 1–4.

—— Committee on Nutrition (1968) *Diet and Heart Disease*, pp. 1–4.

—— Committee on Nutrition (1973) *Diet and Coronary Heart Disease*.

—— Committee on Nutrition (1978) *Diet and Coronary Heart Disease*.

American Medical Association (1977) Statement on American Medical Association to Select Committee on Nutrition and Human Needs 18 April. Washington, DC: US Government Printing Office.

Béhar, M. (1976) Appraisal of the Nutritional Status of Population Groups in Nutrition. *Nutrition in Preventive Medicine*. Geneva: World Health Organization, p. 559.

Council for Agricultural Science and Technology (1977) Dietary Goals for the United States: A commentary. Report No. 71, 30 November.

Department of Health Education and Welfare (1978) Facts of Life and Death. DHEW Publication No. (HRA) 74-1222. Washington, DC.

—— (1979) Healthy People – The Surgeon General's Report on Health Promotion and Disease Prevention. DHEW Publication No. 79-55071, Washington DC: US Government Printing Office.

Dwyer, J. and Mayer, J. (1979) Beyond Economics and Nutrition: The Complex Basis of Food Policy. In J. Mayer and J. Dwyer (eds) *Food and Nutrition Policy in a Changing World*. New York: Oxford University Press, pp. 9–10.

Elwood, P.C. (1981) Methods for the Evaluation of Nutritional Status. In Michael R. Turner (ed) *Nutrition and Health – A Perspective*. New York: Alan R. Liss, pp. 5–20.

Enloe, C.F., Jr (ed). (Nov./Dec. 1977) U.S. Dietary Goals. Twenty commentaries. *Nutr. Today* 12: 11.

Ernst, N. and Levy, R.I. (1980) Diet, Hyperlipidemia and Atherosclerosis. In R.S. Goodhart and M. Shils (eds) *Modern Nutrition in Health and Disease*. Philadelphia: Lea and Febiger.

Grundy, S.M., Bilheimer, D., and Blackburn, H. (1982) Rationale of the Diet – Heart Statement of the American Heart Association. *Circulation* 65 (4): 839A.

Haazland, G.W. (1980) *Feeding Children: Federal Child Nutrition Policies in the 1980's*. Washington, DC: US Government Printing Office.

Habicht, J.P., Meyers, L.D., and Brownie, C. (1982) Indicators for Identifying and Counting the Improperly Nourished. *American Journal of Clinical Nutrition* 35: 1241.

Handler, P. (1979) Dedication address. Northwestern University Cancer Center, 18 May.

Harper, A.E. (1978) Dietary Goals – A Skeptical View. *American Journal of Clinical Nutrition* 31: 310–21.

—— (1981) Dietary Goals In L. Ellenbogen (ed.) *Controversies in Nutrition*. New York: Churchill Livingstone, pp. 63–84.

Hayes, C.D. (ed.) (1982a) *Making Policies for Children: The Policy Determination Literature*. Washington, DC: National Academy Press, pp. 6–7.

—— (ed.) (1982b) *Making Policies for Children: Components of the Policy Formation Process*. Washington, DC: National Academy Press, p. 38.

—— (ed.) (1982c) *Making Policies for Children: Three Cases of Federal Policy Formation*. Washington, DC: National Academy Press, pp. 15–20.

Hegstead, D.M. (1978) Dietary Goals – A Progressive View. *American Journal of Clinical Nutrition* 31: 1504.

Jelliffe, D.P. (1966) The Assessment of the Nutritional Status of the Community. *WHO Monograph Series*, Series no. 53. Geneva: World Health Organization, pp. 63–78.

Kannell, W.B. (1978) Status of Coronary Heart Disease Risk Factors, Perspective. *J. Nutr. Educ.* 10: 10–14.

Kennedy, E. (1983) Evaluating Nutritional Status – Dietary Assessment. In D.M. Paige (ed.) *Manual of Clinical Nutrition*. Pleasantville, NJ: Nutrition Publications, pp. 11: 1–20.

Kritchevsky, D. (1979) Atherosclerosis and Nutrition. In H.H. Draper (ed.) *Advances in Nutrition Research*, vol. 2, pp. 181–98.

Leville, G.A. (1977–78) Establishing and Implementing Dietary Goals. Presented at Food and Agriculture Outlook Conference, USDA, 17 November, 1977; Establishing and Implementing Dietary Goals, National Live Stock and Meat Board, *Food and Nutrition News* 42(2): 1–4.

McNutt, K. (1980) Dietary Advice to the Public. *Nutrition Reviews* 38: 353–60.

Mayer, J. (Nov. 1977) Dietary Goals for the United States. *Family Health*, pp. 39–40.

NAS/NRC, FNB (1979) Research Needs for Establishing Dietary Guidelines for the U.S. Population. Washington, DC: NAS.

National Center for Health Statistics (1979) *Caloric and Selected Nutrient Values for Persons 1–74 Years of Age, United States 1971–1974*. Vital and Health Statistics, Series 11, No. 209. Washington, DC: US Government Printing Office.

National Nutrition Consortium (1980) Guides for a National Nutrition Policy. *Nutrition Reviews* 38 (2): 96.

Neuberger, A. (1981) Introduction. In Michael R. Turner (ed.) *Nutrition and Health – A Perspective*. New York: Alan R. Liss, p. 3.

Oace, S.M. and Ullrich, H.D. (eds) (1977) U.S. Dietary Goals. *J. Nutr. Educ.* 9: 152.

Olson, R.E. (1978) Statement to the Senate Select Committee on Nutrition and Human Needs, July 26. See Senate Select Committee (1977) Clinical Nutrition, An Interface Between Human Ecology and Internal Medicine. *Nutrition Reviews* 36: 161.

Page, I.H., Store, F.J., Corcoran, A.C., Pollack, H., and Wilkinson, C.F. (1957) Atherosclerosis and the Fat Content of the Diet. *Circulation* 16: 163.

Paige, D.M. and Egan, M.C. (1985) Community Nutrition. In Allan W. Walker and John B. Watkins (eds) *Nutrition in Pediatrics – Basic Science and Clinical Application*. Boston: Little, Brown, pp. 183–203.

Pinstrup-Andersen, P. (1983) Estimating the Nutritional Impact of Food Policies: A Note on the Analytical Approach. In *Household*

Food Distribution – Food Policy Symposium Food and Nutrition Bulletin 5 4: 16–21.

Radzikowski, J. and Gale, S. (1984) Requirement for the National Evaluation of School Nutrition Programs. *American Journal of Clinical Nutrition* 40: 365.

Russell, R.M. and Greenberg, L.B. (1983) Evaluating Nutritional Status – Adults. In D.M. Paige (ed) *Manual of Clinical Nutrition*. Pleasantville, NJ: Nutrition Publications, pp. 10.1–16.

Select Committee on Nutrition and Human Needs, US Senate (1977) Dietary Goals for the United States. First edition. Washington DC: US Government Printing Office, Stock no. 052-070-03913-2.

Senate Select Committee on Nutrition and Human Needs (1977) Dietary Goals for the United States – Supplemental Views. Washington, DC: US Government Printing Office.

Simopoulos, A.P. (1979) The Scientific Basis of the "Goals": What Can Be Done Now? *Am. J. Dietet. Assoc.* 74: 539–42.

Trowbridge, F.L. (1983) Evaluating Nutritional Status — Infants and Children. In D.M. Paige (ed.) *Manual of Clinical Nutrition*. Pleasantville, NJ: Nutrition Publications, pp. 9.1–28.

US Department of Agriculture, Agricultural Research Service (1957) Essentials for an Adequate Diet. Home Economics Research Report No. 3. Washington, D.C.: USDA.

—— Science and Education Administration (1979) *Food*. Home and Garden Bulletin No. 228. Washington, D.C.: USDA.

Winikoff, B. (1979) Introduction. In D.P. Jelliffe and E.F. Jelliffe (eds) *Nutrition and Growth*. Vol. 2 of R.B. Alfin-Slater and D. Kritchevsky (eds) *Human Nutrition: A Comprehensive Treatise*. New York: Plenum Press.

Three

Epidemiology and health policy:
coronary heart disease

S. Leonard Syme and

Jack M. Guralnik

Introduction

A major goal of epidemiologic research is to identify factors
involved in the etiology of diseases to prevent or control such
diseases. One of the ways in which research findings lead to
prevention and control programs is by influencing public
policy. The purpose of this paper is to examine the degree to
which epidemiologic research on coronary heart disease (CHD)
has in fact had an impact on public policies regarding this
disease.

To identify links between epidemiologic research and public
policy on CHD is an especially challenging task because this
disease has been of great public concern. In such a circumstance,
it is difficult precisely to identify specific and clearly defined
connections between particular epidemiologic research findings
and resultant policy: research findings often simultaneously

influence both policy and public opinion; in turn, policy and public opinion influence the initiation and direction of research. For this reason, we will make no attempt in this paper to isolate *the* major turning points in policy development as a result of particular research but will instead describe various policies regarding CHD with the understanding that epidemiologic research has been a major, but not the only, influential factor.

In the discussion to follow, an effort will first be made to summarize what is now known about the distribution of CHD in the population and about the major CHD risk factors. Three major risk factors have received most attention by medical researchers, the media, and the general public. These three factors were identified primarily as a result of large epidemiological studies in six communities in the United States and findings from these studies later led to several massive intervention programs. These intervention programs sometimes were aimed at the primary prevention of disease in high risk individuals, sometimes at prevention in the community, and sometimes at secondary prevention in persons who already had suffered a heart attack. While these programs were primarily research-oriented and focused on selected participants, they also have had impacts on policy-makers and the public at large because of enthusiastic media coverage of their findings.

Following a discussion of these research programs, we will then review several public policies that have emerged from this work. Our review will be organized around three central issues. The first issue concerns the dilemma of developing policy recommendations when doubt exists about the quality and completeness of available research data. The second issue is that in policy development some risk factors tend to be more heavily emphasized than others even though this may not be consistent with research evidence. The third issue is that virtually all CHD policy has been directed exclusively towards the individual, with much less consideration given to the full range of policy options that should be considered in the control and prevention of the disease: the unique perspective of epidemiology – to observe the distribution of disease in the community and to generate interventions at that level – has generally not been taken advantage of either in research or in policy development.

The epidemiology of coronary heart disease

Introduction

Arteriosclerotic cardiovascular disease, particularly coronary heart disease (CHD) and stroke, leads to more deaths, disability, and economic loss than any other disease (DHHS 1981). Coronary heart disease has been the leading cause of death in the United States (and many other industrialized countries) since 1950. During the last thirty years, a tremendous amount of research has been devoted to studies of CHD: this research has focused primarily on basic biological mechanisms and on improvements in medical care but considerable research also has been done on the epidemiology of CHD and it is to that body of evidence that this paper is directed.

Descriptive epidemiology

Coronary heart disease has its major impact in the developed countries of the world. Nevertheless, there are enormous differences in CHD among these countries, with mortality rates in 1977 ranging from 102.6 per 100,000 in Japan to 878.0 per 100,000 in Finland (DHHS 1981). Geographic differences in monthly rates also exist within countries. While these international and national differences have been the object of research inquiries, the reasons for such geographic variations remain largely unexplained.

Men have a greater incidence of CHD than women, with men showing a mortality rate two to four times greater than women in most industrialized countries. As with geographic differences, only a small part of this sex difference can be explained by known exogenous risk factors. Men and women also differ in the pattern of clinical manifestations of CHD: women with CHD have angina pectoris more frequently than men with this disease; however, when women have myocardial infarctions, they die from them at a much greater rate than men (DHEW 1968, 1977).

CHD increases with age. However, autopsy studies in less-developed countries have demonstrated that arteriosclerosis may be completely absent in very old people. This is also sometimes seen even in developed countries and suggests that arteriosclerosis may not be an inherent part of the aging process.

Worldwide, significant changes in CHD mortality rates have occurred over time. Explaining these trends has been a challenge to our understanding of this disease. In the United States, CHD mortality seems to have begun its rise in the 1920s (Anderson 1973). There was a well-documented continued and significant increase in mortality in the 1940s and 1950s. In the mid-1960s, mortality rates began to decline in the United States and, in the period from 1968 to 1978 the death rate for CHD dropped 27 per cent (Stamler 1981). While some other countries also show a decline in rates, most countries are experiencing either minimal declines or increases in rates.

A conference on the declining mortality from CHD in the United States was held in 1978. Conclusions from this meeting were that the reasons for the change could not be precisely identified (DHEW 1979b). Because CHD morbidity data is scant and conflicting, it is not known if the decline in mortality has been paralleled by a decline in overall incidence of CHD. If this were the case, a reduction in predisposing risk factors in the population would be implicated as a cause for declining mortality. On the other hand, a greater role for the effects of improved medical care would be implicated by a declining mortality in the face of a stable incidence rate.

Risk factors

In the late 1940s, the great public health impact of CHD was well appreciated, but little was known about factors which put one at increased risk of the disease. The importance of high blood pressure and cigarette smoking was being considered at that time and Ancel Keys had written several influential papers suggesting the importance of dietary fat (Keys 1953). However, for meaningful policy to be developed, it was imperative that these factors be systematically studied and evaluated. The US Public Health Service began to lay plans for a longitudinal study of CHD to follow a large population of people for many years. This study, initiated in Framingham, Massachusetts, was soon followed by several other large studies in Albany, Chicago, Los Angeles, and Minnesota. The importance of several risk factors became apparent as the years went by, and by the late 1950s, elevated serum cholesterol, hypertension, and smoking were recognized as major risk factors for CHD. Results from these studies and from two others which began later were eventually combined into the so-called Pooling Project (Pooling Project Research Group 1978).

By analyzing data obtained from a large number of people, the Pooling Project was able to make a significant contribution to our understanding of CHD epidemiology. Findings from the various studies were found to be generally comparable and predictive indices were refined not only for single risk factors but for risk factors in combination. Meanwhile, numerous other studies were initiated which gave additional information on these risk factors and identified new ones. More recently, research on risk factors has included intervention trials designed to demonstrate the beneficial effects of reducing known risk in affected individuals.

Cholesterol The link between serum cholesterol and CHD was suspected prior to the initiation of the major epidemiological studies of the 1950s. Animal feeding studies had shown that a diet high in cholesterol and saturated fat could raise serum cholesterol and induce atherosclerotic changes. Futher, cholesterol was known to be a major component of atherosclerotic lesions in humans. Following these early studies, numerous longitudinal investigations demonstrated a direct association in most age groups between the level of serum cholesterol and the rate of CHD (Pooling Project 1978). The relationship between dietary intake of cholesterol and serum cholesterol levels has also been examined in a variety of ways (Rifkind 1979; Stamler, 1978). International comparisons show a general tendency for countries with higher fat intake to have higher levels of serum cholesterol and higher rates of CHD (Keys 1980). However, there are many differences between these countries other than dietary intake. Most studies within homogeneous populations in the United States (such as in Framingham) have not shown a correlation between individual dietary fat intake and serum cholesterol level. This result is consistent with the finding that only a fraction of serum cholesterol is derived from the diet, the rest being synthesized in the liver. There have been a few studies, however, which have demonstrated a small but significant relationship between diet and serum cholesterol, the largest of which was the study of Western Electric workers in Chicago (Shekelle *et al.* 1981).

Efforts to demonstrate the beneficial effect for CHD of lowering dietary lipids have been made in several intervention trials (DHEW 1979b). A number of difficulties plagued these studies but ultimately most found no convincing evidence that CHD incidence could be modified by dietary changes. Two exceptions to this findings are notable. An intervention trial in two mental hospitals in Finland showed a lower CHD mortality rate in men on a cholesterol-lowering diet (Miettinen, Turpeinen, and Karvonen 1972). Although the dietary intervention in this study was not extreme, some have questioned whether the results are relevant for free-living populations. A five-year trial in Oslo was done with middle-aged men in which both smoking and diet were modified (Hjermann, Byre, and Holme 1981). Those in the experimental group experienced a lower incidence of both fatal and non-fatal myocardial infarction and sudden death when compared to the control group. The effect of diet modification alone on CHD mortality did not reach statistical significance in this study.

In summary, there is some evidence that diet can affect serum cholesterol and there is little dispute that elevated serum cholesterol is associated with an increased rate of CHD. However, these two relationships do not prove that diet affects heart disease. While intervention trials are useful in establishing a causal link between a risk factor and disease, most have been unable to prove this in studying diet and CHD. Because of the mass of other supportive data, there has been general agreement among the majority of people working in the field that this causal link probably exists, but others have argued there is a lack of solid scientific evidence to support it (Mann 1977). Thus, while it can be said that measuring an individual's cholesterol reflects risk of CHD, one is on less firm ground scientifically in assuming that a change in the person's diet will ultimately affect that risk.

A study to definitively prove that dietary modifications can alter CHD incidence would require a very large sample size and be extremely expensive. Because of this, investigators have sought insights into the effect of cholesterol lowering by the use of drug therapy. Early studies of various drugs were inconclusive because some produced significant side effects. Recent findings from the Lipid Research Clinics (Lipid Research Clinics Program 1984) demonstrated that cholestyramine therapy has a significant effect on lowering both serum cholesterol and CHD incidence in middle-aged hypercholesterolemic men. This study indicates that drug therapy is an effective way to prevent CHD in high risk men and suggests that cholesterol lowering by any means, including diet, might be beneficial.

The lipoprotein fractions of cholesterol have received a great deal of attention in the study of CHD (Inkeles and Eisenberg 1981). Serum lipids circulate in the bloodstream combined with proteins and laboratory methods allow for the separation and analysis of these lipoproteins. An inverse relationship between high density lipoprotein (HDL) cholesterol and CHD has been consistently found. Low density lipoprotein (LDL) cholesterol has a direct relationship with CHD incidence. The predictive power of measuring HDL cholesterol has been found to be greater than measuring total serum cholesterol. Interestingly, certain factors such as exercise and moderate alcohol intake, which are associated with a lowered CHD risk, also are associated with higher levels of HDL cholesterol.

A direct association between serum triglyceride and CHD has been shown. However, this can be entirely explained by the association that triglyceride has with cholesterol and other factors such as body mass and high density lipoproteins (Hulley *et al.* 1980). For this reason, it is unlikely that there is a causal relationship between triglyceride and CHD.

Hypertension Hypertension has emerged as probably the most important risk factor for CHD, both because of its potent effect on arteriosclerosis and its high prevalence in the population. Data from the Pooling Project showed a consistent and significant effect of blood pressure on CHD. Compared to the group with diastolic pressures under 85 mm Hg, those with a diastolic pressure over 105 mm Hg had nearly four times the number of first major coronary events and about three times the rate of CHD deaths. In the Framingham study (Kannell 1975), blood pressures over 140/90 mm Hg were found in 73 per cent of men and 81 per cent of women who died of CHD.

Three large intervention studies dealing with hypertension

have been done, two in the United States and one in Australia (Australian Therapeutic Trial in Mild Hypertension 1980; Hypertension Detection and Follow-up Program Cooperative Group 1979; Veterans Administration Study Group on Antihypertensive Agents 1967, 1970). All of these studies demonstrated significantly fewer strokes in those aggressively treated for hypertension. However, the Veterans Administration and Australian studies were unable to demonstrate a significant decrease in CHD deaths in the treated groups. One difficulty these studies had in showing benefit for CHD is suggested by the authors of the Australian study, who felt that the clear success in preventing stroke early in these trials prohibited them from running long enough to demonstrate a protective effect for CHD. Preliminary analyses of the Hypertension Detection and Follow-Up Program show a decrease in deaths from acute myocardial infarction in the intensively treated group compared to the control group (which received regular care from outside providers). Deaths from other forms of ischemic heart disease, however, were similar in the two groups.

While the benefits of treating moderate and severe hypertension have been generally agreed upon, questions have been raised recently about the overall benefits of drug treatment of mild hypertension (Kaplan 1983; McAllister 1983; Perry and Smith 1978).

Smoking   The relation of smoking to CHD has been firmly established. The Pooling Project found that risk is dose-related to the number of cigarettes smoked per day. More than three times the risk of CHD was seen in those smoking over one pack per day. This risk was found to be independent of the other coronary risk factors. As in most risk factors associated with CHD, the pathological mechanism by which cigarettes exert their deleterious effect remains speculative.

The causal relationship between cigarette smoking and CHD is supported by data on former smokers (DHEW 1979c). Ex-smokers have a lower risk of CHD than if they had continued to smoke. The longer the time an individual has abstained from cigarettes, the more his risk of CHD resembles that of a lifetime non-smoker.

Other risk factors High serum cholesterol, hypertension, and smoking have been focused on as the "big three" risk factors for CHD. They were the first to be clearly identified and have been the risk factors addressed in most intervention studies. However, a variety of other risk factors have emerged from epidemiological research and they have added a great deal to our understanding of CHD.

Numerous dietary and metabolic factors have been examined in relation to CHD. While diabetics have higher lipid levels, higher blood pressures and a greater prevalence of obesity, it has been demonstrated that even after controlling for these risk factors and for cigarette smoking, diabetes still has an independent positive relationship to CHD (Garcia *et al.* 1974). Mild overweight is not a risk factor, but significant obesity leads to a marked increase in CHD through its direct relationship with blood pressure, serum cholesterol and diabetes (Fitzsimmons 1982). The role of dietary salt in hypertension is a complex one. While a fraction of the population may manifest hypertension with moderate salt intake, there is no strong evidence that lowering salt intake in the entire population would lead to a significant decrease in arteriosclerotic cardiovascular disease by diminishing the prevalence of hypertension (Tobian 1979a, b). Moderate alcohol intake is associated with a lower risk of CHD but heavy drinking does not provide a protective advantage and may even lead to increased risk (Evans 1980).

There are rare, simply inherited forms of hypercholesterolemia which are clearly associated with premature arteriosclerosis and death (Robertson 1981). Aside from these, there is evidence from epidemiologic studies that a positive family history for CHD prior to age fifty puts one at increased risk (Voller and Strong 1981). This risk is greater for those with first-degree relatives with premature CHD. The cause of this familial pattern is unclear and may relate to such diverse factors as the genetic determination of cholesterol metabolism and coronary artery anatomy and, perhaps, the familial aggregation of cigarette smoking and behavior patterns.

Epidemiological studies of exercise have been faced with a number of problems, but studies have appeared in the last few years which make a strong case for physical inactivity being a risk factor for CHD (Morris *et al.* 1980; Paffenbarger *et al.*

1978a, 1978b). Varying degrees of risk resulting from physical inactivity have been found. The Framingham study (Kannell and Sorlie, 1979) showed that, in men, lack of exercise is a significant risk factor, independent of other established risk factors, but its effect was found to be smaller than that of the major risk factors. Paffenbarger's study of longshoremen, on the other hand, showed that smoking over one pack per day, elevated systolic blood pressure, and low physical activity were each associated with a two-fold increase in risk (Paffenbarger *et al.* 1978a). Women have not been well studied in this regard. After adjusting for age, the Framingham study found no beneficial effects of exercise on CHD in women.

Three psychosocial factors have been supported by a relatively large body of empirical evidence. People who have experienced life changes have higher rates of CHD than those with fewer such changes, independent of such other CHD risk factors as age, sex, cholesterol, hypertension, smoking, and family history. The largest body of evidence has focused on the importance of job changes, residential mobility, and changes in marital status (Syme 1984).

Second, there is evidence that the absence of social support networks is associated with an increased rate of CHD. In large prospective studies in Alameda County, California (Berkman and Syme 1979) Tecumseh, Michigan (House, Robbins, and Metzner 1982) and Durham County, North Carolina (Blazer 1982) those with fewer social ties had higher mortality rates of CHD than those with more ties, independent of age, sex, relative weight, smoking, alcohol consumption, physical activity, health practices, and health status at baseline. On the other hand, each of these studies has reported some findings not found in the others and some of these findings were not replicated in a recent prospective study of Japanese American men living in Hawaii (Reed *et al.* 1983).

The third psychosocial factor has been identified as type-A behavior. This behavior pattern is characterized in its fully developed form by a chronic sense of time urgency, increased aggressiveness and drive, and competitive hostility. The most compelling evidence on this factor comes from an 8½ year prospective study of 3,524 men in the Western Collaborative Group Study (WCGS). It was found that men with behavior pattern A experience twice as much CHD as those without it after account had been taken of major CHD risk factors (Rosenman, Brand, and Jenkins 1975). The results of the Framingham study, (using a different method of assessing the behavior pattern) are generally consistent with results from the WCGS (Haynes, Feinleib, and Kannell 1980). On the other hand, recent results from the Multiple Risk Factor Intervention Trial found no difference in CHD incidence according to behavior pattern (Shekelle *et al.* 1983). Almost all of this research has been done among employed middle-class white men living in western industrialized countries and it is not clear whether this factor is of similar importance among women, other ethnic groups, and persons living in different cultural settings (Review Panel 1981).

As can be seen, a wide variety of CHD risk factors have been identified and studied. Attempts have been made to combine these risk factors to predict overall CHD risk using multiple logistic equations. However, more than half of CHD incidence cannot be predicted by these equations (Hudes 1982). Further, equations developed for one country have not been successful in predicting CHD in another country (Keys *et al.* 1972). This suggests that although epidemiologic research has contributed a great deal to our understanding of CHD, this disease is still not fully understood.

The development of public policy

After World War II, the tremendous impact of CHD on mortality and morbidity increasingly became recognized. However, lack of knowledge at this time regarding CHD risk factors in large part prevented formulation of specific policies to prevent or control the disease. As previously noted, the major impetus to public policy development came from the large epidemiological studies that began around 1950 in several cities throughout the United States. By the mid-1950s, results began to appear in the scientific and lay literature regarding these risk factors and, by the early 1960s, the importance of elevated serum cholesterol, hypertension, and smoking as risk factors for CHD was generally appreciated.

Data on these risk factors led to a wide-ranging series of programs, projects, and campaigns oriented to the prevention and control of CHD. In 1960, the American Heart Association (AHA) issued its first statement in which smoking was linked to CHD (Ad Hoc Committee on Smoking and Cardiovascular Disease 1960). The first formal position taken by the US government on this question occurred in 1964 when the Surgeon General's Report on Smoking was issued (DHEW 1964). Although this report focused mainly on cancer, it also considered CHD. In this report, it was clear that the impact of smoking on CHD was cause for major concern. In the following year, Congress passed the Federal Cigarette Labeling and Advertising Act. This led to the now familiar warning on cigarette packages and printed advertisements as well as to a ban in 1971 on television and radio advertising.

In 1964, the President's Commission on Heart Disease, Cancer and Stroke was formed to develop a national plan for the prevention and control of these diseases. The following year, the US Congress elected to promote advances in cardio-vascular disease and cancer by passing Public Law 89-239, "Education, Research, Training, and Demonstrations in the Fields of Heart Disease, Cancer, Stroke, and Related Diseases." This law called for the establishment of regional programs and the development of guidelines which would lead to both improved treatment and prevention of CHD. The Surgeon General was given power to pursue these goals and for this purpose established the Inter-Society Commission for Heart Disease Resources. This group issued an influential report (Report of Inter-Society Commission 1970) which outlined the epidemiological knowledge available at that time and which made a strong case for the importance of primary prevention of the disease. Specific recommendations were made in this report for diet modification, elimination of cigarette smoking, and detection and control of hypertension. The diet recommendations were comprehensive and set the tone for most current public policy related to diet. The general goals of these dietary recommendations were:

1 adjustment of caloric intake to achieve and maintain optimal weight;
2 reduction of dietary cholesterol to less than 300 mg per day; and
3 substantial reduction of dietary saturated fat.

Specific objectives were outlined regarding meats, dairy products, baked goods, fats and oils, food labeling, government programs, and public and professional education.

Nutrition recommendations also were the focus of the White House Conference on Nutrition held in 1970. While heart disease prevention was not the main concern of the Conference, the panel assigned to this area issued a strong statement which reflected an approach in agreement with the Inter-Society Commission and which thereby provided emphasis to those recommendations.

In the early 1970s, several major programs dealing with hypertension were initiated by the government. A major effort to treat hypertension was launched in 1972 when the Secretary of Health, Education and Welfare established the National High Blood Pressure Education Program (National Conference on High Blood Pressure Education 1973). This ambitious program called for coordination and expansion of treatment programs in hypertension as well as for continuing research and increased public and professional education. Also that year, the Hypertension Detection and Follow-up Program was begun by the National Heart, Lung, and Blood Institute. This project screened 159,000 people, age 30–69 years, in fourteen communities throughout the United States and eventually identified 10,940 individuals with diastolic blood pressures over 90 mm Hg who were then invited to participate in an intervention program.

All of the preceding activities, research programs, and policy recommendations with regard to CHD culminated in the major governmental decision in 1972 to launch the Multiple-Risk Factor Intervention Trial. It was known at that time that the project would be enormously expensive (planned for about $100,000,000), extraordinarily complex, and difficult to implement. Nevertheless, the feeling at the time was that enough information had already accumulated regarding the etiologic importance of the major CHD risk factors to now take action to see if reducing them would reduce the incidence of the disease. The design of the Trial required the cooperation of over 12,000 high risk men and 250 researchers in 22 clinical centers across the nation. The Trial was scheduled to continue for a period of six years but an additional four years was allowed for planning the trial and analyzing the results. By any standard, this clinical trial has been the most expensive and largest experiment ever designed to change behavior with the hope of preventing disease. This trial clearly reflected a major policy commitment to the study of ways to reduce CHD. The results of the Trial, published in 1982, were disappointing to those supporting its approach to heart disease prevention (Multiple Risk Factor Intervention Trial Research Group 1982). The Trial was unable to demonstrate that the group which received special intervention to reduce serum cholesterol, smoking, and high blood pressure had significantly lower incidence of CHD than the group that received regular care from their physicians.

Since the early 1970s, the nutrition recommendations originally offered by the Inter-Society Commission have been supported by the US Congress but challenged by the National Academy of Sciences. In 1977, Senator McGovern's Select Committee on Nutrition and Human Needs issued its report *Dietary Goals For the United States* (Select Committee on Nutrition and Human Needs 1977). This report made a special effort to give practical advice to those attempting to follow its recommendations. However, in 1980, a break with past public policy regarding diet recommendations occurred which provoked a great deal of controversy. The Food and Nutrition Board of the National Academy of Sciences decided that there should be no specific recommendations about dietary cholesterol for the healthy person with a normal serum cholesterol level (Food and Nutrition Board 1980). After carefully evaluating existing studies, this group felt that conclusive evidence did not exist upon which a public policy should be based. This conclusion went against the recommendations of some twenty government and private groups which had previously developed policies on this issue.

As is evident from the foregoing account, many different agencies, bureaux, and commissions have offered various recommendations and policy statements regarding the prevention and control of CHD. In 1979, the coordination of this effort in preventive medicine at the federal level was assigned to the Office of Disease Prevention and Health Promotion. This Office prepared a book entitled *Healthy People* (DHEW 1979a). The section on heart disease in this volume summarized

for the lay person the most current knowledge then available
on prevention of CHD.

As can be seen, the overwhelming emphasis of public policy
on CHD to date has been that of pronouncements, declarations,
and announcements. These activities have been directed at
both physicians and the lay public. Research aimed at enhancing
knowledge regarding the causes and treatment of CHD also has
been emphasized. On the other hand, relatively less emphasis
has been placed on the establishment of long-term or permanent
community prevention and treatment programs or to fundamental alterations in such matters as food and tobacco
availability or to social factors influencing lifestyle and
behavior.

The path from epidemiology to public policy

The link between epidemiologic research and the formulation
of public policy is never direct. The establishment of public
policy usually relates to a body of information but rarely do the
"facts" lead irrevocably to policy. The same facts often are
seen quite differently by people with different perspectives,
experiences, and priorities. In this section, a range of considerations and influences which have had relevance for CHD
policy formation will be considered. The discussion will be
organized around the following differences in approach to such
policy formulation: (a) differences in the interpretation of
evidence; (b) differences in emphasis on certain specific interventions compared to others; and (c) differences in whether
interventions should be at the individual or community level.

Evidence for policy

The need to generate policy for a complex, chronic disease
such as CHD has meant that decisions often have been made
with incomplete or conflicting evidence. Some have argued
that the magnitude of the CHD problem requires that policy be
created as early as possible, especially if the recommended
interventions are thought not to be harmful. If an airtight
scientific case must be made before we act, they say, we may

have to wait forever. Others have felt that generating policy based on incomplete information may lead to unwanted side effects, wasted energy, and loss of limited resources which could have been used for more important interventions. Furthermore, even when scientific research clearly identifies a risk factor for a disease, there is often insufficient research concerning the actual potential for intervention programs to have an effect on this risk factor.

Because the interpretation of scientific findings is not necessarily a straightforward process, disagreement about the need for policy may arise even when a large body of research exists. This is illustrated by differences that exist between those who feel that enough information now exists about CHD risk factors to initiate vigorous intervention and social change programs and those who feel that not enough is known to proceed with such ambitious interventions. Disagreements also occur in the interpretation of the same data. Thus, as noted above, the prestigious Food and Drug Board of the National Academy of Sciences in 1980 disagreed with past policy in the interpretation of the evidence regarding the need for limitations of dietary cholesterol intake by healthy individuals.

Even when agreement exists regarding the need for policy intervention, differences may arise as to whether or not prior research has adequately explored possible adverse effects that might result from full-scale intervention programs. This is exemplified by the previously mentioned concern that policy recommending drug therapy for mild hypertension may be inappropriate due to side effects of the drugs.

The problem of unintended consequences is further illustrated by current difficulties in producing foods to implement nutrition policy. Most dietary policy has recommended (a) a decrease in dietary saturated fat and cholesterol and (b) the substitution of polyunsaturated fat for saturated fat. The second recommendation has led to tremendous growth in the vegetable oil and margarine industries. While the cholesterol lowering effects of vegetable oils is well known, this desired effect may not have occurred in people consuming the actual products manufactured by this burgeoning industry due to unanticipated effects of the hydrogenation process. Hydrogenation is used in industrial processing of vegetable oils to improve appearance, taste, and texture. This process reduces the amount of linoleic acid and generates trans fatty acids. Linoleic acid is the principal essential fatty acid responsible for the cholesterol lowering effect of vegetable oils. Further, although the data are conflicting, trans fatty acids may raise serum cholesterol.

This situation was reviewed in detail by a government-appointed committee in Canada (Minister of Supply and Services 1980). Surveys found that a significant proportion of margarines contain low levels of linoleic acid and high levels of trans fatty acids. A situation thus exists in which a public policy agreed on by most experts has been translated into a product which may not be beneficial. The Committee recommended regulations which would allow margarines and oil to be labeled useful in atherosclerosis only if their percentage of linoleic acid exceeds a certain amount and if their percentage of trans fatty acids is lower than an established figure.

Yet another example of such unintended consequences is provided by the case of advertising for cigarettes. The banning of cigarette advertising from television and radio seemed to be a logical and effective approach to reduce smoking. When the advertisements left the air, however, the numerous public service announcements educating people about the hazards of cigarettes also were eliminated. Money saved by cigarette companies was then poured into magazine advertisements and sponsorship of sporting events, while the counter-messages were lost. The balance of advertising thus swung clearly in favor of the cigarette industry.

Emphasis of policy

The effort to decrease a nation's risk of CHD cannot give equal emphasis to all possible policy interventions. In a disease such as CHD in which multiple risk factors have been demonstrated, decisions must be made as to how to distribute resources among them. While policy may not explicitly define which risk factors are the most important, resource allocations certainly reflect the risk factors that policy-makers feel should be pursued most intensively. Ideally, these policy-makers should take into account research findings concerning both the relative impact of each risk factor on the disease and our ability actually to alter those factors. In fact, it can be argued that these considerations are not always taken into account. For example, diet has received relatively more attention from policy-makers than other factors. While a strong association exists between cholesterol and CHD, diet itself is not nearly as good a predictor of CHD as either smoking or hypertension. Of these latter two risk factors, it is probably easier to promote long-term compliance in taking anti-hypertensive medication than to effect smoking cessation. It might therefore be argued that the risk factor on which to focus most attention, the one which would perhaps yield the greatest decline in CHD, should have been hypertension rather than diet.

While the three major risk factors for CHD have received a great deal of attention from policy-makers, this has not been the case with the other risk factors. Although it would seem that all risk factors in a disease of this magnitude should be addressed, there are reasons why this has not occurred. Historically, the three major risk factors were the first to be recognized and they therefore received attention early on. Part of this early attention was due to the fact that they were more easily researched than other factors, yielding more clear-cut empirical findings. The major risk factors are also clearly biologically plausible, accounting for both their early recognition and their quick acceptance by the medical community and policy-makers. This has not been the case, for example, with psychosocial risk factors. Compared to psychosocial factors, the major risk factors can be dealt with more directly by physicians, making it easy to generate policy aimed at stimulating physicians to reduce these risk factors in their patients.

Along this same line, the major risk factors seem easy to modify. While this may not truly be the case for diet and smoking, the problems of developing policy to modify exercise, obesity, or psychosocial risk factors have seemed to be more complex and difficult. However, the complexity of these factors may be only part of the reason they have received relatively less attention. Most input in policy formulation comes from physicians who may be unfamiliar and uncomfortable in dealing with risk factors such as stress, physical activity, and obesity. Furthermore, compared to policy which calls for changes a doctor can introduce in his office and under his direct control, policy dealing with psychosocial and behavioral risk factors may involve the need for major social changes – an area in which many physicians feel their intervention is inappropriate.

The ability to implement efforts to alter risk factors has had an impact on policy emphasis. The National High Blood Pressure Education Program has been able directly to provide for the treatment of hypertension. Most smoking policy, on the other hand, has been aimed at simply educating people about this risk factor. The more active approach in hypertension is possible because this policy integrates well into available systems, particularly the existing health care system. The approach to hypertension has involved promotion of increased surveillance and treatment in physicians' offices and clinics and the establishment of new facilities to do this. A similar approach in smoking would mean using medical facilities to institute behavior modification or other suitable smoking cessation programs. This is quite foreign to the medical care system and would obviously be harder to implement than a program dealing with hypertension.

To ease the implementation of dietary policy, the egg has been singled out as the most important dietary item to avoid. Eggs contribute a significant proportion of daily cholesterol intake and are a neat, easy-to-count package for that cholesterol. In contrast, the fat and cholesterol content of meat depends on the type and cut of meat chosen and on the way it is cooked; this makes suggestions for dietary restriction more difficult to formulate. There are those who feel, however, that the risk of eating eggs is overstated, and that people who remove eggs selectively from their diets are losing an inexpensive source of protein and may end up substituting foods of less nutritional value (Vaupel and Graham 1980).

Models for intervention

The link between epidemiological research findings and the formulation of public policy is mediated, as noted, by the ways in which research evidence is interpreted and by the emphasis placed on certain interventions instead of others. A third factor involved in relating research to policy is the choice of intervention models. As implied throughout this paper, virtually all CHD preventive activities have been based on a medical model. As Winkelstein and Marmot (1981) have defined it, a medical model of prevention and control "aims at identifying individuals at higher risk for disease and subsequently treating them by modifying the risk factors." The substantial research effort underway over the last thirty years has been directed toward the discovery of such risk factors, towards the identification of individuals with these factors, and towards the development of various programs to lower these risks in affected individuals. While these programs seem reasonable and useful, it may be that no matter how clever we are in better identifying CHD risk factors, and no matter how energetic we are in developing preventive programs, these efforts cannot hope to have an important impact on the distribution of disease in the community as long as they are based on this one-to-one medical model. Two epidemiologic facts support this view.

Magnitude of the problem   In a disease that affects a large number of people, it must be considered that dealing with sick individuals, one at a time, is of limited value. This is not to deny that affected individuals and their families desire and appreciate such attention but rather to emphasize that from a community perspective this approach cannot hope to deal with massive disease problems. Each year, over 1 million people have heart attacks and over 600,000 die of this disease (DHHS 1982).

Let us examine the medical, one-to-one approach for a disease of this magnitude. While the focus of our discussion thus far has been on CHD risk factors, for the example to follow let us consider the entire spectrum of the problem, including those entering the at-risk population for the first time, those becoming sick for the first time, and those who already have the disease. There are approximately 7 million people in the United States with one or another form of atherosclerotic disease. To examine the medical model in its best light, let us assume that a permanent cure is available for this disease (i.e. 100 per cent effective with no relapses) which can be easily administered by physicians in their offices. If each person with the disease were to visit doctors for a total of twelve hours during one year to receive this permanent cure, this would result in 84 million visiting hours per year. What impact would these visits have on physician time?

In 1979, there were almost 390,000 professionally active physicians in the United States (DHHS 1982). Not all of these physicians would likely treat CHD. If from this number are removed such physicians as pediatricians, dermatologists, surgeons, anesthesiologists, pathologists, radiologists, and psychiatrists, a group of about 150,000 physicians is left. If all of these physicians treated heart diseases, each would contribute 560 hours (84 million divided by 150,000) of time to this treatment each year. Again, making the most favorable assumptions about the time available to these physicians for treatment, let us stipulate that all of these 150,000 physicians work forty hours every week for fifty weeks a year. Since each physician then works approximately 2,000 hours per year, treatment of these patients who have heart disease would take about 28 per cent (560 divided by 2,000) of each physician's time.

The difficulty with this solution is that an enormous number of people will continue to become ill with CHD for the first time because the treatment program described above does nothing to deal with all the people "at risk" of becoming ill. We could justifiably assume that about 40 per cent of those people over the age of thirty in the United States at this time are "at risk." If these individuals went to doctors for help to lower their risk, the impact on physician time would be staggering. Using 1980 population figures, over 45 million people would be included in this "at risk" group. We could further assume that each of these people would require an average of six hours of physician time per year to maintain lower levels of blood pressure, serum cholesterol, blood glucose, body weight, and so on. To care for these "at risk" persons would take 91 per cent of the time of the 150,000 physicians in the country each and every year.

Even if this were considered a justifiable use of physician time, it must be noted that such a program has done nothing to reduce the flow of new people into the "at risk" population. Thus, while we have virtually exhausted physician resources, we have not "solved" the problem because we have not altered those forces in society that continuously provide new "at risk" persons into the population. If we assumed that 1 per cent of the healthy over-thirty population become "at risk" each year, we would add approximately 1,132,300 new "at risk" patients to the population each year.

It must be noted that this scenario is based on conservative figures because it assumes a cure "once and for all" for all those with CHD and assumes a completely successful program with no recurrences. The conclusion to be derived from this example must be that a one-to-one approach is of value to the patient, his family, and friends but does little to alter the distribution of disease in the population. Even with a "cure" for CHD available, a one-to-one approach exhausts most of the physician resources available in the community and does nothing to address those factors that have caused the problem in the first place.

Changes in behavior   Much of the emphasis on serum cholesterol, blood pressure, and cigarette smoking has been based on the implicit assumption that it would be easier to take pills and to change eating and smoking behavior than it would be to change the community or environment. In fact, it has proven to be extraordinarily difficult to bring about these behavior changes.

For example, an enormous number of programs have been established since the early 1960s to help people quit smoking. Also enormous is the range of techniques and approaches which have been developed to help people quit. Three general conclusions can be reached about these efforts:

1 No one cessation technique or approach is clearly superior to any other.
2 Most people who join cessation programs do not quit smoking.
3 Of those who do quit, most do not remain off cigarettes for any substantial period of time   (Syme and Alcalay 1982).

In addition to difficulties in smoking cessation, we have had little success in getting people to lower the fat or salt content of their diet (Kirscht and Rosenstock 1977). The vast majority of people who try to lose weight and maintain losses fail in their efforts. One of the major problems in these cessation programs is that we have viewed these behaviors almost exclusively as problems of the individual. Thus, virtually all smoking cessation programs have been directed at the individual smoker. It is true that cigarette smoking is an individual behavior: individuals begin to smoke, they become regular smokers, and they quit smoking. However, this behavior occurs in a social and cultural context. Smoking behavior is neither random nor idiosyncratic but exhibits patterned consistencies by age, race, sex, occupation, education, and marital status. By focusing on the individual's motivations and perceptions, we neglect some of the most important influences on this behavior (Leventhal and Cleary 1980). A wide variety of components of the social and cultural environment influence smoking behavior (Dekker 1975). These components include the cultural associations between smoking and relaxation, adulthood, sexual attractiveness, and emancipation; the socioeconomic structure of tobacco production, processing, distribution, and legislation; explicit advertising on the part of the tobacco industry based on cultural values that favor smoking; subtle but effective advertising by such influential persons as film stars and TV personalities; and the influence of parents, siblings, peers, and significant persons. Unless these components are considered in smoking cessation programs, we ignore a social environment that implicitly encourages people to start and continue smoking.

While it is true that only individuals can begin and quit smoking, it also is true:

1 that the tobacco industry has gone to extraordinary lengths to create an atmosphere where smoking is considered attractive and desirable behavior;
2 that many teenagers face so much peer pressure to smoke that many find it easier to smoke than to refrain;
3 that smoking still is perceived as attractive, social behavior that helps people establish links with others; and
4 that cigarettes are advertised everywhere and are always easily accessible.

These circumstances provide a climate that encourages smoking and that makes it acceptable, easy, and convenient. Virtually all smoking cessation programs ignore these issues and focus instead on the individual, his beliefs, his habits, his perceptions and desires. It is perhaps not surprising that success rates in these programs are as low as they are.

Winkelstein and Marmot (1981) have described two approaches as alternatives to the medical model. They describe the "Public Health Model" as involving health education and community organization directed at entire communities. They review two community programs aimed at the prevention of CHD. One, the North Karelia Project, was initiated in 1972 and involved extensive health education activities as well as provision of prevention clinics, training prgrams, and patient advice services (Salonen, Puska, and Mustaniemi 1979). The other intervention program, the Stanford Heart Disease Prevention Project, began at about the same time and emphasized an extensive health education media campaign as well as face-to-face educational interventions (Farquhar 1978). In both projects, the intervention communities showed a significant reduction in CHD risk factors compared to control communities.

The major strength of such public health approaches is logistic. These programs affect very large numbers of people in the community at a fraction of the cost of such one-to-one programs as the Multiple Risk Factor Intervention Trial and the Hypertension Detection and Follow-up Program. In addition, evidence available to date suggests that they are at least as effective as medical interventions in bringing about behavior change. In the end, however, this model still focuses on the individual as the prime target of educational and treatment programs.

The third alternative approach described by Winkelstein and Marmot (1981) is the "Ecological Model." In this model, structural changes are introduced in the community that, indirectly, result in behavior change and risk reduction. In this approach, no direct effort is made to change individual behavior or health status. This approach has been used to lower highway fatalities. Thus, it has been argued that it is more cost-effective in reducing highway fatalities to (a) build safer cars, (b) build safer highways, and (c) lower speed limits than it is to educate drivers, one at a time, in safer driving techniques. Similarly, it may be more useful to change the cost and availability of healthful foods than it is to educate people about better nutrition. The same argument could be made for having less accessible and more expensive cigarettes. If it is true that those with poor social support networks have higher rates of CHD, it would perhaps be easier to introduce relatively simple changes in work and living arrangements than it would be to urge people to "be more friendly."

One of the criticisms of the ecological model is that it pre-empts individual freedom and choice by limiting options and by allowing the few to dictate to the many. In fact, the ecologic approach can be seen in precisely the opposite way – as increasing freedom of choice and options. For example, teenagers can hardly be considered free agents when the tobacco industry exerts enormous pressure on them to smoke. By providing structural alternatives, teenagers would have more options for making choices than are now possible. Similarly, when a food market has a wide selection of unhealthful foods prominently and attractively displayed at cheap prices, the consumer hardly has a full range of options available. The structural pressures now in place often favor unhealthful interests; the introduction of healthful structural changes can be seen as redressing the balance and thereby providing true freedom of choice.

Discussion

Epidemiologic research has played a major role in the momentous effort to understand, prevent, and treat CHD which has taken place during the past thirty years. This research has provided the rationale for almost all of the community and individual intervention programs that have been established in a number of countries. Consonant with the magnitude of the CHD problem, a great deal of public policy has been generated. The role of epidemiology in the formation of this policy has been central.

This is not to say that epidemiologic research findings have been translated into policy as effectively or rationally as one might have wished. More efficient and effective policy recommendations might have resulted if epidemiologic research findings had been more thoughtfully considered in deciding which risk factors to emphasize and whether to approach the problem using medical or community intervention models. This criticism must be tempered, of course, by recognizing that CHD mortality rates have been declining dramatically in recent years in some countries. Unfortunately, the impact of CHD policies on this decline is not clear.

While some have claimed that this decline is due to the aggressive implementation of specific policy directed towards CHD, the reasons for the decline appear to be more complex. For example, the dramatic decline of CHD mortality in the United States is not unique to this disease but is paralleled by a similar decline in mortality rates from other diseases. Mortality rates from CHD between 1968 and 1976 in the United States dropped 21 per cent and 28 per cent in men and women respectively. Excluding mortality from CHD and cancer, the mortality rate from all other causes of death declined 20 per cent and 25 per cent in the same time period for men and women respectively (DHEW 1979b).

Several considerations outside the scientific realm play a role in determining whether policy can effectively address the problems it aims to deal with. In certain situations, while intervention to reduce a risk factor may be indicated, public policy may simply not be the best approach. The number of people regularly exercising in the US has increased dramatically in the last fifteen years. This has occurred for a variety of reasons, with the role of public policy being quite minor. When free enterprise leads to the marketing of such things as exercise facilities and smoking cessation programs there may be less need for public policy. However, assuming this approach will deal with the entire problem is a mistake since those most in need of intervention frequently do not participate in private programs.

Even when epidemiologic studies clearly identify disease risk factors, there are many political forces at work as the path toward policy formation is traversed. While the effects of cigarette smoking were appreciated in the 1950s, health advocates in Congress were unable to generate policy due to opposition of tobacco forces. In 1962, to avoid accusations of bias, various medical associations, government agencies, and the Tobacco Institute were invited to participate in the selection process for the Surgeon General's Advisory Committee on Smoking and Health. The Committee's deliberations were held in closed meetings with high security, minimizing the effects of outside influence (Schumann 1981). It is interesting that, while most of the decisions of the Committee were purely scientific, these security measures were necessary to deal with the charged political atmosphere surrounding this issue. The meat, dairy, and egg industries have historically played roles similar to the tobacco industry in attempting to influence health policy. When the Framingham study was unable to find a significant relationship between diet and serum cholesterol, a media campaign by these industries made certain that these findings were well publicized.

A coordinated preventive effort to deal with CHD is clearly desirable. Epidemiologic research has pointed out that risk factors tend to cluster in certain individuals and in certain subgroups in the population. Further, it has been further demonstrated that there is a synergistic effect when multiple risk factors occur together. There is thus some logic in focusing policy not on particular risk factors but on an integrated approach dealing with high risk people and groups.

Implementation of this approach has been problematic. Not only is an integrated effort lacking in CHD intervention programs, but fragmentation occurs in policy efforts to deal with single risk factors. This is evident at many levels of government. There are various committees and subcommittees in Congress dealing with such things as hypertension, smoking, and nutrition. Hypertension programs exist in NIH and other parts of the Department of Health and Human Services (DHHS). School nutrition education is dealt with in the DHHS as well as in the Office of Education. In an attempt to coordinate disease prevention efforts, the Office of Disease Prevention and Health Promotion was established, but it has been limited by underfunding and lack of power to influence activities in other agencies.

While a great deal of epidemiologic research has been done on CHD there is a clear need for a continued effort. We have attempted to make the case that while valuable policies have been created using the medical model approach, the greatest potential for future policy lies in a more balanced approach that gives considerably more attention to community and ecological approaches. Futher epidemiologic research on these types of interventions is essential to the formation of rational and effective policy. While it would be of value to continue the search for new risk factors, it is perhaps even more important at this time to use epidemiologic tools to determine optimal ways of reducing known risk factors. This approach includes such strategies as pinpointing different types of high risk populations and determining which interventions are most effective in reducing such risk.

The problems and difficulties identified in this paper on the link between epidemiology and policy regarding CHD must be kept in perspective. CHD is the first non-infectious disease to have received such intensive and massive attention from governmental agencies, the public, and the scientific and medical community. The effort to generate effective public policy from epidemiologic research has been a challenging task. That all has not gone smoothly is in large part attributable to the fact that there had been little prior experience in dealing with a chronic, non-infectious disease at the national level. In a sense, the situation for CHD serves as a model for other diseases. Hopefully, as our experience accumulates, so will our wisdom.

Acknowledgements

The authors wish to acknowledge the valuable contributions of Susan P. Ehrlich and Warren Winkelstein, Jr. in the preparation of this paper.

References

Ad Hoc Committe on Smoking and Cardiovascular Disease (1960) Cigarette Smoking and Cardiovascular Diseases. *Circulation* 22: 160–66.

Anderson, T.W. (1973) Mortality from Ischemic Heart Disease. Changes in Middle-aged Men since 1900. *Journal of the American Medical Association* 224: 336–38.

Australian Therapeutic Trial in Mild Hypertension. Report by the Management Committee (1980) *Lancet* 1: 1261–267.

Berkman, L.F. and Syme, S.L. (1979) Social Networks, Host Resistance, and Mortality: A Nine-year Follow-up Study of Alameda County Residents. *American Journal of Epidemiology* 109: 186–204.

Blazer, D. (1982) Social Support and Mortality in an Elderly Community Population. *American Journal of Epidemiology* 115: 684–94.

Dekker, E. (1975) Youth Culture and Influences on the Smoking Behavior of Young People. In *Smoking and Health. Proceedings of the Third World Conference*. Washington, DC: Department of Health Education and Welfare.

Department of Health and Human Services (1981) Report of the Working Group on Arteriosclerosis of the National Heart, Lung and Blood Institute. US Department of Health and Human Services.

—— (1982) *Health – United States 1982*. Publication No. (PHS) 82-1232.

Department of Health Education and Welfare (1964) *Smoking and Health*. Report of the Advisory Committee to the Surgeon General of the Public Health Service. Public Health Service Publication No. 1103.

—— (1968) The Framingham Study, Section 6.

—— (1977) The Framingham Study, Section 32. Publication No. 77-1247.

—— (1979a) The Surgeon General's Report on Health Promotion and Disease Prevention: *Healthy People, Background Papers*. Publication No. 79-55071.

—— (1979b) *Proceedings of the Conference on the Decline in Coronary Heart Disease Mortality*. NIH Publication No. 79-1610.

—— (1979c) *Smoking and Health: A Report of the Surgeon General*. DHEW Publication No. 79-50066.

Evans, D.A. (1980) Alcohol and Coronary Heart Disease. *American Heart Journal* 100: 584–86.

Farquhar, J.W. (1978) The Community-based Model of Life-style Intervention Trials. *American Journal of Epidemiology* 108: 103–11.

Fitzsimmons, S. (1982) Is Fat Bad: Health Risks of Thinness, Overweight, and Obesity. Paper presented at Pacific Medical Center Conference on Obesity and Health: Myths and Realities. San Francisco, 5 Nov.

Food and Nutrition Board, Division of Biological Sciences Assembly of Life Science (1980) *Toward Healthful Diets*. Washington, DC: US Government Printing Office.

Garcia, M.J., McNamara, P.M., Gordon, T., *et al*. (1974) Morbidity and Mortality in Diabetes in the Framingham Population. Sixteen Year Follow-up Study. *Diabetes* 23: 105–11.

Haynes, S.G., Feinleib, M., and Kannell, W.B. (1980) The Relationship of Psychosocial Factors to Coronary Heart Disease in the Framingham Study: Eight-year Incidence of Coronary Heart Disease. *American Journal of Epidemiology* 111: 37–58.

Hjerman, I., Velve Byre, K., and Holme, I. (1981) Effect of Diet and Smoking Intervention on the Incidence of Coronary Heart Disease. *Lancet* 2: 1303–310.

House, J.S., Robbins, C., and Metzner, H.L. (1982) The Association of Social Relationships and Activities with Mortality: Prospective Evidence from the Tecumseh Community Health Study. *American Journal of Epidemiology* 116: 123–40.

Hudes, M.L. (1982) Improvements in Screening Effectiveness and Efficiency from Increasing the Number of Predictors in Logistic Risk Analysis. Unpublished doctoral dissertation. Berkeley, California: University of California.

Hulley, S.B., Rosenman, R.H., Bawol, R.D., *et al.* (1980) Epidemiology as a Guide to Clinical Decisions: The Association Between Trigycleride and Coronary Heart Disease. *New England Journal of Medicine* 302: 1383–389.

Hypertension Detection and Follow-Up Program Cooperative Group (1979) Five-Year Findings of the Hypertension Detection and Follow-Up Program. *Journal of the American Medical Association* 242: 2562-571.

Inkeles, S. and Eisenberg, D. (1981) Hyperlipidemia and Coronary Atherosclerosis: A Review. *Medicine* 60: 110–23.

Kannell, W.B. (1975) Role of Blood Pressure in Cardiovascular Disease: The Framingham Study. *Angiology* 26: 1–14.

Kannell, W.B. and Sorlie, P. (1979) Some Health Benefits of Physical Activity: The Framingham Study. *Archives of Internal Medicine* 139: 857–61.

Kaplan, N. (1983) Therapy for Mild Hypertension, Toward a More Balanced View. *JAMA* 249: 365–67.

Keys. A. (1980) *Seven Countries*. Cambridge, Mass.: Harvard University Press.

Keys, A. (1953) Prediction and Possible Prevention of Coronary Heart Disease. *American Journal of Public Health* 43: 1399–407.

Keys, A., Aravanis C., Blackburn, H.W., *et al.* (1972) Probability of Middle-Aged Men Developing Coronary Heart Disease in Five Years. *Circulation* 45: 815–29.

Kirscht, J.P. and Rosenstock, I.M. (1977) Patient Adherence to Anti-hypertensive Medical Regimens. *Journal of Community Health* 3: 115–24.

Leventhal, H. and Cleary, P.D. (1980) The Smoking Problem: A Review of the Research and Theory in Behavioral Risk Modification. *Psychological Bulletin* 88: 370–405.

Lipid Research Clinics Program (1984) The Lipid Research Clinic's Coronary Primary Prevention Trial Results: 1. Reduction in Incidence of Coronary Heart Disease. *Journal of the American Medical Association* 251: 351–64.

McAllister, N.H. (1983) Should We Treat 'Mild' Hypertension? *Journal of the American Medical Association* 249: 39–382.

Mann, G.V. (1977) Diet-heart: End of an Era. *New England Journal of Medicine* 297: 644–49.

Miettinen, M., Turpeinen, O., and Karvonen, M.J. (1972) Effect of Cholesterol-lowering Diet on Mortality from Coronary Heart Disease and Other Causes. *Lancet* 2: 835–38.

Minister of Supply and Services (1980) Report of the Ad Hoc Committee on the Composition of Special Margarines. Ottawa, Canada.

Morris, J.N., Pollard, R., Everitt, M.G., *et al.* (1980) Vigorous Exercise in Leisure-time: Protection Against Coronary Heart Disease. *Lancet* 2: 1207–210.

Multiple Risk Factor Intervention Trial Research Group (1982) Multiple Risk Factor Intervention Trial: Risk Factor Changes and Mortality Results. *Journal of the American Medical Association* 248: 1465–477.

National Conference on High Blood Pressure Education (1973) National Heart and Lung Institute. DHEW. No. 73-486.

Paffenbarger, R.S., Brand, R.J., Sholts, R.I., *et al.* (1978a) Energy Expenditure, Cigarette Smoking and Blood Pressure Level as Related to Death from Specific Diseases. *American Journal of Epidemiology* 108: 12–18.

Paffenbarger, R.S., Wing, A.L., and Hyde, R.J. (1978b) Physical Activity as an Index of Heart Attack Risk in College Alumni. *American Journal of Epidemiology* 108: 161–75.

Perry, H.M. and Smith, W.M. (eds) (1978) *Mild Hypertension: To Treat or Not To Treat*. New York: New York Academy of Sciences.

Pooling Project Research Group (1978) Relationship of Blood Pressure, Serum Cholesterol, Smoking Habit, Relative Weight and ECG Abnormalities to Incidence of Major Coronary Events: Final Report of the Pooling Project. *Journal of Chronic Disease* (special issue) 31: 201–306.

Reed, D., McGee, D., Yano, K., Feinleib, M. (1983) Social Networks and Coronary Heart Disease Among Japanese Men in Hawaii. *American Journal of Epidemiology* 117: 384–96.

Report of the Inter-Society Commission for Heart Disease Resources (1970, Revised 1972) Primary Prevention of Atherosclerotic Diseases. *Circulation* 42: A55–A95.

Review Panel on Coronary-Prone Behavior and Coronary Heart Disease (1981) Coronary-prone Behavior and Coronary Heart Disease: A Critical Review. *Circulation* 63: 1199–215.

Rifkind, B.M. (1979) Current Status of the Role of Dietary Treatment in the Prevention and Management of CHD. *Med. Clin. N. Amer.* 63: 911–25.

Robertson, F.W. (1981) the Genetic Component in Coronary Heart Disease – A Review. *Genetic Research* 37: 1–16.

Rosenman, R.H., Brand, R.H., and Jenkins, C.D. (1975) Coronary Heart Disease in the Western Collaborative Group Study: Final Follow-up Experience of Eight and a Half Years. *JAMA* 233: 872–77.

Salonen, J.T., Puska, P., and Mustaniemi, H. (1979) Changes in Morbidity and Mortality During Comprehensive Community Programmes to Control Cardiovascular Diseases During 1972–7 in North Karelia. *British Medical Journal* 2: 1178–183.

Schumann, L.M. (1981) the Origins of the Report of the Advisory Committee on Smoking and Health to the Surgeon General. *Journal of Public Health Policy* 2: 19–27.

Select Committee on Nutrition and Human Needs, US Senate (1977) Dietary Goals for the United States. 2nd edition. Washington, DC: US Government Printing Office.

Shekelle, R., Hulley, S., Neaton, J., *et al.* (1983) Type A Behavior and Risk of Coronary Death in MRFIT. Paper read at 23rd Annual Conference on Cardiovascular Disease Epidemiology. San Diego, California.

Shekelle, R.B., Shyrock, A.M., Paul, O., *et al.* (1981) Diet, Serum Cholesterol and Death from Coronary Heart Disease. The Western Electric Study. *New England Journal of Medicine* 304: 65–70.

Stamler, J. (1978) Lifestyles, Major Risk Factors, Proof and Public Policy. *Circulation* 58: 3–19.

Stamler, J. (1981) Primary Prevention of Coronary Heart Disease: The Last 20 Years. *American Journal of Cardiology* 47: 722–35.

Syme, S.L. (1984) Sociocultural Factors and Disease Etiology. In D. Gentry (ed) *Handbook of Behavioral Medicine*, NY: Guilford Press.

Syme, S.L. and Alcalay, R. (1982) Control of Cigarette Smoking from a Social Perspective. *Annual Review of Public Health* 3: 179–99.

Tobian, L. (1979a) Relationship of Salt to Hypertension. *American Journal of Clinical Nutrition* 32 (12 suppl.): 2739–748.

—— (1979b) Dietary Salt (Sodium) and Hypertension. *American Journal of Clinical Nutrition* 32 (12 suppl.): 2659–663.

Vaupel, J.W. and Graham, J.D. (1980) Egg in Your Bier? *Public Interest* 58: 3–17.

Veterans' Administration Cooperative Study Group on Antihypertensive Agents (1967) Effects of Treatment on Morbidity in Hypertension – Results in Patients with Diastolic Blood Pressures Averaging 115 through 129 mm Hg. *Journal of the American Medical Association* 202: 1028–034.

—— (1970) Effects of Treatment on Morbidity in Hypertension. II. Results in Patients with Diastolic Blood Pressure Averaging 90 through 114 mm Hg. *Journal of the American Medical Association* 213: 1143–152.

Voller, R.D. and Strong, W.B. (1981) Pediatric Aspects of Atherosclerosis. *American Heart Journal* 101: 815–36.

Winkelstein, W. and Marmot, M. (1981) Primary Prevention of Ischemic Heart Disease: Evaluation of Community Interventions. *Annual Review of Public Health* 2: 253–76.

Four

Cancer epidemiology and
health policy

Marianne N. Prout,

Theodore Colton, and

Robert A. Smith

I

Scientific uncertainties of both the mechanisms of carcinogenesis and the precipitations of pathogenesis into clinical
cancer make the translation of epidemiologic data on cancer
into policies and actions to control or prevent cancer deaths
especially complex. The classical distinctions between primary,
secondary, and tertiary prevention help us to define policy
goals, but in reality the temporal relationships between
preventive activities and cancer development are rarely known.
We first review briefly how current theories of the causes and
development of cancers affect priorities for prevention.

One best views the cancers, like many other chronic
diseases, as the clinical end result of a long causal chain
composed of many links. The first step in this causal chain,
initiation, requires the formation of an inheritable change in
DNA, that is something must alter the cell's genetic material
such that this altered cell has the capability of reproduction
into malignant cells. Although this initial event can theoretically

occur after just a small single exposure to a particular carcinogen, the probability of such a change increases with increasing doses and repeated exposures to this carcinogen or with several exposures to a multiplicity of carcinogens. While such an alteration in DNA (which rarely is inherited) constitutes a prerequisite for the formation of cancer, it is not sufficient. The altered cells must undergo prompting to reproduce in order to create a clinically significant mass of abnormal cells. Factors which affect this process bear the label of *promoters*. This process of cell division is generally very slow: *Table 4.1* illustrates the exponential growth process. Starting from a single cell, twenty doubling times (or cell division times) must elapse to create a 1 mm mass of cells, a process that would require twenty years of efficient cell division for many common cancers. Very aggressive cancers such as the usual lung cancer would still require five years of promotion of efficient cell division. The body does not lack defenses against the formation of cancers. Each step along the slow evolution to clinical cancer could be undone, from excision and repair of damaged DNA to cytocidal immunologic response against emerging cancer cells. As a consequence, in the simplest of views on prevention of cancer one must at least consider initiators, promoters, and host defenses.

Table 4.1 *Growth of a solid tumor and clinical state.*

doublings	cells	size	clinical state
0	1	< 1 mm	undectectable
20	10^6	1 mm	undectectable
30	10^9	1 cm	detectable
35	$10^{10.5}$	3 cm	average Dx
40	10^{12}	10 cm	death

Several biologic realities limit the alternatives for prevention of cancer deaths. Cancer is many diseases. Although the generic category of "cancer" is the second commonest cause of death in the United States, each of the more than 200 individual cancer sites has low incidence. This statistical problem translates into low predictive values with major consequences for cancer screening, as we shall see later, and with unfavorable cost benefit assessments for many policies designed to reduce risks of specific cancers.

The pathologic classification of these different cancers follows lines of anatomic site and histologic appearance, rather than etiology. Correspondingly, each site of cancer has, in general, its own rather unique epidemiologic pattern. The development of health policies for cancer control likewise mandates knowledge of the epidemiology of the particular cancers of interest.

The long latent periods between carcinogenic insults and the occurrence of clinical disease limit the role of short-term studies to assess the impact of preventive measures on human cancer and necessitate reliance on intermediate outcome measures. Typically, 20–40 years elapse between exposures and clinical cancer. The long latency also complicates our views of cancer prevalence. Generally, prevalence is used in public health to define persons with detectable pre-clinical disease who could be diagnosed by screening programs.

Clinical cancer is a rare event. Each cancer site not only has low prevalence and involves long latency periods (with considerable opportunities for synergistic and antagonistic events in the interim) but, at a cellular level, entails extremely low probability that a cancer emerges from the billions of cell divisions that occur in one's lifetime.

An understanding of the natural history of each type of cancer is essential to developing health policies to control cancer mortality and morbidity. *Figure 4.1* shows typical five year survivals for various cancer sites. In general, cancers that grow rapidly (short doubling times) and metastasize quickly (spread to other parts of the body) have low survivals, exceptions include those cancers (for example, testicular cancer and childhood leukemia) where effective systemic therapy prevails.

II

The facts that cancer represents over 200 diseases, that there are multiple, interrelated causes for each cancer site, and that we have only partial knowledge of the etiology for each cancer type mean that there is no one single best strategy for cancer prevention. One must consider at least three approaches, roughly corresponding to primary, secondary, and tertiary

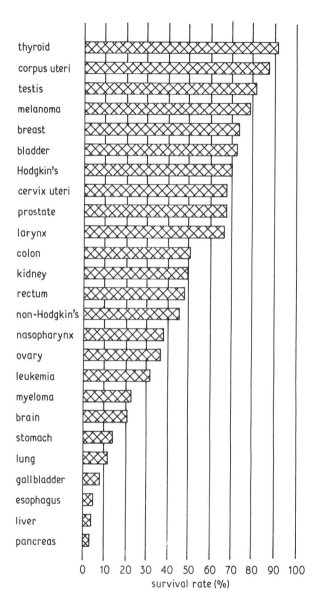

Figure 4.1 Site-specific five year relative survival rates for white male and female cancer patients, based on SEER data for 1973–80 are profiled graphically.

Source: National Cancer Advisory Board (1984)

prevention, for each cancer site. Cancers for which there is no effective treatment would require a primary prevention approach. Cancers amenable to effective treatment when detected early suggest prevention through screening programs. Cancers amenable to effective treatment but not to screening or primary prevention suggest an approach of prompt referral to comprehensive treatment and rehabilitation facilities.

Figure 4.2 shows a time line for development of clinical cancers following exposure to carcinogens. Tests available to identify whether events leading to cancer have occurred in an individual appear below the line. Most of elapsed time consists of a latent period of 8–40 years during which tests reveal neither carcinogen nor detectable cancer. Weinstein (1982) has reviewed the areas of research regarding the tests listed to evaluate whether biologic effects have occurred from carcinogen exposure (DNA-adducts, urine mutagenicity, chromosomal breaks).

Epidemiology can play a major role in the evaluation of the effectiveness of various strategies to reduce cancer mortality. The long latent period makes such studies not only costly but subject to considerable intervening and confounding events. Discouragingly, by the time adequate data collection efforts have reached completion, the prevention strategy under scrutiny may have become obsolete.

In cancer, randomized clinical trials have served as the basis for assessing the effectiveness of new therapeutic modalities. These trials have typically lasted 5–10 years and have generally involved multi-institutional efforts. Even in this favorable setting many debates remain regarding risk versus benefit for various subgroups (for example the effectiveness of adjuvant chemotherapy for women with post-menopausal breast cancer).

Only one randomized trial, the HIP of New York study of mammography and breast cancer, has demonstrated the effectiveness of cancer screening (Shapiro *et al.* 1982). Even in this "best case" situation, disagreement on screening policy continues. For other cancer sites the evidence on screening effectiveness is even less certain and the definition and implementation of screening programs is even more tenuous. National consensus conferences have addressed screening specifically for breast, cervical, and colo-rectal cancers.

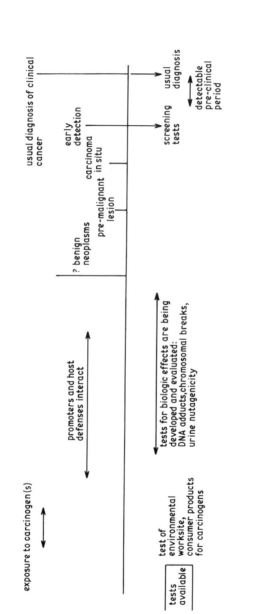

Figure 4.2 Development of clinical cancer after carcinogen exposure

The intellectual appeal of primary prevention as the intervention to be emphasized must be tempered in view of the large knowledge gaps. Although many risk factors have been proposed in the development of cancers of various sites, the important converse that removal of the risk factor results in prevention of cancer has rarely been demonstrated. For cigarette smoking and in menopausal use of estrogens, present knowledge has demonstrated decreases in rates of lung cancer and endometrial cancer within five years of removal of the risk factor. For most risk factors, however, total elimination of the factor is unlikely and a precise timing of removal of the factor is unknown. The anticipated beneficial outcome will likely entail a 10–30 year delay and, because of the low incidence rate of most cancer sites, adequate demonstration of an effect will require studying large populations.

Biologically, a primary prevention strategy has greatest appeal for those cancers with poor survival and unfavorable natural history, such as lung cancer. Screening programs seem reasonable for those cancers with a favorable natural history (that is long period of localized growth compatible with a long detectable pre-clinical period), effective therapy for early disease, but with poor overall survival, such as melanoma. To circumvent the low prevalence and poor predictive value of each cancer site, high risk groups which might have a prevalence rate of up to 100 times the general population are targeted for screening programs. Squamous cell cancers of the head and neck region, which develop in heavy smokers and drinkers, exemplify this approach. Childhood leukemia represents a disease with unknown etiologies and unfavorable natural history, for which we are unable to devise primary and secondary prevention strategies. Fortunately, therapeutic advances have resulted in marked improvements in long-term survival; successful rehabilitation and elimination of workplace prejudice towards cancer survivors have now become problems for national policy with these patients.

Finally, with many cancers our current state of knowledge regarding etiology, risk factors, early detection, and treatment is, at best, inadequate for comprehensive prevention programs. An understanding of when *not* to set policy and mustering the courage to admit to areas of ignorance become essential components of progress. The controversies surrounding AIDS dramatize the policy problems that occur whenever "cancer clusters" or new sources of carcinogen exposures emerge. What risks are acceptable? What level of knowledge mandates the imposition of restrictions? Who should bear the costs? Who should decide? The public perception of cancer as a dreaded disease translates into political incentives to develop popular programs, usually treatment based, as national policies. Policies which offend powerful constituencies, such as restriction on tobacco use, are subject to political constraints and often emerge as local initiatives.

III

Descriptive epidemiology

A clear picture of cancer incidence by site among specific age, sex, and racial groups is the first step in setting cancer policy priorities. Cancer incidence data for the United States was collected in three national cancer surveys (1937–39, 1947–48, and 1969–71) for approximately 10 per cent of the population, and since 1974 has been continuously collected under the National Cancer Institute's Surveillance, Epidemiology, and End Results (SEER) program for a 10 per cent sample of the US population. In general, the common cancers increase steadily with age. For example, the incidence rate of colorectal cancer doubles with each decade from age forty until age seventy. Therefore although the incidence rate of cancers has generally been level or decreasing (with the exception of lung cancers and melanoma), the public's perception of cancer as a greater health problem now than forty years ago accurately reflects the total increase in cancer cases in an aging population. *Tables 4.2* and *4.3* show the mortality for the leading cancer sites in men and women in specific age groups. Note that the absolute number of cases rises with each increasing age group. The data in these tables points up one of the conflicts in cancer policy priorities: should resources be directed in proportion to the number of deaths caused by specific cancers or should excess resources be focused on preventing the smaller number of cancer deaths in young people?

Cancer sites and mortality rates also vary by racial and

Table 4.2 *Mortality for the five leading cancer sites for males by age group, United States, 1981*

all ages	under 15	15–34	35–54	55–74	75 +
all cancer 227,885	*all cancer* 1,213	*all cancer* 3,883	*all cancer* 25,978	*all cancer* 128,036	*all cancer* 68,141
lung 76,764	leukemia 485	leukemia 772	lung 9,847	lung 49,594	lung 17,143
colon and rectum 25,899	brain and CNS 248	brain and CNS 412	colon and rectum 2,221	colon and rectum 13,918	prostate 13,374
prostate 23,370	non-Hodgkin's lymphomas 101	non-Hodgkin's lymphomas 362	pancreas 1,245	prostate 9.651	colon and rectum 9,527
pancreas 11,191	connective tissue 54	Hodgkin's disease 306	brain and CNS 1,119	pancreas 6,588	pancreas 3,308
leukemia 9,078	bone 50	skin 276	leukemia 1,005	stomach 4,635	bladder 3,245

Source: Vital Statistics of the United States, 1981. *Ca-A Cancer Journal for Clinicians* 35 (Jan./Feb. 1985): 21.

Table 4.3 *Mortality for the five leading cancer sites for females by age group, United States, 1981.*

all ages	under 15	15–34	35–54	55–74	75 +
all cancer 194,209	*all cancer* 928	*all cancer* 3,554	*all cancer* 26,652	*all cancer* 96,880	*all cancer* 66,177
breast 36,483	leukemia 345	breast 665	breast 7,947	breast 18,645	colon and rectum 13,178
lung 29,797	brain and CNS 209	leukemia 508	lung 4,754	lung 18,571	breast 9,219
colon and rectum 27,350	connective tissue 52	uterus 346	colon and rectum 2,037	colon and rectum 11,981	lung 6,369
ovary 11,006	other lymphomas 51	brain and CNS 308	uterus 1,825	ovary 6,160	pancreas 4,482
uterus 10,718	bone 43	skin 213	ovary 1,805	uterus 5,394	uterus 3,149

Source: Vital Statistics of the United States, 1981. *Ca-A Cancer Journal for Clinicians* 35 (Jan./Feb. 1985): 21.

ethnic groups, defying a simplistic approach to cancer control in the heterogeneous US population. *Figures 4.3* and *4.4* contrast probabilities of dying of specific cancers for blacks and whites in the United States. Studies to elucidate reasons for these differences in mortality have suggested complex reasons

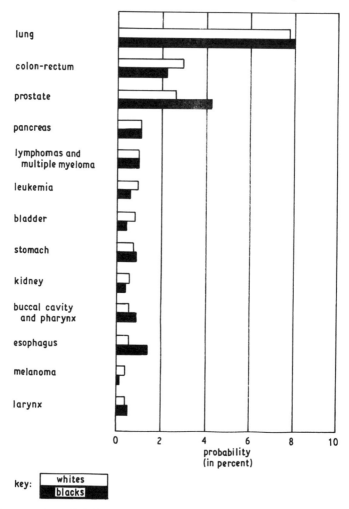

Figure 4.3 Probability at birth of eventually dying of cancer of selected sites, white and black males – United States, 1985.

Source: Ca-A Cancer Journal for Clinicians 35 (Jan/Feb. 1985): 46.

including varying exposures to carcinogens, promoters and inhibitors of carcinogenesis, and access to and utilization of health care. A few studies have attempted to look at socio-economic classes rather than racial groups and indicate that lower socio-economic status carries the increased cancer risk.

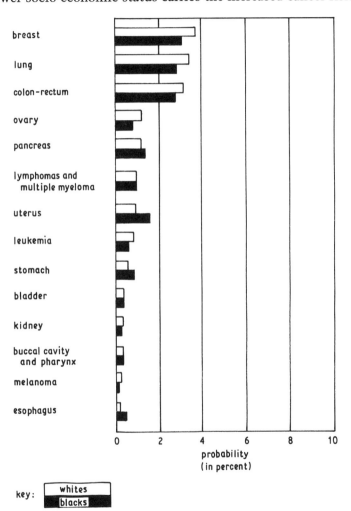

Figure 4.4 Probability at birth of eventually dying of cancer of selected sites, white and black females – United States, 1985.

Source: Ca-A Cancer Journal for Clinicians 35 (Jan/Feb 1985): 77.

Overall cancer mortality rates are useful to define specific cancers as major health problems in specific groups, but additional information is required to indicate which approaches might reduce these cancer deaths. Survival rates of diagnosed cases, generally at five years, and especially survival rates by stage at the time of diagnosis, can help define whether:

1 effective therapy exists for every stage;
2 effective therapy is available only for early stages and therefore early detection should be emphasized; or
3 no effective therapy is evident.

Using the SEER data, trends in stage at diagnosis can be correlated with trends in survival and with programs to promote early detection (National Cancer Advisory Board 1984). For example, secular trends show an increase in the incidence of melanoma, a modest increase in mortality from melanoma, and a steady increase in survival rates of melanoma patients. These trends correlate with many professional and public articles on suspicious skin lesions.

Careful examination of data from descriptive epidemiology has often suggested clues to etiology. *Figures 4.5* and *4.6* show changes in cancer mortality in US males and females over a fifty year period. The dramatic decrease in stomach cancer has spawned many hypotheses for dietary changes that produced this decrement. The dramatic increase in lung cancers, first in men and then women, followed at a twenty year lag the increases in cigarette sales to these groups. Detailed etiologic investigations have been directed to sub-populations within the United States who are at low risk for several cancers.

Finally, dramatic international variations in cancer rates and the changes in cancer rates experienced by migrant populations have also guided inquiries into risk factors for specific cancer sites. *Table 4.4* reflects some of these major international variations (OTA 1981). The substantial differences in breast and colon cancer mortality rates between Japan and the United States have fed multiple dietary hypotheses, providing a veritable feast of possible etiological morsels for investigators to digest. The substantial but delayed increase in these cancer rates among Japanese who have migrated to the United States has reinforced the notion that specific diets are associated with increased cancer rates. The converse, that decreased breast and

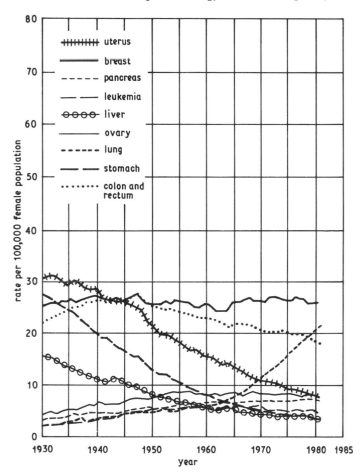

Figure 4.5 Age-adjusted cancer death rates for selected sites, females, United States, 1930–82.

Sources of data: US National Center for Health Statistics and US Bureau of the Census. Adjusted to the age distribution of the 1970 US census population (*Ca-A Cancer Journal for Clinicians* 35 (Jan/Feb. 1985): 24).

colon cancer rates can result from broad-scale adoption of Japanese dietary practices, is untested.

Descriptive cancer epidemiology, in summary, can be used to define major cancer problems for specific groups and to generate specific hypotheses about risk factors for further

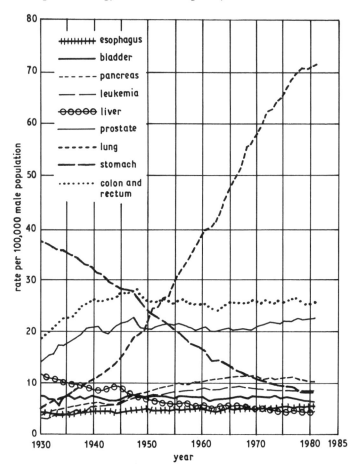

Figure 4.6 Age-adjusted cancer death rates for selected sites, males, United States, 1930–82.

Sources of data: US National Center for Health Statistics and US Bureau of the Census. Adjusted to the age distribution of the 1970 US census population (*Ca- A Cancer Journal for Clinicians* 35 (Jan./Feb. 1985): 25).

testing. The broad ranges of cancer mortality rates have been used to support the theory that cancers are not an inevitable consequence of old age or an inherent genetic defect expressing itself in old age. Intensive studies of specific risk factors and their implications for policies to control cancer mortality will be reviewed next.

Table 4.4 *Range of incidence rates for common cancers among males (and for certain cancers among females)*

site of origin of cancer	high incidence area	sex	cumulative incidence[a] % in high incidence area	ratio of highest rate to lowest rate[b]	low incidence area
Skin (chiefly non-melanoma)	Australia, Queensland	♂	> 20	> 200	India, Bombay
Esophagus	Iran, northeast section	♂	20	300	Nigeria
Lung and bronchus	England	♂	11	35	Nigeria
Stomach	Japan	♂	11	25	Uganda
Cervix uteri	Colombia	♀	10	15	Israel: Jewish
Prostate	United States: blacks	♂	9	40	Japan
Liver	Mozambique	♂♀	8	100	England
Breast	Canada, British Columbia	♀	7	7	Israel: non-Jewish
Colon	United States, Connecticut	♂♀	3	10	Nigeria
Corpus uteri	United States, California	♀	3	30	Japan
Buccal cavity	India, Bombay	♂	2	25	Denmark
Rectum	Denmark	♂	2	20	Nigeria
Bladder	United States, Connecticut	♂	2	6	Japan
Ovary	Denmark	♀	2	6	Japan
Nasopharynx	Singapore: Chinese	♂	2	40	England
Pancreas	New Zealand: Maori	♂	2	8	India, Bombay
Larynx	Brazil, São Paulo	♂	2	10	Japan
Pharynx	India, Bombay	♂	2	20	Denmark
Penis	Parts of Uganda	♂	1	300	Israel: Jewish

Source: Doll and Peto 1981: 1199

Notes:

[a] By age 75 years in the absence of other causes of death.

[b] At ages 35–64 years standardized for age as in IARC (1976). At these ages, even the data from cancer registries in poor countries are likely to be reasonably reliable (although at older ages serious underreporting may affect the data).

IV

Epidemiology of risk factors for cancer

The US Congress mandated the Office of Technology Assessment (OTA) to examine the methods used to generate data on various factors associated with cancer in the United States. The OTA, in turn, commissioned Sir Richard Doll and Richard Peto to undertake this assessment. Their report and subsequent paper and paperback (OTA 1981) summarizing their meticulous investigation has been widely circulated and much debated.

Table 4.5 summarizes the categories of risk factors used in the OTA report and the range of estimates of the percentage of US cancers associated with each factor.

Tobacco   Few, if any, would deny that tobacco deserves first place among risk factors for cancer; it certainly is the most extensively studied risk factor. To keep in perspective the many adverse health consequences of cigarette tobacco, coronary heart disease is the major type of excess mortality among smokers. This does not contradict the fact that heavy cigarette smoking has a much stronger relationship with lung cancer than with coronary heart disease (CHD). In fact, the risk of lung cancer and CHD as a consequence of heavy smoking have often appeared as the illustration to clarify epidemiologically the distinction between relative and attributable risks. For heavy smoking, the relative risk of lung cancer is considerably higher than that of CHD, indicating a much stronger relationship of heavy smoking and lung cancer. Since, however, lung cancer is a relatively rare disease in the population while CHD is rather common, with the cessation of smoking we would see more instances of CHD prevented than lung cancers prevented. In other words, although a weaker relationship obtains between smoking and CHD, the attributable risk with heavy cigarette smoking and CHD exceeds that with heavy cigarette smoking and lung cancer. Cancer mortality rates for male smokers, however, are approximately double those of non-smokers. Female smokers experience cancer mortality rates 30 per cent higher than female non-smokers (DHHS 1982).

Several different cancer sites are associated with cigarette smoking. Lung cancer is the most common; 15 per cent of heavy male smokers will develop lung cancer during their lifetimes. The relative risk for lung cancer among smokers varies with total dose (usually cited as pack-years = number of packs per day × number of years) from ten to twenty-five-fold increased over non-smokers. There are estimates that cessation of cigarette smoking will prevent over 85 per cent of lung cancers. The synergism of cigarette smoking with other respiratory carcinogens, most notably asbestos, has created conflicts over which "contributing cause" one should have avoided and who bears the responsibility for prevention of lung cancer. There should be no confusion, however, that lung cancer – the number *one* cause of cancer death in men and women in the United States and the sole cause of the epidemic of age-standardized cancer mortality – is for the most part avoidable by prevention of smoking. Clear evidence also exists for reduction in risk of lung cancer 2–5 years after smoking cessation.

Squamous cell cancers of the larynx, oral cavity, and esophagus are associated with cigarette smoking and alcohol consumption, risk factors that act synergistically to create relative risks of twenty-fold and greater among heavy abusers. Again, there are estimates that over 85 per cent of these less common cancers are attributable to cigarettes. Smoking cessation is known to diminish risks for these cancers.

Several studies have also associated bladder, kidney, and pancreatic cancers with cigarette smoking. The magnitude of relative risks for these sites is 1.5 to 3-fold and the effects of smoking cessation for cancers at these sites remain undocumented.

The cancer risk for so-called "passive smokers", non-smokers who are exposed in their immediate environment to mainstream and sidestream smoke from smokers, remains unresolved (Symposium 1984). Several studies have shown some slight elevations in lung cancer rates among smoker's spouses. The potential policy, not to mention political, implications of health hazards that smokers impose on non-smokers have added to the anticipated difficulties in demonstrating low-level cancer risks from this ubiquitous exposure.

Smokeless tobacco has been associated with increased risk for cancers of the gum and cheek, but not for lung cancer. Pipe

Table 4.5 *Estimates of the percentage of total cancer associated with various factors*

factor	estimate %	time period to which estimate applies	author
tobacco			
US mortality, males and females combined	30	1977	Doll and Peto (93)
US male mortality population	25–35	1960–72	Hammond and Seldman (155)
US female mortality	5–10	1960–72	Hammond and Seldman (155)
various populations	24–38	—	Enstrom (100)
US male incidence	43	1980	US Surgeon General (287)
US female incidence	18	1980	US Surgeon General (287)
US male mortality	51	1980	US Surgeon General (287)
US female mortality	26	1980	US Surgeon General (287)
male cancers, England	30	1968–72	Higginson and Muir (166)
female cancers, England	7	1968–72	Higginson and Muir (166)
US male incidence	28	1976	Wynder and Gori (368)
US female incidence	8	1976	Wynder and Gori (368)
alcohol			
mortality of males and females combined	4–5	1978	OTA based on Schottenfeld (323)
US male mortality	14	1974	Rothman (313)
US female mortality	12	1974	Rothman (313)

US mortality, males and females combined (approximately 4.6% for males and 1% for females)	3	1977	Doll and Peto (193)
US male incidence	4	1976	Wynder and Gori (368)
US female incidence	1	1976	Wynder and Gori (368)
male cancers, England (tobacco/alcohol)	5	1968–72	Higginson and Muir (166)
female cancers, England (tobacco/alcohol)	3	1968–72	Higginson and Muir (166)
diet			
US male incidence	40	1976	Wynder and Gori (368)
US female incidence	60	1976	Wynder and Gori (368)
US mortality, males and females combined	35	1977	Doll and Peto (93)
occupation			
US male incidence	4	1976	Wynder and Gori (368)
US female incidence	2	1976	Wynder and Gori (368)
male cancers, England	6	1968–72	Higginson and Muir (166)
female cancers, England	2	1968–72	Higginson and Muir (166)
US male cancers	< 15	not specified	Cole (62)
US female cancers	< 5	not specified	Cole (62)
US incidence, males and females combined	2.3–38	near term and future	HEW (82)
US male mortality	6.8	1977	Doll and Peto (93)
US female mortality	1.2	1977	Doll and Peto (93)

Source: OTA 1981: 108–09

and cigar smokers have been shown to have a higher risk of
lung cancer than non-smokers but somewhat less than cigarette
smokers.

Nutrition and diet   Considerable controversy pertains to the
role of diet in the causation of cancer. Doll and Peto's estimate
that 35 per cent of cancers in the United States might be
attributable to dietary factors has received more attention than
the uncertainty they expressed by ascribing a range of 10–70
per cent. One must appreciate three major problem areas in
setting nutritional goals for cancer prevention:

1 The conflicts in epidemiologic data.
2 The imprecisions in defining an individual's or group's diet.
3 The potential trade-offs in health problems that could result
   from major dietary changes.

Ecologic studies of international variations in site specific
cancer rates and per capita dietary fat consumption yield
correlation coefficients up to 85 per cent for cancers of the
colon, breast, and endometrium. Migrant studies show secular
trends which also associate dietary fat with these cancer rates.
Analytic studies of individuals, mostly of the case-control
types, however, fail to demonstrate consistent relationships.
Various proponents have viewed dietary fat as a cause, a
promoter, or a proxy for the causes of these cancers.

Most dietary components interrelate in complex ways. Total
calorie intake often correlates with fat consumption; fat-
soluble vitamin (A, D, E, and K) stores may vary with wide
ranges in dietary fat; many populations on low fat diets also
ingest large amounts of fiber in substitution for fats. The type
of cooking technique may dramatically change fat content and
introduce carcinogens. *Table 4.6* itemizes the many potential
pathways for diet to affect cancer rates.

The National Academy of Sciences (NAS) Committee on
Diet, Nutrition, and Cancer in their assessment of the
available epidemiologic and laboratory evidence found (1982)
that the relationship between high dietary fat consumption
and cancer was the dietary association most likely to be causal.
Their recommendations, however, also encompassed the less
well-substantiated links of fiber and vitamin intake to cancers.
Although the role of high fiber diets in reducing colon cancer

has undergone extensive study, no relationship has emerged among those studies that actually quantified fiber consumption. The role of fiber *per se* versus other constituents in high fiber foods for reduction of cancer risk remains unsettled.

The NAS committee recommended an emphasis on vitamin and mineral intake through consumption of fresh fruits and vegetables. This advice accommodates the epidemiologic and experimental studies that show inverse relationships between vitamin A and selenium intake and risk of cancer. At the time of writing, the NCI has embarked on a series of clinical trials of supplementations of these two micro-nutrients under careful medical supervision to define both optimum doses and the potential for human cancer prevention. The Public Health Service's objectives for nutrition (1983) encompass dietary fat reduction and increased fiber consumption. The quick commercial use of the fiber recommendations despite the inadequacy of data may require corrective public education about the uncertainties of dietary changes to prevent cancer.

Reproductive and sexual factors   Doll and Peto (1981) have estimated an upper bound of 7 per cent of cancers preventable by changes in reproductive and sexual factors. This category is rather broad in scope since it includes risk factors such as early onset of sexual intercourse, late or no childbearing, numerous sexual partners, early menarche, and late menopause.

Many studies have shown an increase in risk of breast cancer among women with early menarche (relative risk 1.5 for menarche < 13 years versus > 14 years of age) and late menopause (relative risk 2.0 for > 55 years versus < 45). The close relationship of lean body mass and onset of menarche suggests at least some partial linkage of these factors with diet. Late age at first childbirth also increases risk for breast cancer and is a more apparently modifiable risk factor. Miller and Bulbrook have suggested: "A population that achieved a 5-year reduction in age at first delivery might achieve a 30 per cent reduction in incidence of breast cancer." We know of no data currently available which supports a social policy to encourage early childbirth as a means to decrease the incidence of breast cancer. Despite secular trends of steady decreases in median age at menarche, increases in age at menopause, and changes in

Table 4.6 *Some currently attractive hypothetical or actual ways in which diet may affect the incidence of cancer.*

possible ways or means	example[a]
Ingestion of powerful, direct-acting carcinogens or their precursors	Carcinogens in natural foodstuffs (plant products)
	Carcinogens produced in cooking
	Carcinogens produced in stored food by microorganisms (bacterial and fungal)
Affecting the formation of carcinogens in the body	Providing substrates for the formation of carcinogens in the body (e.g. nitrites, nitrates, secondary amines)
	Altering intake or excretion of cholesterol and bile acids (and hence the production of carcinogenic metabolites in the bowel)
	Altering the bacterial flora of the bowel (and hence the capacity to form carcinogenic metabolites)
Affecting transport, activation, or deactivation of carcinogens	Altering concentration in, or duration of contact with, feces
	Altering transport of carcinogens to stem cells
	Induction or inhibition of enzymes (which affect carcinogen metabolism or catabolism

	Deactivation, or prevention of formation, of short-lived intracellular species (e.g. by use of selenium, vitamin E, or otherwise trapping free radicals; by use of b-carotene or otherwise quenching singlet oxygen; by use of other antioxidants)
Affecting "promotion" of cells (that are already initiated)[b]	Vitamin A deficiency (clinical or subclinical) Retinol (Binding Protein) (hormonal and other factors determine blood RBP, though vitamin A intake may not affect it much) Otherwise affecting stem cell differentiation (carotenoids? determinants of lipid "profile"?)
Overnutrition	Age at menarche Adipose-tissue-derived estrogens Other effects

Source: OTA 1981: 77.
[a] There may be considerable overlap between many of the entries in this table.
[b] Or more generally, affecting the probability that a partially transformed stem cell will become fully transformed and will proliferate successfully into cancer.

childbearing practices, the incidence rate of breast cancer has remained essentially level.

Epidemiologic studies have linked carcinoma of the cervix with early age at first intercourse and multiple sexual partners; the older studies defined high risk groups as < 20 years of age at first intercourse and two or more partners. The utility of these criteria for defining high risk women in the United States today is less certain. The effectiveness of early detection and treatment for cervical cancer and the marked decline in cervical cancer mortality rates in the United States over the past fifty years constitute a notable success story in cancer control. Recommendations of sexual prohibitions as a means for primary prevention of cervical cancer appear unnecessary.

In contrast, AIDS (acquired immune deficiency syndrome), with its expression of Kaposi's sarcoma and lymphomas, has rapidly emerged as a mortality risk in homosexuals, hemophiliacs, and IV drug abusers. Until the development of an effective vaccine or therapy, medical and public health recommendations must primarily focus on sexual practices and illegal drug use.

Infections   Internationally, the role of infections in causing cancers is extremely important. In parts of China and Africa, liver cancer associated with hepatitis B infection is one of the most frequent cancers. Burkitt's lymphoma in Africa and nasopharyngeal carcinoma in China have been linked to infection with Epstein-Barr virus. Even in these strongly linked settings, one requires many cofactors and special host circumstances to traverse the course from acute to chronic infection to expression of clinical cancer. In the United States, viruses remain suspect as major factors in the development of cervical cancer, penile cancer, acute lymphocytic leukemia of children, and, most recently, AIDS.

Our current knowledge of how and in whom common infectious agents rarely produce cancers suggests the inappropriateness of those infection control measures classically utilized for acute infections as a means of cancer prevention. Although it is uncertain whether vaccines against a single virus will effectively prevent any of these cancers, large-scale trials of vaccination against HBV to prevent liver cancer are at this writing underway in Africa. With the development in the future of effective vaccines that would also prevent viral-related cancers we might subsequently avoid 5–10 per cent of US cancer deaths.

Alcohol Alcohol is a well-defined risk factor for specific cancer sites: squamous cell carcinomas of the head and neck region and esophagus and hepatocellular carcinomas. There is poor understanding, however, of the role of alcohol in the formation of these cancers; in animal studies alcohol *per se* is not a carcinogen. Epidemiologic data suggest strong synergism between alcohol and tobacco with relative risks for heavy abusers of both tobacco and alcohol of 60–90 compared to non-smoking and non-drinking groups. Whether alcohol promotes cancer growth or acts indirectly through nutritional and immunologic mechanisms is uncertain but may be important for prevention of these cancers.

Geophysical factors Ultraviolet and ionizing radiation contribute the 3 per cent of US cancers ascribed to geophysical factors, with skin cancers resulting from excessive sunlight exposure of fair-skinned individuals constituting the bulk of these cancers. The most common skin cancers, basal cell and squamous cell carcinomas, rarely metastasize or cause death. The incidence of the highly malignant skin cancer type, melanoma, has increased almost two-fold in the past ten years without an increase in mortality because of increases in case survival rates. Commercial marketing of successful sunblockers coupled with increasing public and professional awareness of relationships between sun and skin cancer may explain part of these data. Melanoma, however, is poorly linked to an individual's (as opposed to a population's) sun exposure. The improved survival in melanoma might also relate to professional recognition of recently defined precursors of melanoma.

A considerable literature exists in regard to ionizing radiation exposures. In the overview perspective of this chapter, ionizing radiation is a well-recognized carcinogen but not a current major risk factor for cancers in the United States. The largest source of ionizing radiation for the typical person in the United States is natural background, and about half of that dose comes from cosmic radiation (Harley *et al.* 1975). The second largest source for the US population is medical and dental X-rays (Brown, Shaver and Lamel 1980). The largest occupationally exposed group (approximately 1 million workers) are medical technical personnel.

Occupation   The contribution of occupational exposures to carcinogens to the total cancer mortality in the United States has been a highly controversial issue. Estimates of the percentage of cancers attributable to occupation have ranged from 2 to 50 per cent. Three major sources of uncertainty arise in the use of epidemiologic studies of occupational cancer risks to set cancer policies for workers.

1 Today's epidemiologic data reflect exposures of 20–40 years ago because of the long latency between carcinogen exposure and the occurrence of clinical cancer. Industry frequently points out dramatic decreases in levels of exposure to known carcinogens and proposes that epidemiologic studies overestimate the risk. The converse is also true: risk assessments based on contemporary epidemiologic data may not reflect or predict cancer occurrence from exposures to new chemicals or combinations of chemicals.

2 Synergistic action between carcinogenic exposures clouds the attribution of risk to occupational exposures. For example, the relative risk for lung cancer in non-smoking asbestos workers is approximately three times that for non-smoking, non-exposed workers. Smokers exposed to asbestos have a relative risk virtually multiplicative, i.e. up to seventy-five times the risk for non-smokers not exposed to asbestos. Synergism has also been noted in epidemiologic studies of uranium miners who smoke. Currently the courts are wrestling with legal claims of "cause" in such situations with an inherent interwined pathobiology. Theoretically synergism could also occur between familial predisposition to cancer and occupational carcinogen exposures or between several carcinogens each at exposure levels estimated individually as having minimal risk.

3 Considerable gaps in knowledge pervade the area of occupational cancer since the past has seen little routine collection of data on both occupational exposure to carcinogens and subsequent rates of occurrence of cancer. Epidemiologic studies have appeared mainly in plants or industries that

have a high index of suspicion for occurrence of occupational cancers.

Doll and Peto's conservative estimate of 4–5 per cent of US cancers attributable to occupational exposures thus could reflect a much higher risk in a subset of occupations (OTA 1981).

Table 4.7 summarizes the cancer sites associated with occupational exposures. *Table 4.8* illustrates the occupational exposures for which epidemiologic data suggest carcinogenicity (Schottenfeld 1982).

Environment   The limitations noted with the use of epidemiologic data for occupational cancers as a basis for formulation of cancer policies in the work-place pose even greater problems in regard to environmental policies. Not surprisingly, the variety of studies that have attempted to correlate air or water pollution with cancer rates have shown minimally elevated or no increased risks. These studies cannot demonstrate effects on vulnerable subgroups or the effects of current exposures. The evolution of chemical production in the United States has outstripped the evolution of knowledge of health effects. Time has seen the creation of approximately 5 million chemical formulations with some 66,000 in regular use in the United States – and 700 new chemicals are being added yearly. Less than 1,000 chemicals have undergone testing for carcinogenicity and current testing capacity can evaluate fewer than 250 per year. Thus even though the current estimate of US cancers attributable to environmental exposures or consumer products is less than 3 per cent, and even though US cancer rates over time have remained generally stable (except for lung cancer), complacency should not be the policy.

The process of defining carcinogens remains difficult; controversy prevails on the respective roles of evidence from human epidemiologic studies, animal bioassays, and short-term *in vitro* tests as a basis for establishment of policies for carcinogen control. Epidemiologic studies, in particular, suffer considerable limitations in their ability to detect modest increases in risk, say of the magnitude of relative risk of 1.3 or below. Many epidemiologists would, in fact, consider 1.3 as the lower limit of relative risk capable of detection even in a large study. One

Table 4.7 *Cancer sites for which relationships with occupational exposures are well-established in human studies*

site	agent or industrial process	references
Bladder	Benzidine, β-naphthylamine, 4-Aminobiphenyl (xenylamine)	Rehn 1895; Ferguson et al. 1934; Scott 1952; Case et al. 1954; Melick et al. 1955; Vigliani and Barsotti 1961; Lieben 1963; Goldwater et al, 1965; Mancuso and El-Attar 1967; Melick et al 1971; Zavon et al. 1973; Tsuchiya et al. 1975
	Manufacture of certain dyes (e.g. auramine and magenta)	Case and Pearson 1954
	Gas retorts	Doll et al. 1965; Doll et al. 1972
	Rubber and cable-making industries	Case and Hosker 1954; Davies 1965
Blood (leukemia)	Benzene	Girard et al. 1971; Aksoy et al. 1974; Vigliani 1976; Infante et al. 1977
	X-radiation	Warren 1956; Seltser and Sartwell 1965; Warren and Lombard 1966; Matanoski et al, 1975
Bone	Radium, Mesothorium	Martland 1931, Polednak et al, 1978
Larynx	Ethanol (ethyl alcohol) manufacture by strong acid process (diethyl sulfate?)	Lynch et al. 1979
	Isopropyl alcohol manufacture by strong acid process (diisopropyl sulfate?)	Weil et al. 1952; Eckardt 1974
	Mustard gas	Wade et al. 1968
Liver (angiosarcoma)	Arsenic (inorganic compounds)	Roth 1958
	Vinyl chloride	Creech and Johnson 1974; Waxweiler et al. 1976; Spirtes and Kaminski 1978

Lung, bronchus	Arsenic (inorganic compounds)	Hill and Faning 1948; Roth 1958; Galy et al. 1963; Lee and Fraumeni, 1969; Ott et al. 1974; Milham and Strong 1974; Kuratsune et al. 1974; Tokudome and Kuratsune 1976; Rencher et al. 1977; Pinto et al. 1978; Axelson et al. 1978; Mabuchi et al. 1980
	Asbestos	Merewether 1949; Doll 1955; Mancuso and Coulter 1963; Selikoff et al. 1964; Jacob and Anspach 1965; Lieben 1966; Enterline and Kendrick 1967; Selikoff et al. 1968; Knox et al. 1968; Newhouse 1969; Tabershaw et al. 1970; Elmes and Simpson 1971; Fletcher 1972; Selikoff et al. 1972; Newhouse et al. 1972; Enterline et al. 1973; Selikoff et al. 1973; Edge 1976; Martischnig et al. 1977; Peto et al. 1977; Robinson et al. 1979; McDonald et al. 1980; Selikoff et al. 1980
	Bis(chloromethyl) ether	Figueros et al. 1973; Lemen et al. 1976; DeFonso and Kelton 1976; Pasternack et al. 1977
	Chromium compounds	Machie and Gregorius 1948; Baetjer 1950b; Mancuso and Hueper 1951; Brinton et al. 1952; Bidstrup and Case 1956; Enterline 1974; Langard and Norseth 1975; Royle 1975; Michel-Briand and Simonin 1977; Davies 1978; Hayes et al. 1979; Dalager et al. 1980

Source: Schottenfeld and Fraumeni 1982: 320

Table 4.8 Industrial materials for which epidemiologic studies suggest carcinogencity

material	site(s)	references
acrylonitrile	lung	O'Berg 1980
asbestos	colon, rectum	Selikoff et al. 1973
	esophagus	Selikoff et al. 1973
	larynx	Stell and McGill 1973; Shettigara and Morgan 1975
	stomach	Selikoff et al. 1973
beryllium	lung	Mancuso 1980; Wagoner et al, 1980
cadmium	lung	Lemen et al. 1976
	prostate	Potts 1965; Kipling and Waterhouse 1967; Lemen et al. 1976
coke oven emissions	kidney	Redmond et al. 1972
	prostate	Redmond et al. 1972
cutting oils	lung, digestive organs	Waterhouse 1972
	stomach, large intestine	Decouflé 1978
	stomach	Jarvholm et al. 1981
ethylene oxide/ethylene dichloride	blood (leukemia)	Hogstedt et al. 1979
	stomach	Hogstedt et al. 1979
lead	lung	Cooper and Gaffey 1975
polychlorinated biphenyls	skin (melanoma)	Bahn et al. 1976
vinyl chloride	brain	Waxweiler et al. 1976
	lung	Waxweiler et al. 1976

Source: Schottenfeld and Fraumeni 1982: 323

might view risks of this magnitude as the "noise within the system" where one cannot dismiss, beyond reasonable doubt, uncontrolled confounding as a plausible explanation of the observed result. In addition, rarely do the findings of a single epidemiologic study serve as the basis for policy decisions. One of the important criteria in proceeding epidemiologically from association to causation is consistency of the association in different populations and with different methodologies. With the price tag of each individual epidemiologic study of an alleged environmental carcinogen exceeding the $1 million mark, epidemiologic studies in human populations do not seem to serve routinely as the most feasible and cost-efficient route for generating the requisite data base of evidence for regulation of potential environmental carcinogens.

Bioassays are laboratory experiments involving administration of potential carcinogens to animals. The usual criticisms of bioassay evidence are: the use of doses considerably higher than those involving human exposures, deployment of routes of ingestion different from those of human exposures, and the testing on non-primate species. Even standard bioassays using rats and mice exposed to high doses are expensive; the use of primates or of low doses with large numbers of rats and mice becomes prohibitively expensive. Short-term tests of *in vitro* systems such as the Ames test for mutagenicity are quick and relatively cheap ($1,000–$3,000 to screen each chemical). The results of chemicals evaluated by both bioassays and short-term tests have shown substantial correlations. Unfortunately, there are too few human epidemiologic studies involving chemicals to obtain a handle on their association with short-term tests and bioassays of these same chemicals (OTA 1981).

Medical therapies and procedures The last group of risk factors includes a variety of drugs and X-rays used for diagnosis, treatment, or prevention of medical ailments. Because of FDA testing requirements for drugs and devices and the fact that exposed population groups are often readily identifiable for the conduct of studies (both prospective and historical), cancer risks are often known. With the risk known, the essential questions become whether the risk is acceptable and more specifically, whether the potential medical benefits for the therapies and procedures outweigh their attendant subsequent cancer risk.

Table 4.9 lists several drugs associated with increased cancer risks (Schottenfeld 1982). An example of current controversy includes the proper use of chemotherapy and radiation therapy in the treatment of Hodgkin's disease. Contemporary therapy allows for effective treatment of this cancer, but treatment-induced second malignancies appear in up to 15 per cent of treatment survivors.

Controversy prevails regarding the proper balance between therapeutic and carcinogenic effects of treatment for this malignancy. The role of post-menopausal estrogens seems clear both as a prophylactic for osteoporosis and as a risk factor for endometrial cancers. Again, the balance of benefits remains a difficult question: bone fractures secondary to osteoporosis constitute an important source of morbidity and mortality in elderly women. Can one detect endometrial cancers early and treat them such that their subsequent morbidity and mortality is less than that attendant upon the treatment of fractures as a consequence of osteoporosis?

Although medical treatments represent a small portion of total US cancers, they highlight the problems of clinical decision-making and the determination of acceptable risk–benefit ratios, even when one has available reasonably firm estimates of risk and benefit.

Table 4.9 *Drugs associated with cancer in humans*

drug	malignancy
Drugs established as human carcinogens	
Radioactive drugs:	Organs where concentrated:
Phosphorus (P^{32})	Acute leukemia, osteosarcoma,
Radium	nasal sinus carcinoma,
Mesothorium	angiosarcoma of the liver
Thorotrast	
Chlornaphazine	Bladder cancer
Arsenic	Skin cancer
Methoxypsoralen	Skin cancer
Alkylating agents:	Acute non-lymphocytic leukemia
Melphalan, chlorambucil,	other sites?
dihydroxybusulfan,	
busulphan, and others	
Cyclophosphamide	Bladder cancer

drug	malignancy
Immunosuppressive agents – Azothioprine	Lymphoma, skin cancer, soft tissue sarcoma melanoma? liver and gallbladder? lung adeno-carcinoma?
Androgenic-anabolic steroids	Hepatocellular carcinoma
Steroid contraceptives	Endometrial carcinoma, liver tumors (benign) breast cancer? cervical cancer? ovarian cancer? choriocarcinoma? melanoma?
Estrogens:	
DES (prenatal)	Vaginal adenocarcinoma
Conjugated estrogens	Endometrial carcinoma breast cancer? ovarian cancer?
Phenacetin-containing drugs	Renal pelvis carcinoma bladder cancer?

Suspect drugs for which human evidence of carcinogenicity is either inconclusive or conflicting

Chloramphenicol	Leukemia
Iron Dextran	Soft tissue sarcoma (site of injection)
Dilantin	Lymphoma
Phenobarbital	Brain tumors, liver cancer
Amphetamines	Lymphoma
Reserpine	Breast cancer
Progesterone (Depo-Provera)	Cervical cancer
Phenylbutazone	Leukemia
Crude tar ointment	Skin cancer
Clofibrate	Gastrointestinal and respiratory malignancies

Suspect drugs for which human studies have as yet not yielded evidence of carcinogenicity
Isoniazid
Metronidazole
Antimetabolites (methotrexate, 5-Fluorouracil)

Suspect drugs as yet unevaluated in humans
Dapsone
Griseofulvin
Phenothiazines
Oxytetracycline
Chloroquin
Source: Hoover and Fraumeni:(173)

V

Public policies and cancer

The range of public policies that have evolved and could evolve from epidemiologic data on cancer is enormous. The complexity of the cancer data has created reactive, complex, chaotic, and often contradictory policies at multiple levels of government and by multiple professional groups. Cancer policies may be aimed at intervening at different stages of the disease or specific population groups.

Policies for primary prevention are directed toward the control of carcinogens and the reduction of risk factors. Although there is no single federal cancer policy generally accepted in the United States, the federal government has issued several major documents that address the definition and regulation of carcinogens (*Table 4.10*).

Table 4.10 *Cancer policy* (February, 1985)

1 *Major documents*	
a EPA: Proposed Guidelines for Carcinogen Risk Assessment. Fed. Reg. 49, 46294-46301	23 November, 1984
b NTP: Ad Hoc Panel on Chemical Carcinogenesis Testing and Evaluation	17 August, 1984
c Office of Science and Technology: Chemical Carcinogens; Notice of Review of the Science and Its Associated Principles. Fed. Reg. 49, 21594-21661	22 May, 1984
d IARC Monographs: Evaluation of the Carcinogenic Risk of Chemicals to Humans	October, 1982
e OSHA: Identification, Classification, and Regulation of Potential Occupational Carcinogens	22 January, 1980
2 *States*	
a California: Carcinogen Policy, A Policy for Reducing the Risk of Cancer – draft criticisms and responses of Staff of DOHS	December, 1982 23 August, 1983
b Pennsylvania: The Pennsylvania Cancer Plan	March, 1983
c Louisiana: Environment and Health in Louisiana: The Cancer Problem	March, 1984

Several additional states are writing state-wide cancer policies and a federal policy may finally emerge in reaction to multiple, varying state policies. The Intergovernmental Health Policy Project (1984) identified thirty-three states with statutes on occupational or environmental carcinogens. Why is a cancer policy needed? An effective policy should clarify criteria to evaluate the scientific literature on cancer, including the quality of the data and their utility for human risk assessment. A policy should establish criteria for incorporating qualitative and quantitative data of carcinogenicity from epidemiologic and animal studies and short-term tests. A cancer policy should set criteria in advance for the magnitude of risk that would require a regulatory response. Ideally such a policy could be applied when new cancer risks become suspect with a substance already in use and with evaluation of new substances.

While an assortment of cancer policies have attempted to address the problems of chemical carcinogens, the major primary risk factors for cancer, namely tobacco and diet, fall within the category of "lifestyle" risks. The emergence of effective lobbies for non-smokers' "rights to clean air" may effect both statutory and judicial restraints on smokers. Seven states limit smoking in the work-place by statutes. Swingle (1980) has extensively reviewed potential judicial remedies of involuntary exposure to cigarette smoke. Nutrition constitutes the focus of review and consensus statements by the National Academy of Science.

The American Cancer Society has emphasized secondary prevention ("Seven Warning Signals" and "Guidelines for the Cancer-related Checkup" (1980)). Many other professional groups have recommended specific schedules of health examinations for the early detection of cancers, including the widely cited reports of a Canadian Task Force and the Institute of Medicine. In addition, eight states have statutes requiring education of the public on risks of women exposed to diethylstilbestrol (DES) *in utero* and three states require hospitals to offer pap smears to female patients. Assessment of the effectiveness of policy statements and statutes on cancer screening and early detection poses considerable difficulty. Several studies have estimated compliance with such recommendations in various health care settings and have found wide ranges in utilization of early detection tests (Battista 1983; Survey of Physicians 1985). For example, 8–20 per cent of women receive mammography according to guidelines, 10–50 per cent of patients have fecal occult blood testing performed, whereas approximately 75 per cent of women have pap smears. The role of federal policy becomes most apparent in the tertiary prevention of cancer (*Decade of Discovery* 1981). The National Cancer Act of 1971 resulted in major increases in comprehensive cancer centers (from three to over twenty), in the number of practicing medical oncologists (from a few hundred to over 3,000), and major expenditures for cancer research. (The National Cancer Institute budget increased from $230 million in 1971 to $1 billion in 1980). Although we cannot ascertain the effects of these expenditures on changes in survival for specific cancer sites, case survival rates offer a rough guide to the effectiveness of this predominantly treat-ment-oriented research thrust. Certainly, major therapeutic gains have accrued in testicular cancer, childhood leukemia, and Hodgkin's disease; the bulk of cancers among older persons, however, has seen only minor improvements in survival. For the increasing number of young people who have survived cancer, policies affecting rehabilitation assume great importance. Several states have addressed job discrimination against recovered cancer patients. Although interpretation of the Vocational Rehabilitation Act of 1973 includes cancer patients, surveys show that few patients have cognizance of their eligibility for rehabilitation. Eligibility for various types of insurance is another major obstacle in rehabilitation.

Policies can also be directed at reducing cancer mortality among specific target populations. Universal policies seek to decrease cancer risks or improve cancer care for the entire population. Statutes and regulations for the control of carcinogens in the environment and in consumer products fall into this category. An example is the elimination of asbestos in the manufacturing of blow dryers. Health education about the hazards of cigarettes and statutes that establish cancer registries for populations are additional examples of policies applicable to entire populations. Selective policies direct their efforts toward special risk groups defined by occupation, place of residence, sex, and so on. Examples include state-mandated cervical cancer screening of female hospital patients in certain age groups, monitoring of workers exposed to radiation by dosimeter badges, and ironically, special warnings to persons who purchase cigarettes through the labelling of cigarette packages. Indicated policies address not groups at high risk but specific individuals at risk for specific cancers, for example women exposed to DES *in utero*.

Statutory and regulatory approaches have been enacted at federal, state, and local levels, often with contradictory goals and requirements. The report to the OTA classified the federal statutes according to their goals. "No risk" laws allow no exposure to chemicals shown as carcinogenic in animals; the Delaney clause of the Food, Drug, and Cosmetic Act and the Resource Conservation and Recovery Act exemplify this approach. The "technology-based" laws mandate consideration of technical and economic feasibility in setting exposure limits, such as in the Clean Water Act and Clean Air Act. "Balancing" laws require control of "unreasonable risks", as in the Consumer Product Safety Act. The Intergovernmental Health Policy Project recently reviewed legislation affecting cancer prevention in all fifty states. The plethora of policies is confusing, but the most frequent areas addressed by state legislatures included smoking, education, dedicated taxes, and cancer registries. Less frequently, specific statutes have addressed cancer screening procedures or the control of occupational or environmental carcinogens. Many local communities actively regulate smoking in public facilities.

Conclusion

Because of the complexities and uncertainties surounding the variety of diseases within the rubric of "cancer," we must design policies directed against cancer which can incorporate increased knowledge. Epidemiologic evidence will continue to indicate problem areas, to refine and reformulate etiologic hypotheses, and especially to monitor the effectiveness of different policies.

What kind of national cancer policy might we formulate to encompass the diverse data from cancer epidemiology? First, a nationally accepted process should be developed for the evaluation of new data from epidemiologic and laboratory studies. Second, we have to learn how to develop policy within the context of uncertainties. We need to decide on the level of risks we will tolerate in our daily lives and for future generations. The purpose of a national policy would not be to formulate an artificial consensus on a one shot basis but to develop established procedures whereby administrative decisions as to what constitutes "acceptable risk" or "unreasonable risk" are continually scrutinized and in accord with the values of an enlightened public.

References

Battista, R. (1983) Adult Cancer Prevention in Primary Care: Patterns of Practice in Quebec. *American Journal of Public Health* 73: 1036–039.

Board of Scientific Counselors (1984) Report of the Ad Hoc Panel on Chemical Carcinogenesis Testing and Evaluation of the National Toxicology Program. US Government Printing Office 4,726: 421–32.

Brown, R.F., Shaver, J.W., and Lamel, D.A. (1980) The Selection of Patients for X-ray Examinations. *FDA*: 80-8104.

Cervical Cancer Screening: The Pap Smear. National Institutes of Health Consensus, Development Conference Summary. (1980) Washington, DC: US Government Printing Office: 0-341, 1321–3201.

Committee on Diet, Nutrition and Cancer, Assembly of Life Science, National Research Council (1982) *Diet, Nutrition and Cancer.* Washington, DC: National Academy Press.

Coping with Cancer. NIH Publication No. 80-2080: 3–97.

Decade of Discovery. Advances in Cancer Research (1971–1981). NIH Publication No. 81-2323.

Department of Health and Human Services, Office on Smoking and Health (1982) *The Health Consequences of Smoking: Cancer. A Report of the Surgeon General.*

Department of Health Education and Welfare *Atlas of Cancer Mortality.* For U.S. Counties (1950–1969). DHEW No. 75-780.

Department of Labor, Occupational Safety and Health Administration (1986) *Identification, Classification and Regulation of Potential Occupational Carcinogens.* Fed. Reg. 45, 5001–296.

Devesa, S., Silverman, D. (1978) Cancer Incidence and Mortality Trends in the U.S. 1935–74. *Journal of National Cancer Institute* 60: 545–71.

Doll, R. and Peto, R. (1981) *The Causes of Cancer.* Oxford: Oxford University Press.

Guidelines for the Cancer-related Check-up (1980) *Ca-A Cancer Journal for Clinicians* 30: 194–240.

Harley, J., Holtzman, R., Lowder, W., Moeller, D., Tanner, A., and Wogman, N. (1975) Natural Background Radiation in the United States. Washington, DC: National Council on Radiation Protection and Measurements, Report No. 43.

Intergovernmental Health Policy Project (1984) *State Legislated Actions Affecting Cancer Prevention: A Fifty State Profile.* NIH Publication No. 84-2686.

Kyle, R. (1982) Second Malignancies Associated with Chemotherapeutic Agents. *Seminars in Oncology* 9: 131–42.

National Cancer Advisory Board (1984) *Annual Cancer Statistics Reivew.* Prepared by Demographic Analysis Section Biometry Branch, Division of Cancer Prevention and Control.

NIH/NCI (1978) Consensus Development Meeting on Breast Cancer Screening. *Preventive Medicine* 7: 269–78.

Office of Science and Technology (1984) Chemical Carcinogens. (1984) Notice of Review of the Science and Its Associated Principles. *Fed. Reg.* 49, 21594–1661.

Office of Technology Assessment, Environment Office (1981) Assessment of Technologies for Determining Cancer Risks. Washington, DC.

Periodic Health Examination: Report of a Task Force to the Conference of Deputy Ministers of Health (1980) Hull, Quebec: Canadian Government Publishing Center.

Preventive Services for the Well Population (1978) Report of the Institute of Medicine, National Academy of Science. Healthy People (appendices). Washington, DC: DHEW.

Public Health Service Implementation Plans for Attaining the Objectives for the Nation. *Public Health Reports*, supplement to Sept.–Oct. 1983.

Rogers, E., Goldkind, L., and Goldkind, S. (1982) Increasing Frequency of Esophageal Cancer Among Black Male Veterans. *Cancer* 49: 610–17.

Rothman, K. and Poole, C. (1985) Science and Policy Making. *American Journal of Public Health* 75: 340–41.

Sandler, D., Everson, R., Wilcox, A., and Browder, J. (1985) Cancer Risk in Adulthood from Early Life Exposure to Parents' Smoking. *American Journal of Public Health* 75: 487–92.

Schottenfeld, D., (1982) Cancer Risks of Medical Treatment. *Ca-A Cancer Journal for Clinicians* 32: 258–79.

Schottenfeld, D. and Fraumeni, J. (ed.) (1982) *Cancer Epidemiology and Prevention.* Philadelphia: W.B. Saunders.

Schottenfeld, D. and Haas, J. (1979) Carcinogens in the Workplace. *Ca-A Cancer Journal for Clinicians* 29: 144–68.

Screening and Early Detection of Colorectal Cancer. Consensus Development Conference Proceedings. (1979) NIH No. 80-2075.

Shapiro. S., Venet, W., Stax, P., Venet, L., Roeser, R. (1982) Ten to Fourteen-year Effect of Screening on Breast Cancer Mortality. *Journal of National Cancer Institute* 69: 349.

Silverberg, E. (1985) Cancer Statistics. *Ca-A Cancer Journal for Clinicians* 35: 19–35.

Survey of Physicians' Attitudes in Early Cancer Detection (1985) *Ca-A Cancer Journal for Clinicians* 35: 197–213.

Swingle, M. (1980) the Legal Conflict Between Smokers and Non-smokers; The Majestic Vice versus the Right to Clean Air. *Missouri Law Review* 45: 444–75.

Symposium: Medical Perspectives on Passive Smoking (1984) *Preventive Medicine* 13: 557–30.

Weinstein, B. (1982) The Scientific Basis for Carcinogen Detection and Primary Cancer Prevention. *Ca-A Cancer Journal for Clinicians* 32: 348–62.

Willet, W. and MacMahon, B. (1984) Diet and Cancer – An Overview. *NEJM* 310: 633–38, 697–703.

Five

Epidemiology in occupational health policy

Ian T. T. Higgins

Introduction

Safe working conditions, the aim of humanitarian employers in the nineteenth century, are now considered in most developed industrial countries, to be a basic human right. Recognized by enlightened management to be sound policy, the identification and elimination of risks of accidents and occupational diseases are mandated by laws which are enforced by federal and other agencies.

Epidemiology contributes to knowledge about the impact of occupation on health by identifying hazards and estimating their significance, relating hazards to disease and impairment, quantifying such relationships, and, in particular, summarizing them in the form of dose/response curves. Valid, accurate and complete dose/response curves provide a sound basis for recommending safe working conditions. These recommendations, with or without further policy modifications, are frequently used as the scientific basis for legal standards. Further observations designed to assess the adequacy of any standards which are imposed are additional examples of the important role of epidemiology in occupational health. Thus, ongoing monitoring of the environment to ensure that the standards are adhered to and surveillance of the health of the workers to confirm that the standards provide adequate protection are essential.

Attention has usually been drawn to an occupational hazard by the occurrence of disease resulting from exposure to high concentrations of the causative agent. The occurrence of toxic poisoning from exposure to heavy metals, such as lead, mercury, arsenic, cadmium, or of respiratory disease from inhalation of inorganic or organic dusts, or of cancer from chromates, nickel, aniline dyes, or ionizing radiation provide illustrative examples.

Often the consequences of such high exposures are clinically obvious or indeed obvious to lay persons with no particular clinical knowledge. Most of the specific classical occupational diseases have been identified without much help from epidemiology. Increasingly, however, concern is with less obvious hazards in the work-place and with occupation as a factor in the causation of diseases which can affect people irrespective of their jobs – with the effects of exposure to low concentrations or with effects which may ensue after a long delay, or with such conditions as chronic bronchitis, coronary heart disease or arthritis, or with a possible occupational component in cancer of the lung, urinary bladder, or at other sites. Here an epidemiological approach is essential. The relationship of occupational and other factors to the disease of interest is a central concern in occupational epidemiology.

A simple example of the value of epidemiology in identifying, quantifying, and controlling an occupational hazard involved an outbreak of illness among a group of detectives working for the Lancashire Constabulary in England (Agate and Buckell 1949). The epidemic involved seven men out of a group of thirty-two detectives. The symptoms comprised tremor and an unusual degree of nervousness, embarrassment, and vasomotor instability, which was particularly troublesome when the subject was watched. These symptoms were diagnosed as being those characteristic of mercury intoxication and a source of exposure to mercury was therefore sought. All of the detectives spent a considerable amount of their time investigating crimes, in the course of which they searched for fingerprints. The standard method for bringing out fingerprints at that time in Britain was to dust suspect areas with gray powder, a mixture of mercury and chalk. The powder was liberally applied with a brush and the excess removed by blowing it away. This resulted in a cloud of dust, which could be readily inhaled. Considerable exposure was confirmed in all thirty-two men from urinary mercury measurements. The occurrence of intoxication varied with the degree of exposure. Six out of the seven men affected had spent 250 or more hours during the previous year on detective duties. Furthermore, in individual subjects the frequency of the symptoms could sometimes be shown to vary with the number of crimes being investigated. It was estimated that 90 per cent of all finger-printing carried out in Britain used gray powder and consequently a large potential problem existed. Rubber gloves were sometimes worn by the detectives when engaged in fingerprinting, but clearly although some absorption through the skin may have occurred, this was of secondary importance to inhalation. Respirators were considered as a possible means of controlling the hazard, but were decided to be impracticable. Instead, substitution of a powder which contained no mercury was instituted. Not only did this eliminate the risk of mercurialism, but the substitute also proved more effective than the substance it replaced, since it was found to fluoresce better in ultra-violet light. This simple example illustrates the identification of the hazard, some assessment of its magnitude, both actual and potential, an estimate of dose/response relationships, and the institution of control measures.

Occupational mortality and morbidity

Often identification of a hazard depends on the chance observation of a cluster of cases of some disease. Regular review of mortality and morbidity records should introduce system into the search for hazards and reduce the need to rely on chance in their identification. Good occupational records of mortality were recognized by William Farr (1975) to be essential to the assessment of occupational health in Britain in the latter half of the nineteenth century. The Registrar

General's Decennial Occupational Mortality Supplements have provided some degree of monitoring of occupations in Britain ever since. However, groups of concern often lie within the broad categories of occupations used. Consequently the supplement is often of limited value in identifying hazards. Death, too, is a late index of adversity. Information on morbidity is required. It should be the policy of large industrial organizations to keep accurate, reliable, up-to-date records of the health of their employees. Sufficiently detailed analyses of these records should be carried out to monitor the health of subgroups of especial interest within the whole. Such subgroups might include employees exposed to chemicals which are known to have adverse health consequences in high concentrations, but which are believed to be safe in the present situation, and others exposed to new substances the full extent of whose actions may still be imperfectly known.

The Occupational Survey

Once the possibility of an occupational hazard has been raised and any available records which might throw any light on the situation have been reviewed, the most direct approach to defining the problem and assessing its magnitude, as well as exploring the relationship between the hazard and any causative factors, is to conduct an epidemiological survey. While any of the standard epidemiological descriptive or analytic methods may be useful in particular circumstances, cross-sectional or prevalence studies of specific diseases or functional derangements and historical cohort mortality studies have perhaps proved particularly valuable as a first step in assessing occupational hazards. A central aim of such studies is to establish the relationship between exposure and response. Persons are categorized by some measure of working exposure and these categories are related to the frequency or severity of disease. A good illustration of this procedure can be seen from the study of mercury poisoning in the felt hat industry conducted by the US Public Health Service during the 1940s (Neal *et al.* 1942). In this study, currently employed workers were questioned and examined for evidence of disease. Concurrently measurements were made at representative sites within the plants of the concentrations of mercury in the air. Occupational histories were taken from each employee. By combining current concentration with duration of each job, an estimate of lifetime work exposure could be made. Prevalence of disease was then related to lifetime work exposure to develop dose/response curves. *Table 5.1* shows the relationship between mercury exposure and evidence of mercury poisoning. The greater the estimated dosage the greater the likelihood (prevalence) of mercury intoxication. The table suggests that persons exposed to less than 80 $\mu g/m^3$ in the air they breathed showed no signs of mercury intoxication even after years of employment. This suggests that 80 $\mu g/m^3$ of mercury is a safe level of exposure. In fact, the authors noted that no case of mercury intoxication occurred in persons who were exposed only to concentrations of less than 100 $\mu g/m^3$. They, therefore, accepted 100 $\mu g/m^3$ as a critical threshold exposure and recommended an occupational standard of 100 $\mu g/m^3$ for mercury. This standard remained in force for twenty-five years.

Table 5.1 *Mercurialism in the felt hat industry*

duration of work (yr)	mercury concentrations ($\mu g/m^3$)							
	0–79		80–159		160–239		240 +	
	no.	%	no.	%	no.	%	no.	%
0–9	36	0	76	1.3	80	3.8	30	6.7
10–19	10	0	31	6.5	80	17.5	27	14.8
20 +	20	0	20	10.0	77	23.4	24	54.2

Source: Neal *et al.* (1942)

Byssinosis, a condition resulting from inhalation of vegetable dusts from cotton, flax, or soft hemp, provides another illustration of the use of epidemiological evidence in formulating policy. Studies in the cotton mills of Lancashire during the early 1950s (Schilling 1956), revealed the extent of the problem and indicated clearly where in the mills the main hazards of exposure lay. The gradient of risk, highest in those working on or near the carding engines and declining steadily in those engaged in processing cotton as the distance from the carding machines increased pointed clearly to the source of the problem and indicated where preventive measures – enclosure, dust suppression and the use of respirators – were needed. Equally important, however, were the activities which led to conclusions about safe working dust concentrations. As in the case of mercury intoxication, occupational histories combined with environmental monitoring permitted categorization of the workers by exposure and duration of employment. The frequency of byssinosis found in these categories provided the dose/response relationship (*Table 5.2*) from which policy recommendations were made (*Table 5.3*).

Table 5.2 *Dose/response relationship prevalence of byssinosis*

duration of exposure (years)	concentration of dust (mg/m^3)					
	no.	0 – byssinosis %	no.	1 – byssinosis %	no.	2.5 and over byssinosis %
0 –	31	0 –	116	1.7	62	32.3
10 –	23	0 –	59	8.5	48	47.9
20 –	18	0 –	41	12.2	8	75.0
30 –	9	0 –	34	14.7	9	33.3
total	81	0 –	250	6.8	127	40.9

Source: Roach and Schilling 1960

Table 5.3 *Conclusions drawn by Roach and Shilling (1960)*

concentration of total dust	conclusions and recommendations
I under 100 mg/100 m^3	safe with medical supervision of workers
II 100–250 mg/100 m^3	dust control desirable and medical supervision essential
III more than 250 mg/100 m^3	dust control and medical supervision essential

These two illustrations refer to relatively acute medical conditions, though each requires some time to develop. An example where time is more important is the development of asbestosis from exposure to asbestos dust. In 1938 the US Public Health Service published the results of a study of four asbestos textile plants. The prevalence of asbestosis which was found in the employees was related to the average lifetime

Table 5.4 *Prevalence of ground glass opacities on chest radiograph by concentration of dust and duration of exposure*

duration of exposure (years)	concentration mp/ft³			
	< 5	*5 –*	*10 –*	*20 +*
< 5	0/82 (0)	0/68 (0)	3/50 (6)	6/80 (8)
5 –	0/19 (0)	7/36 (19)	3/18 (17)	17/28 (61)
10 –	0/4 (0)	7/13 (54)	4/13 (31)	8/14 (57)
15 +	0/0 (0)	4/6 (67)	2/4 (50)	3/5 (60)

For each group: Number with opacities
Number in the group
Prevalence in parentheses (%)
Source: Dreesen *et al.* (1938)

exposure and the duration of employment. *Table 5.4* presents the findings for one index of asbestosis (ground glass opacity in the chest radiograph) – fairly unequivocal evidence of the presence of the disease. It will be seen that the prevalence of ground glass opacities increased with both exposure and duration, that is with lifetime dosage of dust. No cases of ground glass opacities were observed in this study in workers exposed to concentrations of less than 5 million particles per cubic foot. On the basis of this evidence, the authors drew the conclusion that exposures to dust concentrations of less than 5 mp/ft³ would not lead to the development of asbestosis and that 5 mp/ft³ would therefore be a suitable maximal allowable concentration for this industry. A standard of 5 mp/ft³ was therefore promulgated. It remained in force for over thirty years. It should be stressed that this standard was for the prevention of asbestosis and not for the prevention of lung cancer or mesothelioma, the relation of which to asbestos dust was not recognized in 1938. It is obvious in retrospect that the recommendation and the standard which resulted from it were wrong. Indeed, with the wisdom of hindsight, it is easy to criticize the judgment which led to the 5 mp/ft³ standard for the prevention of asbestosis. Apart from the small numbers available, which make any firm predictions uncertain, evidence was available to the authors and indeed reported in the paper, which made it unlikely that the 5 mp/ft³ standard would be adequate to prevent the disease completely. Thus, the authors noted that there were three cases of questionable asbestosis which occurred with exposures of less than 5 mp/ft^3. We should almost certainly accept these three cases as having early asbestosis nowadays; but in reaching a standard, or safe exposure level, in 1938 they were ignored. In summary, this experience illustrates the use of epidemiology to set policy but unfortunately the conclusions drawn from the epidemiology were wrong. Clearly it is important that policy decisions be based not on sound evidence, but correct interpretation of that evidence.

It is obviously undesirable to rely on a single study to reach a decision on safety. The need for replication is better recognized nowadays than it was in the 1930s. Until replication is carried out, however, one study may be all the evidence which is available and the best that can be made of the data must be made. In retrospect, it seems extraordinary that thirty years had to pass before further attempts were made to evaluate safe levels of asbestos in the work-place. Follow-up of the study population after a few years would have been of great interest and would no doubt have thrown light on points which were uncertain at the time of the initial study. Indeed, a follow-up of mortality of the cohort would, even at this late date, be of great interest, particularly in view of the light that it might shed on the problems of lung cancer and mesothelioma. Unfortunately, the records which were obtained in 1938 have apparently been destroyed. It cannot be too strongly stated that priceless records should be cherished and preserved and never come near a shredder. Or to be more up to date, the data tapes and the raw data should be deposited in some bomb-proof archives. This clearly raises one of the most pressing issues epidemiology has to face, namely the issue of confidentiality. Surely the benefits of the availability of records of great value would be worth the small sacrifice of confidentiality that would be needed were such archives to become frequent.

A threshold limit value or maximal allowable concentration may need to be reduced as more knowledge becomes available. The more recent history of the acceptable concentration of asbestos in the work-place is illustrative. In 1968, some thirty years after the publication of the US Public Health Service, monograph already mentioned, the British Occupational Hygiene Society (BOHS) reconsidered the evidence on exposure to asbestos and the risk of asbestosis. The experience of a textile factory in the north of England provided the data from which a dose/response curve (*Figure 5.1*) was derived. During the 1960s, the method which was used to measure the concentration of asbestos in the work-place was changed and the result was no longer expressed in mp/ft^3, but instead fibers per cubic centimeter (fb/cm^3), or in fibers per milliliter (fb/ml). The average lifetime working-shift concentration was combined with the number of years of exposure to obtain an estimate for each worker of the lifetime dosage of asbestos received. The result was expressed as fiber-years per ml (fb-yrs/ml) by multiplying the mean fibers/ml by the number of years of exposure. *Figure 5.1* indicates that 1% of the employees might be expected to have developed the earliest signs of asbestosis after exposure to 112 fb-yrs/ml of asbestos. This is equivalent

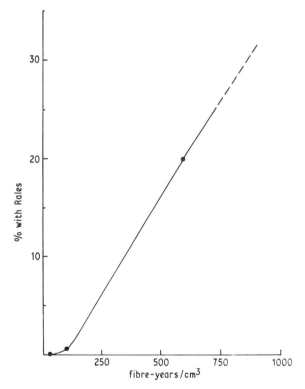

Figure 5.1 Dose/response to chrysotile asbestos exposure

Source: Roach (1970)

to an exposure of 2.2 fb/ml each work-shift for fifty years or 4.4 fb/ml each work-shift for twenty-five years. On the basis of this evidence, a Threshold Limit Value – Time Weighted Average (TLV TWA) – the average concentration for a normal eight hour work day and forty hour work week, to which nearly all workers may be repeatedly exposed, day after day, without adverse health effect – was set at 2 fb/ml. This is the basis for the current asbestos standard in the United States. Again, the results of epidemiology clearly affected public health policy.

It is interesting to compare the dose/response relationships found in the BOHS study with those which can be extracted from the Public Health Service study when this is analyzed using the composite dosage of time and duration which is now policy in these kinds of studies. *Figure 5.2* is based on the

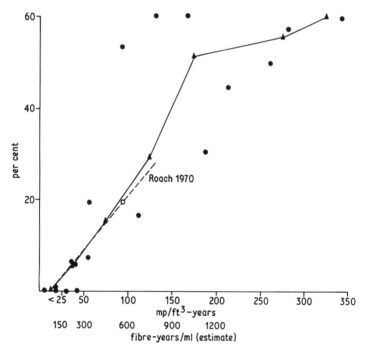

Figure 5.2 Prevalence of asbestosis (ground glass opacities) by cumulative lifetime exposure

Source: Public Health Service Study (Dreesen *et al.* 1938) and Roach (1970)

assumption that the means of the exposure and duration categories best represent cumulative dose. Thus, those exposed to less than 5 mp/ft^3 for less than 5 years are assumed to be exposed to 2.5 mp/ft^3 for 2.5 years; those exposed to 5–9 mp/ft^3 for 5–9 years to 7.5 mp/ft^3 for 7.5 years, etc. At the extremes, those exposed to 20 mp/ft^3 and over for 15 years and over were assumed to be exposed to 22.5 for 17.5 years. The graph suggests that approximately 2.5 per cent of the population might show ground glass opacities after exposure to 25 mp/ft^3 years. It is not easy to convert mp/ft^3 into fibers/ml though a figure of 5 has been suggested for textile workers (McDonald 1982). If the conversion factor of 1 mp/ft^3 = 5 fb/ml is accepted, then 25 mp/ft^3-yrs is equivalent to 125 fiber-years/ml, which equates to 2 fb-yrs/ml for 50 years, not very different from the figure reached by BOHS.

Safety margins

A later paper (Berry *et al.* 1979) however, cast doubt on the adequacy of the levels reached in 1968 to protect health with the result that permissible exposures have been revised downwards. This raises the difficult question of safety margins. To what extent should they be incorporated into standards? Should they be wide or narrow? How much does this depend on the particular outcome being studied? One view is that it is better to accept a standard in the vicinity of the putative threshold concentration and through monitoring and surveillance to confirm that this is adequate, or if such confirmation is not forthcoming to revise the standard downwards. Another view is that any safety margin should be wide enough to cover all uncertainty. The difficulty with this approach is that if an excessively low concentration is specified, it will never be known whether such stringency was needed or not. Clearly which view one adopts depends on the degree of hazard and the severity of the disease for which regulatory policy is being formulated. Far more latitude about the accuracy of a safety standard can be permitted for a disease that is mild and reversible than for one which is likely to be progressive or fatal. It should also be noted that the basis for the 2 fb/ml

concentration was asbestosis, not lung cancer and not mesothelioma.

Problems raised by cancer

One of the most serious difficulties encountered in deciding
policy on permissible exposures where cancer may result is
due to the current uncertainty about the shape of any
dose/response relationships. The problem may again be most
clearly illustrated from experience with asbestos. Exposure to
all types of asbestos is now generally recognized to be a hazard
for respiratory cancer. The evidence indicates clearly that the
risk of cancer increases with increasing cumulative lifetime
dose. A few quantitative dose/response curves have been
derived from the occupational cohorts which have been
followed (*Figure 5.3*). All these dose/response curves are

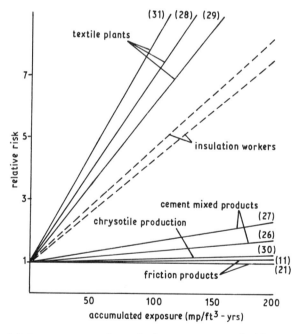

Figure 5.3 Lung cancer risks and asbestos exposure in 10 occupational
          cohorts.

Source: McDonald (1984)

compatible with the view that there is no threshold below which there can be said to be no increased risk. On the contrary, all are compatible with a progressive linear increase in risk from the lowest to the highest dosage. Unfortunately, there seems no way that either epidemiology or animal experiment can illuminate the critical lower end of the dose/response curve. Policy is increasingly being based on the assumption that the best estimate of cancer risk is a linear, no threshold model (see Chapter 4).

This means that some degree of risk has to be accepted, that it is no longer sensible to maintain that absolute safety is possible, and that a decision has to be taken on what risk is acceptable. Such decisions must be taken in full recognition of the fact that most estimates of risk are based on averages and that some persons may experience risks which may be two or three orders of magnitude above the averages.

Elimination of hazard by banning or substitution

Policy decisions considered so far concern the degree to which some dangerous substance can be more or less safely used. It is sometimes possible, as in the case of the Lancashire detectives, to eliminate hazardous substances from use. Usually, some alternative safe substance is substituted. Needless to say, if this can be done satisfactorily, occupational policy should be to substitute rather than to try, by all the engineering ingenuity that can be brought to bear, to continue to use the substance. A great deal of effort has been devoted to the replacement of asbestos by safer substitutes. Unfortunately, the characteristics which make a substance valuable may be just those characteristics which contribute to its hazardous nature. The substitution of asbestos by manmade mineral fibers offers hope of elimination of much asbestos. But the question has to be faced: Will the MMF turn out to have the hazardous properties of asbestos? It should be policy to conduct studies to find out as soon as possible – and preferably before a substitute is instituted – just what hazards may be anticipated.

**Failure of prevention, early detection of disease.
Screening**

Should preventive measures fail, it is clearly desirable to detect
disease as soon as possible at a stage when its progression can
be arrested or reversed and serious disablement avoided. It is
the policy of many industrial organizations to conduct pre-
employment and periodic medical examinations to attain this
desirable aim. It has become increasingly obvious that these
examinations are time consuming and costly and efforts have
been made to limit tests to those which are simple, reproducible,
and valid. So far as possible, tests should be suitable for
application by technicians. Epidemiology has an important
role in evaluating such programs. Not only is epidemiology
needed for assessing the claims and assumptions on which
such programs are based, it is also needed in assessing the
suitability of tests and ensuring their appropriate standardization.
Apart from determining if the program or tests are worth doing
at all, epidemiology is in a good position to determine how
frequently a particular test found to be useful should be
repeated.

**The importance of epidemiology for understanding the
natural history of disease**

Epidemiology is essential for a sound knowledge of the natural
history of disease. Important areas of inquiry are into the
factors which influence the progression or remission of
disease, the development of complications, and the risk of
mortality. But it is also often the case that only through
epidemiological study, specifically long-term observations,
that the significance of criteria used as a basis for diagnosis can
be evaluated. Coal workers' pneumoconiosis provides many
examples which illustrate the application of epidemiology to
the definition and natural history of disease and the policy
decisions which can arise from them. It was suggested in the
1940s that two different processes were involved in this
disease:

1 Simple pneumoconiosis which involved the accumulation
   of coal mine dust in the lungs.

2 Progressive massive fibrosis (PMF), which in addition to simple accumulation of dust, comprised dense, collagenous scarring with a tendency to progression irrespective of any further dust accumulation.

Early epidemiological studies indicated that simple pneumoconiosis only developed and progressed in the presence of dust exposure (Fletcher 1948) and later studies that the degree of abnormality was fairly well correlated with the total amount of dust in the lungs. Dose/response curves based on occupational histories and environmental measurements of dust concentration and the degree of abnormality revealed by a chest radiograph, were found to be compatible with an S-shaped or sigmoid curve indicating that with increasing dust dosage an increasing proportion of any work group would have radiographs showing abnormality (Oldham and Roach 1952). It was first believed that PMF occurred mainly in association with advanced degrees of simple pneumoconiosis (category 3) though subsequently it was found that the risk was also raised in workers with well-defined category 2. Later studies indicated an increasing risk of PMF with increasing background of simple pneumoconiosis. It was also widely believed in the 1940s that miners with category 3 pneumoconiosis were seriously disabled and had a markedly increased mortality compared with miners without such changes. It is probably true to say that this view is still widely held by many politicians and others today.

Epidemiological studies have shown that while advanced PMF is a disabling and lethal condition, simple pneumoconiosis is not. Nor do the earlier stages of PMF (category A and early B) constitute the sort of hazard often credited to them. On the other hand, chronic obstructive lung disease (chronic bronchitis and emphysema) appears to be excessive in coal miners and accounts for a major part of the disability often attributed to pneumoconiosis of "black lung" as it is often called. The most important factor in the development and progression of chronic obstructive lung disease is cigarette smoking; but exposure to the respiratory irritants, including coal mine dust, also contributes to some extent.

Many questions of policy follow from these epidemiological studies. Foremost is the question what is the maximum permissible concentration of coal dust in the mines? A long-term prospective study has led to the development of a dose/response curve in British coal mines (*Figure 5.1*). This has provided a sound basis for defining a maximal permissible concentration of coal mine dust to which coal miners may be exposed at work. The argument justifying this maximal dust concentration at work was developed as follows.

Probability estimates were made of the risk of developing pneumoconiosis over a working lifetime of thirty-five years depending on the mean dust exposures received. The relationship between these mean values and those measurements used for routine dust control was considered. Information on dust levels which were available from all British pits was used to assess the likely impact of the adoption of various possible standards and the probability of attainment with current technology evaluated. Extensive information on prevalence and progression of pneumoconiosis provided the necessary medical background to the decisions which had to be made. An 8 mg/m^3 standard for coal faces was chosen as the maximum respirable dust concentration in the return airway during the whole working shift. Such a concentration would be equivalent to an average concentration of 4.3 mg/m^3. If a man was to be exposed to such a concentration over a thirty-five year working lifetime, he would have a 3.4 per cent chance of developing category 2 simple pneumoconiosis, which was considered to be an acceptable risk of any small risk of disability and premature mortality which might result. Additional safeguards through regular periodic chest radiographs and lung function tests were, however, also incorporated to improve these theoretical projections. A great many years of epidemiological and other research were needed before a sound scientific basis was available for these policy decisions (Jacobsen *et al.* 1971).

Important questions of policy also involve the advice that should be given to individual coal miners with evidence of pneumoconiosis. Clearly this advice will depend in part on the stage of the disease, but it will also depend on other considerations, such as age and the potential for obtaining an alternative job. A man with simple pneumoconiosis can on the whole be reassured. Epidemiology has shown that he is unlikely to become disabled or die prematurely because of his disease. He does have an increased risk of developing PMF, but this is uncommon in the UK and US and should not be exaggerated. Epidemiology has shown moreover that whether the miner with simple pneumoconiosis continues in the mines or leaves them, makes little difference to his liability to develop PMF. This indicates that he should not be advised to leave mining immediately and seek alternative employment outside the mines, advice which in the elderly miner may be difficult to follow or totally impracticable.

Intervention and its effectiveness

Epidemiology has an important role to play in demonstrating that measures taken to eliminate some hazard are effective. Indeed perhaps the most effective way to confirm that a suspected hazard is the real cause of some disease or other condition under investigation is to show that removal of the hazard or its elimination leads to a reduction or elimination of the disease that the hazard is believed to cause. An excellent example of the use of epidemiological observations to confirm the control of a hazard can be seen in the nickel refining industry (Doll, Morgan, and Speizer 1970) (*Table 5.5*). A very thorough reorganization of the refinery took place in 1925. The table shows the elimination of the cancer risk for workers who entered the refinery after this date. Many changes which might have influenced the cancer outcome were made at the time of the reorganization of the refinery. Thus, it is not possible to

Table 5.5 *Cancer risks before and after reorganization*

year of first employment	before 1925	1925–44
no. of men	563.0	282.0
person/years	5854.0	4081.0
no. of deaths from nasal sinus cancer		
observed	39.0	0.0
expected	0.107	0.036
proportion obs./exp.	364.0	
no. of deaths from lung cancer		
observed	105.0	8.0
expected	13.9	6.1
proportion obs./exp.	7.5	1.3

Source: Doll *et al.* 1970

determine precisely which change was responsible for the improvement. It has been noted, however, that exposure to nickel carbonyl, the only type of exposure to nickel for which compensation was allowed in Britain at that time, was substantially unchanged in the clean-up and therefore, cannot have been the main cause of the disease.

Examples of the use of epidemiology to confirm the efficacy of preventive measures are rather hard to find. All too frequently studies are carried out, hazards are revealed, standards are set, but no follow-up is made to ensure their adequacy. It is sound policy to continue monitoring and surveillance to show clearly that standards are maintained and, furthermore, that they are effective in achieving their aims.

Compensation for occupational disease

When prevention fails and occupational disease develops, and particularly when this results in disablement, compensation for any loss of faculty or capacity to enjoy life which has been caused needs consideration. Epidemiology provides crucial information that is needed for policy decisions on compensation. The degree to which disablement may be due to occupational exposures or to personal behavior and other non-occupational factors, or the likelihood that some occupational exposure accounts for the development of some type of cancer are examples which can be assessed adequately only by considering epidemiological evidence. It should be accepted policy to settle compensation claims, on the basis of scientific evidence, equitably and promptly and reasonably uniformly in different parts of the country. Such settlement seems unlikely by the adversarial system currently in vogue, which would appear to be designed to ensure costly inefficiency. Fifteen years of experience with the Federal Coal Mine Health and Safety legislation provides ample support for this statement. Recently a number of suggestions have been made for improving the compensation of occupational respiratory disease and for setting up the sort of mechanisms which would facilitate procedures for doing so. A committee of the American Thoracic Society presented some suggestions on compensation for respiratory disease and recently these have again been outlined (Weill 1983). In essence, the medical issues which have to be resolved are diagnosis, causation, and impairment. Diagnosis depends on sound medical practice irrespective of underlying likely cause or causes. Causes need to be assessed based on evidence from epidemiologic studies of exposed populations. Impairment depends on valid tests of function. Guidelines must be established to facilitate each of these steps. A procedure which would result in a workable assessment of individual claimants would consist of:

1 a national panel of experts to develop and maintain the guidelines;
2 a series of regional panels responsible for the day-to-day assessments of individual cases; and finally
3 some system that would permit appeal of the medical decision of the regional panels.

A system somewhat along these lines has been in operation in Britain for pneumoconiosis for the past thirty years, and works fairly well.

References

Agate, J.N., and Buckell, M. (1949) Mercury Poisoning from Fingerprint Photography. *Lancet* 2: 451–54.

Berry, G., Gilson, J.C., Holmes, S., Lewinsohn, H.C., and Roach, S.A. (1979) Asbestosis: A Study of Dose-Response Relationships in an Asbestos Textile Factory. *British Journal of Industrial Medicine* 36: 98–112.

Dement, J.M., Harris, R.L., Symons, M.J., and Shy, C. (1982) Estimates of Dose Response for Respiratory Cancer Among Chrysotile Asbestos Textile Workers. *Ann. Occup. Hyg.* 26: 869–83.

Doll, R., Morgan, L.G., and Speizer, F.E. (1970) Cancer of the Lung and Nasal Sinuses in Nickel Workers. *British Journal of Cancer* 24: 623–32.

Dreesen, W.C., Dallavalle, J.M., Edwards, T.I., and Miller, J.W. (1938) A Study of Asbestos in the Asbestos Textile Industry. *Public Health Bulletin* 241–46.

Farr, W. (1975) *Vital Statistics: A Memorial Volume of Selections from the Reports and Writings of William Farr.* (New York Academy of Medicine.) Metuchen, NJ: Scarecrow, pp. 394 *et seq.*

Fletcher, C.M. (1948) Pneumoconiosis of Coal-Miners. *British Medical Journal* 1: 1015–022, 1065-074.

Henderson, V.I. and Enterline, P.E. (1979) Asbestos Exposure: Factors Associated with Excess Cancer and Respiratory Disease Mortality. *Annals of the New York Academy of Science* 330: 117–26.

Jacobsen, M., Rae, S., Walton, W.H., and Rogan, J.M. (1971) The Relation Between Pneumoconiosis and Dust Exposure in British Coal Mines. In W.H. Walton (ed.) *Inhaled Particles II*. Old Woking, Surrey: Unwin Bros., pp. 903–19.

McDonald, J.C. (1984) Mineral Fibers and Cancer. *Annals of Academy of Medicine of Singapore* 13 (2/supplement): 345–52.

McDonald, J.C., Liddell, F.D.K., Gibbs, G.W., Eyssen, G.E., and McDonald, A.D. (1980) Dust Exposure and Mortality in Chrysotile Mining, 1919–1975. *British Journal of Industrial Medicine* 37: 11–24.

Neal, P.A., Flinn, R.H., Edwards, T.I., Reinhardt, W.H., Hough, J.W., Dallavalle, J.M., Goldman, F.H., Armstrong, D.W., Gray, A.S., Coleman, A.L., and Postman, B.F. (1942) Mercurialism in the Felt Hat Industry. *U.S. Public Health Bulletin* No. 263.

Oldham, P.D. and Roach, S.A. (1952) A Sampling Procedure for Measuring Industrial Dust Exposure. *British Journal of Industrial Medicine* 9: 112.

Roach, S.A. (1970) Hygiene Standards for Asbestos. *Annals of Occupational Hygiene* 13: 7–15.

Roach, S.A. and Schilling, R.S.F. (1960) A Clinical and Environmental Study of Byssinosis in the Lancashire Cotton Industry. *British Journal of Industrial Medicine* 17: 1–9.

Schilling, R.S.F. (1956) Byssinosis in Cotton and Other Textile Workers. *Lancet* 2: 261–65, 319–24.

Weill, H. (1983) Asbestos-associated Diseases: Science, Public Policy, and Litigation. *Chest* 84 (5): 601–08.

Weill, H., Hughes, J., and Waggenspack, C. (1979) Influence of Dose and Fibre Type on Respiratory Malignancy Risk in Asbestos Cement Manufacturing. *American Review of Respiratory Diseases* 120: 345–54.

Six

Injuries

*Susan P. Baker, Stephen P. Teret,
and Erich M. Daub*

Injury Control is the science of reducing the number and
severity of injuries and their sequelae. Successful injury
control depends upon knowledge of the epidemiology of
injuries and the application of that knowledge to public policy.
This chapter will discuss and provide examples of the non-use,
the effective use, and the potential use of epidemiology in
formulating health policy related to injury control.

The term "injury," from the Latin "in + jus" meaning "not
right," refers to human damage from acute exposure to
physical and chemical agents. Although many diseases are also
caused by non-biological agents (e.g. asbestos, tobacco), injuries
differ in that usually the exposure is sudden and the damage is
quickly apparent (Haddon 1980). The epidemiological triad is
the same as for other health problems: injury results when a
susceptible *host* is exposed to above-threshold doses of an
agent. The interaction occurs in a particular *environment* that
permits, or even fosters, the resulting damage. The etiologic
agents of most injuries are various forms of energy: mechanical
energy (which causes more than four-fifths of all injuries),

thermal energy or heat, electricity, chemicals, and ionizing radiation. In addition, some types of injury such as drowning and frostbite result from acute insufficiency of oxygen, heat, or other essentials. Generally, etiologic agents are conveyed to the host by *vectors* (e.g. biting animals, boxing opponents) or, more commonly, by non-living *vehicles* of energy such as motor vehicles, bullets, high-voltage power lines, and hot water. Often the understanding and control of these vehicles and vectors is basic to the control of injuries.

Before discussing the high risk human hosts and the environments in which they are injured, it is necessary to consider ways in which injuries differ from other health problems.

Injuries versus diseases

There are no basic scientific distinctions between injuries and diseases, but the two differ greatly in the attitudes held toward them generally and the degree to which policies and decisions are based on scientific evidence.

Until recent years, injuries were considered in the context of "accidents," a term with connotations of fate, luck, and even inevitability. The emphasis was placed on human error, perhaps because many behaviors are obviously related to injuries (driving too fast, swimming in hazardous waters, leaving children unattended). In the case of diseases, on the other hand, the relevant human behavior is usually far removed in time. For example, the role of eating uncooked vegetables or consuming alcohol may not be apparent when symptoms of the resulting amebiasis or cirrhosis are manifest.

In recent years, increasing emphasis has been placed on injuries and their prevention. Yet inappropriate attention to "accidents" and the behaviors surrounding them continues to dominate the thinking of the general public and of many health professionals and policy-makers. Emphasis on "fault" – with the corollary notion of people "getting what they deserve" – is fostered by reliance on police data as a major source of information on injury producing events. This is especially true of motor vehicle crashes and assaults, which together cause half of all injury-related deaths. Since police data are collected for the primary purpose of establishing who is at fault and who should be punished, it is hardly surprising that behavioral approaches have dominated traditional thinking regarding injury prevention (Baker 1983).

The discrepancy in attitudes toward injuries and diseases is evident in the work-place. According to one textbook on occupational health, occupational diseases have specific causes and can be prevented by such measures as "substitution, enclosure, removal at source, segregation, and what may broadly be called good housekeeping" (Waldron 1976: 245). Although this is equally true of injuries, the same text states that the most important means for preventing occupational "accidents" "is to inculcate an attitude of mind in those at risk which makes them aware of the necessity to comply with safety measures" (Waldron 1976: 237).

Unlike diseases, injuries have often been regarded as being outside the scope of biomedical interests. This is reflected in the dearth of attention that injuries receive from health agencies, from the National Institutes of Health, and in schools of medicine and public health (Committee on Trauma Research 1985). Further evidence is the relegation of many injury problems to non-health agencies. Motor vehicles, airplanes, and other forms of transportation cause more than 50,000 deaths and some 4 million injuries each year; responsibility for preventing these injuries falls primarily within the province of state and federal departments of transportation. Dual responsibilities for public safety and for fostering an industry (such as aviation) places conflicting demands on agencies such as the Federal Aviation Administration, which has been slow to upgrade thirty-year-old standards for airplane crashworthiness (National Transportation Safety Board 1980).

Three major injury producing hazards come under the federal jurisdiction of the Department of Treasury: firearms, which are second only to motor vehicles in the number of injury deaths they cause; cigarettes, the ignition source in almost half of all fatal house fires; and alcohol, which is involved in roughly half of all fatal crashes, homicides, and adult drownings, and in substantial proportions of most other types of injury events. The importance of alcohol, tobacco, and firearms as revenue producing agents often seems to outweigh their importance as injury producing agents.

An overview of injury epidemiology

Size of the problem

Injuries cause 150,000 deaths each year in the United States, or approximately one death out of every twelve. They are the leading cause of death from age one to forty-four. From age one to thirty-four, which is almost half the average lifespan, motor vehicle injuries alone are the number one cause of death. Because injury death rates are especially high relative to diseases during the first four and a half decades of life (*Figure 6.1*), they cause great loss of potential years of life: each year, premature death from injuries causes the loss of 3.4 million years of life, a figure greater than that for cancer and heart disease combined (Committee on Trauma Research 1985).

The size of the injury problem is also expressed in the 60 million non-fatal injuries per year in the United States and in

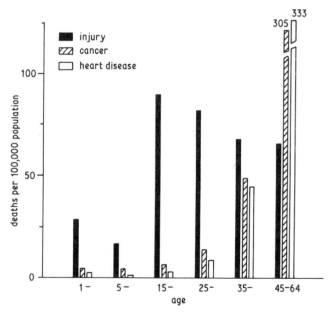

Figure 6.1 Death rates by cause and age, 1980

Source: Reprinted with permission of the publisher, from S. P. Baker, B. O'Neill, and R. S. Karpf, *The Injury Fact Book* (Lexington, Massachusetts: Lexington Books, 1984), p. 9.

the number of hospital admissions: about 3.6 million admissions per year, with an average length of stay of 7.4 days. Of all injuries, fractures of the hip account for the largest number of hospital admissions (Haupt and Graves 1982) – more than 200,000 per year, requiring an average hospital stay of twenty-one days. For ages sixty-five and older, hip fractures alone result in 3.6 million days of hospitalization annually in short-stay hospitals and a Medicare bill of $1.5 billion (Baker and Harvey 1985). The additional care required in extended care facilities and at home is largely unmeasured, as are the resulting disability, loss of independence, and changes in lifestyle.

In addition to hospital and nursing home care, injuries require pre-hospital emergency care, emergency room services, and rehabilitation. The number of physician contacts for injuries, about 70 million per year, represents 7 per cent of all physician contacts (Committee on Trauma Research 1985).

The costs of injuries are correspondingly great. When both direct and indirect costs are considered, motor vehicle-related injuries alone cost an estimated $35 billion annually. A conservative estimate of the annual cost for all injuries is at $75–$100 billion (Committee on Trauma Research 1985).

In view of the long-term and acute care demands on the health care system, it is especially important that adequate funding for prevention and epidemiologic research on injuries be available. This is far from the case (*Figure 6.2*). A number of federal agencies, such as the National Highway Traffic Safety Administration, Veterans Administration, and National Institutes of Health (NIH), support some research on injury – but the injury-related expenditure from *all* such agencies is only one-ninth of the billion dollar budget of the National Cancer Institute. Less than 2 per cent of the total NIH budget is directly related to injuries.

Funding, where available, is spotty: more than $2 million has been spent to study the psychological effects of the Three Mile Island near-disaster, but virtually no funding is available for research on injuries from firearms, which are the second leading cause of death for young adults. With no central, responsible agency and relatively little funding available, there are large and tragic gaps in research programs to reduce the burden of injury (Committee on Trauma Research 1985).

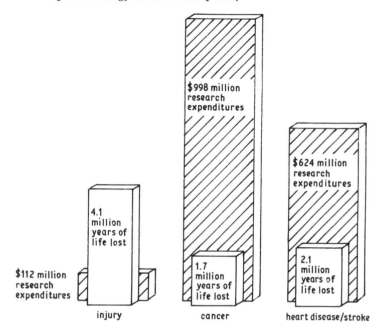

Figure 6.2 Preretirement years of life lost annually and federal
research expenditures for major causes of death in the
United States

Source: Reprinted with permission of the publisher, from Committee on
Trauma Research, *Injury in America: A Continuing Public Health Problem*
(Washington, DC: National Academy Press, 1985), p. 108.

Circumstances of injury

Injuries are often subdivided on the basis of presumed intent
into unintentional, suicidal, and assaultive or homicidal
injuries. About two-thirds of all injury deaths, or approximately
94,000 annually, are considered unintentional (*Table 6.1*); the
remainder are almost equally divided between homicide
(22,000) and suicide (28,000), with the intent not determined in
about 2,000. Motor vehicle crashes are the largest sub-category,
causing 45,000 deaths each year.

Hospital admissions, unfortunately, usually are not categorized
by either the intent or the circumstances of injury (Smith, in
press). Estimates based on several sources indicate that the
largest numbers of hospital admissions for injuries are from

Table 6.1 *Major categories of injury deaths in 1982 in the United States*[a]

injury category	unintentional	suicide	homicide	undetermined	total
motor vehicles (traffic)	44,713	57	b	16	44,786
firearms	1,756	16,575	14,117[c]	540	32,988
falls and jumps	12,077	797	12	127	13,013
drowning	6,351	530	85	387	7,353
poisoning by solids or liquids	3,474	2,943	22	787	7,226
fire and burns	5,364[d]	147	242	151	5,904
suffocation, hanging, and strangulation	881	4,061	977	81	6,000
cutting	118	409	4,365	36	4,928
poisoning by motor vehicle carbon monoxide	596	2,032	b	163	2,791
Other	18,752[e]	691	2,528	924	22,895
Total	94,082	28,242	22,348	3,212	147,884

Notes:
[a] Unpublished data from National Center for Health Statistics.
[b] Rare events not separately identified in mortality statistics.
[c] Includes 276 firearm deaths termed "legal intervention."
[d] Includes 4,200 deaths from house fires, primarily attributable to carbon monoxide poisoning rather than burns.
[e] Includes about 2,600 deaths from surgical and medical complications and misadventures, 1,700 from airplane crashes, 1,400 deaths from machinery, 1,100 deaths from non-traffic motor vehicle crashes, 1,000 electrocutions, and 1,000 deaths caused by falling objects.

falls, motor vehicle crashes, poisonings, and burns (Baker and
Harvey 1985; Haupt and Graves 1982; Smith 1985). Shootings
and drownings are less important causes of hospitalization, but
rank second and fifth, respectively, as causes of injury death. In
addition, firearms are a major cause of spinal cord injury,
exceeded only by motor vehicle crashes and falls (Kraus *et al.*
1975). Other major causes of injury death include airplane
crashes (which cause 1,500 deaths annually, more than 80 per
cent of them from crashes of private planes) and machinery
(about 1,500 deaths, half from farm machinery) (Baker, O'Neill,
and Karpf 1984).

Changes over time

During the past half century, the decline in injury death rates
in the United States has been modest compared with the
virtual elimination of many infectious diseases. Among children
ages one to four, the death rate from all diseases in 1930 was
eight times the death rate from injuries; by 1980 the two rates
were almost equal in this age group (Baker, O'Neill, and Karpf
1984).

For the population as a whole, the death rate from all
unintentional injuries declined by 59 per cent between 1930
and 1980. The decline was far from uniform, however;
decreases of 80 per cent or more occurred in deaths per 100,000
population from non-farm machinery, elevators, and poisoning
by gas piped into homes. In each of these cases, thousands of
lives have been saved by "passive" approaches that automatically
reduced exposure to lethal agents – for example, through
regulations requiring the "guarding" of fixed machinery,
standards for elevator safety, and elimination of carbon
monoxide from domestic piped gas (Baker, O'Neill, and Karpf
1984).

At the opposite extreme, the death rate from farm machinery
has increased by 44 per cent since 1930. This change reflects
increases in both the use and the lethality of farm machinery,
which has not been subject to the regulatory mechanisms that
reduced deaths from elevators and fixed machinery even as
their numbers and use increased.

High risk groups

Peaks in age-specific rates are especially prominent for four age groups. During the first few years of life, children of both sexes have high death rates, especially as motor vehicle occupants or pedestrians and from drowning and housefires.

Teenagers and young adults have extremely high death rates as motor vehicle occupants, with a peak at age eighteen (*Figure 6.3*). Although much lower than the occupant death rates, high death rates are also seen at this age from motorcycles, drowning, poisoning, and homicide. Pronounced peaks are generally seen only for males, except in the case of motor vehicle occupant, motorcyclist, and strangulation death rates, which peak for females at about age eighteen. The high death rates in male teenagers and young adults generally reflect increased participation in hazardous activities and the use of high energy products such as firearms and motorcycles. Adjustment for the amount of driving accentuates the high occupant death rate in this group, indicating the importance of age-related differences in speed of travel, alcohol-impaired driving, and other factors that influence occupant death rates (Baker, O'Neill, and Karpf 1984).

At about age 45–54, female death rates are very high for all modes of suicide (*Figure 6.4*). A peak at this age is not seen among males for any cause of injury.

In the elderly, suicide rates increase for males but not for females. Death rates increase among the elderly for many unintentional injuries including falls, burns, and pedestrian injuries (*Figure 6.5*). The dramatic increase in the unintentional injury death rate in the elderly is mainly due to falls, which by age 75–84 account for half of all unintentional injury deaths. The high death rate in the elderly reflects not only an increased propensity to fall but also lower injury thresholds, especially because of osteoporosis, and greater likelihood of fatal complications. Not only death rates but hospitalization rates for hip fractures increase dramatically in the elderly of both sexes (Baker, O'Neill, and Karpf 1984).

In addition to age and sex, economic factors are strongly related to injury death rates. The median rental value (Mierley and Baker 1983) and the per capita income of area of residence

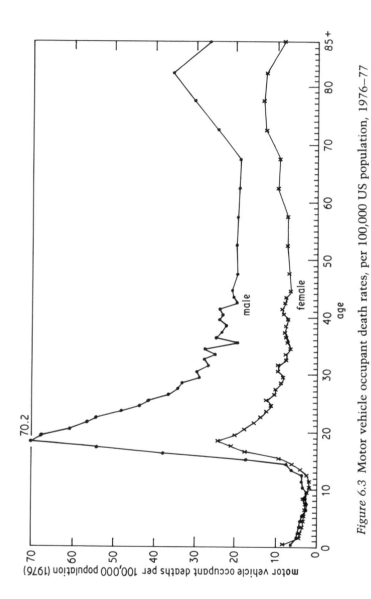

Figure 6.3 Motor vehicle occupant death rates, per 100,000 US population, 1976–77

Source: Insurance Institute for Highway Safety

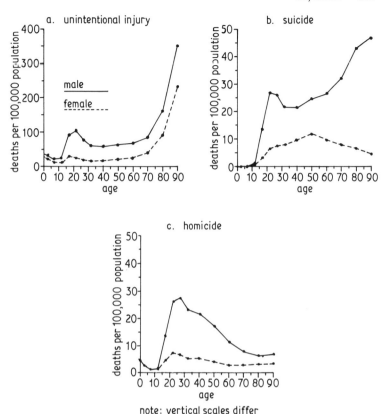

Figure 6.4: Death rates from unintentional injury, suicide, and
homicide by age and sex, 1977–79

Source: Reprinted with permission of the publisher, from S. P. Baker,
B. O'Neill, and R. S. Karpf, *The Injury Fact Book* (Lexington, Massachusetts:
Lexington Books, 1984), p. 19.

(Baker, O'Neill, and Karpf 1984) vary inversely with injury
death rates. For both whites and blacks, unintentional injury
death rates are twice as high in low income areas as in areas of
high per capita income. Among the specific injury categories
showing an especially strong relationship to low income are
motor vehicle occupant deaths, house fires, homicide, and
firearm deaths regardless of intent.

Racial groups differ in their injury death rates, with Asian
Americans having the lowest death rates from unintentional

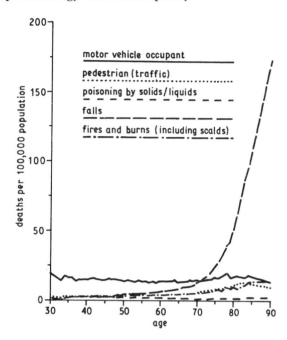

Figure 6.5 Death rates from unintentional injury by age and cause, for ages 30 and older, 1977–79

Source: Reprinted with permission of the publisher, from S. P. Baker, B. O'Neill, and R. S. Karpf, *The Injury Fact Book* (Lexington, Massachusetts: Lexington Books, 1984), p. 43.

injury, homicide, and suicide. Whites and native Americans have the highest suicide rates and native Americans the highest rates of unintentional injury, while blacks have the highest rates of homicidal death. Many of the racial differences reflect economic imbalances and differences in place of residence. In illustration, the unadjusted death rate from heroin poisoning is twice as high in blacks as in whites, but when urban/rural differences are controlled for there is little racial difference. (In other words, the higher death rate in blacks appears to be associated with the fact that blacks are more likely than whites to live in very large cities, where the heroin death rate is twenty-five times the rate for the most rural areas (Baker, O'Neill, and Karpf 1984).)

Other categories of injury death with especially high rates in urban areas are suicide by jumping and homicide by stabbing or strangulation. Typically, however, injury death rates are highest in rural areas: motor vehicle occupant death rates are four times as high in the most rural areas as in the largest cities, and the non-motor vehicle unintentional injury death rate is almost twice as high in rural areas. The rural:urban ratio of death rates is 8:1 or greater for farm machinery, lightning, and natural disaster (Baker, O'Neill, and Karpf 1984).

State-specific death rates for most causes of injury often vary by a factor of ten or more. In general, northeastern states have the lowest rates and southern and western states the highest. Often, variations in state-specific injury death rates point to needed countermeasures. In the mountain states, for example, the high rates of death from motor vehicle overturns (*Figure 6.6*) underscore the need for roads and roadsides designed to reduce the likelihood that out-of-control vehicles will roll down embankments.

Protecting high risk groups

Groups of people who are at greatest risk of serious injury – such as male teenagers, the elderly, young children, people in low income areas, and those who consume excessive amounts of alcohol – tend to be less likely than other people to take steps to protect themselves against injury. Seat belt use, for example, is especially low in population groups with high crash rates: teenagers, people in low income areas, drivers under the influence of alcohol, and drivers who engage in high risk behaviors such as tailgating and driving through red lights (Baker, O'Neill, and Karpf 1984; Robertson 1983; Williams, Wells, and Lund 1983). Similarly, seat belt use by occupants of cars involved in crashes is least common in the highest speed crashes, where the decelerative forces and risk of injury are correspondingly high.

The fact that the very people who are most apt to need protection are also the least likely to take preventive steps has important implications for public policy. Traditionally, attempts to prevent injuries have focused on educational and informational approaches that require extra effort or non-customary behaviors, such as wearing seat belts, storing poisons in child proof areas, or going out of one's way to cross streets at the safest times and

places. Educational approaches, while an essential component
of injury control, are likely to protect only the small minority
of people who are both well informed and highly motivated to
take the necessary precautions.

From properly designed consumer products to safe water

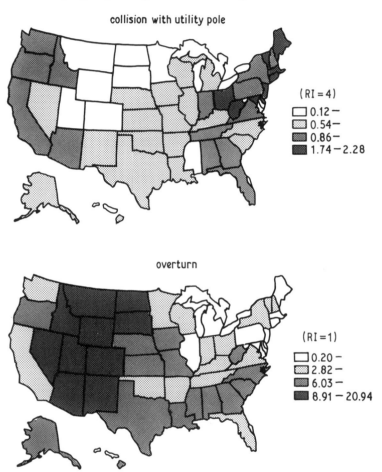

Figure 6.6 Death rates from motor vehicle crashes by state and type
of crash, per billion vehicle miles, 1979–81

Source: Reprinted with permission of the publisher, from S. P. Baker,
B. O'Neill, and R. S. Karpf, *The Injury Fact Book* (Lexington, Massachusetts:
Lexington Books, 1984), p. 225.

supplies, community-oriented methods of protection have the greatest chance of protecting the health of the public (Barry 1975). In order to protect the people who are at greatest risk of injury, preventive measures must provide built-in, automatic (passive) protection as exemplified by household fuses, flame resistant clothing, and laminated windshields. The protection provided to the public by these particular measures is now taken for granted, just as pasteurized milk and low cholesterol foods are widely accepted as providing automatic protection against various diseases without requiring repeated action by the individuals who are to be protected.

The *frequency* with which individuals must take action is an important determinant of whether a protective measure will succeed (Baker 1981; Robertson 1983). Vaccination programs, for example, succeed partly because vaccination is an infrequent matter rather than an oft-repeated chore. Smallpox and other infectious diseases would still be major problems if their control depended upon each individual repeating an action 100,000 times in a lifetime – a conservative estimate of the number of times each person needs to fasten or unfasten a seat belt in order to receive lifetime benefits.

In addition, the *amount of effort* required is important: parents who buy car seats for their children generally do not attach seats properly to the car when that requires special effort, such as installation of an attachment point for a tether strap (Baker 1980; Williams 1979). As a result, the majority of children traveling in such seats are not adequately protected.

These general principles of injury prevention are discussed elsewhere in greater detail (Baker 1981; Haddon and Baker 1981; Robertson 1983; Waller 1985). Before we describe specific examples of epidemiologic knowledge relevant to public policy on injury control, three points deserve emphasis:

1 Sound public health policy requires that effective preventive measures be given preference over approaches that are not likely to succeed.
2 Measures that successfully protect the people who are at greatest risk of injury will generally provide protection to the entire population. On the other hand, the reverse is *not* true: measures that may succeed with the people who are at *least* risk – the well-educated, economically advantaged, and

those not inclined toward hazardous activities – often give little protection to the people in high risk groups.
3 Educational efforts, if their effect is to be maximized, must be focused on influencing the decision-makers: Legislators, regulators, designers, manufacturers, health planners, administrators, and others whose decisions and actions determine the likelihood of injury for large segments of the population.

The epidemiology of injuries in relation to specific public policies

Motorcycle helmet laws

The history of motorcycle helmet laws in the United States presents an example of policy based not on the epidemiology of injuries, but on the political strength of a vocal minority interest group.

Motorcycle travel is a relatively hazardous form of travel. The mileage death rate for motorcycle riders in 1980 was estimated to be twenty-one deaths per 100 million person-miles. This compares with an automobile occupant death rate of 1.3 per 100 million person-miles of travel (Baker, O'Neill, and Karpf 1984). Head injury, the leading cause of death in motorcycle crashes, often can be effectively prevented or reduced to non-disabling levels by the wearing of a helmet.

In an effort to reduce the rising death rate of motorcyclists, the United States Secretary of Commerce in 1967 issued a requirement that states enact compulsory motorcycle helmet laws, or face a substantial reduction in federal highway funding. With this strong incentive, forty-nine states enacted helmet laws between the years 1966 and 1975.

The laws came under attack as improper intrusions into the individual freedoms of motorcyclists. In the US Senate, it was argued that the laws were "an outrageous example of an overbearing, overprotective bureaucracy, gratuitously trying to restrict the freedom of choice of the individual and using the clout of Federal money to try to impose its view on a State government" (121 Congressional Record, 1975).

Congress forbade the withholding of highway funds as a

penalty to states without a helmet law. As a result, twenty-seven states repealed or materially weakened their helmet laws between the years 1976 and 1979. The effect of such repeals was a clear reversal of the declining death rate produced by the laws' enactment. *Figure 6.7*, adapted from the National Highway Traffic Safety Administration's 1980 *Report to Congress on the Effect of Motorcycle Helmet Use Law Repeal*, portrays a compelling picture of the efficacy of helmet laws and the result of their repeal (US Department of Transportation 1980).

Figure 6.7 Motorcyclist deaths per 10,000 motorcycles by year, 1962–81

Source: Reprinted with permission of the publisher, from S. P. Baker, B. O'Neill, and R. S. Karpf, *The Injury Fact Book* (Lexington, Massachusetts: Lexington Books, 1984), p. 261.

An analysis by Watson, Zador, and Wilks (1980) of the effect of helmet law repeals showed a 39 per cent increase in motorcyclist deaths in states with repealed laws. These deaths and other severe, non-fatal injuries result in substantial costs to society. A review of sixty-five motorcyclist patients admitted in fiscal year 1977 to the Maryland Institute for Emergency Medical Services showed that 40 per cent of the patients did not pay for their hospital costs through their own finances or insurance (Insurance Institute for Highway Safety 1980).

Not only have helmet laws been proved to be epidemiologic-ally sound, but they also have been regularly sustained as constitutional by appellate courts. Mandatory helmet laws have been upheld by the highest courts in twenty-five states, and the US Supreme Court has refused to overturn such decisions.

In spite of the efficacy and legality of helmet laws, the majority of states are now without them. This is a result of strong lobbying by motorcyclists who are able to convince legislators that they deserve the freedom to ride helmetless and assume the risk of injury.

This case illustrates the fact that epidemiologic data proving the efficacy of an intervention can be outweighed by the arguments of a vocal, well-organized, but minority opposition to injury control policy.

Air bags

The process of translating epidemiologic information into public policy has been slow and flawed in the area of occupant protection and motor vehicle crashes. By the mid-1960s, it was appreciated that most injuries in motor vehicle crashes result from the impact of the human body with the interior of the vehicle. Most of these injuries could be prevented or reduced by changing the design of the vehicle. The US Senate was cognizant of this information when its Senate Commerce Committee wrote in 1966:

> "For too many years, the public's concern over the safe driving habits and capacity of the driver (the 'nut behind the wheel') was permitted to overshadow the role of the car itself. The 'second collision' – the impact of the individual within the vehicle against the steering wheel, dashboard, windshield, etc. – has been largely neglected. The Committee was greatly impressed by the critical distinction between the causes of the accident itself and causes of the resulting death or injury."   (Senate Report 1966: 2,710)

In 1966 the United States Congress enacted the National Traffic and Motor Vehicle Safety Act, with the stated purpose of reducing "traffic accidents and deaths and injuries to persons resulting from traffic accidents" (15 USC 1381). In its consideration of this legislation, the Senate Commerce Committee reported:

"It should not be necessary to call again the grim roll of Americans lost and maimed on the nation's highways. Yet the compelling need for the strong automobile safety legislation which the Commerce Committee is today reporting lies embodied in those statistics: 1.6 million dead since the coming of the automobile; over 50,000 to die this year."
(Senate Report 1966: 2,709)

The Act ordered the establishment of safety standards for motor vehicles and equipment. These standards were to be minimum standards for motor vehicle or equipment performance; the standards had to be practicable, meet the need for motor vehicle safety, and provide objective criteria.

During the 1960s the automobile manufacturers and suppliers to manufacturers developed the air bag system as an effective method of automatic protection for those involved in frontal or semi-frontal motor vehicle crashes, which cause the majority of occupant deaths and severe injuries. Air bags are inflatable cushions that are stored unobtrusively in the steering wheel and instrument panel. When crash sensors indicate that a frontal or semi-frontal crash has occurred at or above a specified speed, the air bags are instantly and automatically inflated with harmless nitrogen gas.

Impressed with the potential for saving lives with air bags, the government announced on 2 July, 1969 its intention to develop a rule regarding air bags. The notice described the "enormous advantages" of air bags over traditional restraint systems, and stated that "Because of the protection such a restraint system would provide, it is desirable that the system be provided in new motor vehicles as soon as possible, and not later than January 1, 1972" (34 Federal Register 1969).

As soon as the government made obvious its intention to mandate the installation of automatic protection in cars, the automobile manufacturers began to object to this form of regulation. Ford Motor Company, having stated in 1968 that its air bag system provided "significant advantages over existing restraint systems" (Kemmerer, Chute, and Hass 1968), by August, 1969 testified that "it would be prudent to delay wide application [of air bag systems] until we have had further experience with the concept" (Transcript 1969).

For more than fifteen years following the government's first attempt to regulate the installation of automatic protection in cars, this issue has been bitterly fought in Congress, in regulatory agencies, and in the courts. Scientific evidence as to the efficacy of air bags and epidemiologic evidence as to the number of lives that would be saved by the installation of air bags in cars has been irrefutable. Air bags have been extensively tested under laboratory conditions to insure that they provide the desired protection, would not deploy inadvertently, and would not damage hearing or make steering impossible after inflation. Volunteers protected by air bags were uninjured by decelerative forces simulating thirty-one miles per hour barrier impacts (double the speed at which volunteers can be tested wearing standard seat belts).

Approximately 12,000 air bag equipped cars were produced during the mid-1970s and have provided more than 1 billion miles of on-the-road evidence that air bags give good protection in crashes without adverse effects.

In 1981, the National Highway Traffic Safety Administration rescinded the standard which would have required automatic protection in automobiles, as part of the administration's deregulation campaign. This action was contested in the courts by the insurance industry, and was ultimately condemned by the Supreme Court. In a unanimous opinion, the Supreme Court said: "For a decade, the automobile industry waged the regulatory equivalent of war against the airbag and lost – the inflatable restraint was proven sufficiently effective" (Motor Vehicle Manufacturers Association v. State Farm Mutual 1982). The Department of Transportation was ordered to reconsider the automatic protection standard.

In 1984, the Department of Transportation issued a revised automatic protection standard which orders the phasing in of some form of automatic restraints over a period of years. However, the standard provides that if states comprising two-thirds of the United States population pass mandatory seat belt use laws effective by 1 September, 1989, the requirement for automatic protection will be rescinded (Teret 1985). As of this writing, the revised standard is being fought in the courts.

For more than fifteen years, strong public health advocacy efforts have been unable to achieve effective legislation and regulation that puts air bags in cars. Over that period of time, the absence of air bags has contributed to more than 400,000 deaths and millions of serious injuries. Because of this lack of effective legislation and regulation, public health figures have looked to litigation as a possible answer to the problem. Product liability lawsuits brought against car manufacturers by crash victims whose injuries would have been averted by the presence of an air bag may convince manufacturers to offer air bags. At some point, it becomes economically prudent to invest in prevention rather than to pay the penalties for neglect.

In 1982, an article was published in *Trial*, the magazine of the Association of Trial Lawyers of America, suggesting that car manufacturers are liable for failure to provide air bags (Teret and Downey 1982). In 1984, the first case involving air bag liability was settled by a car manufacturer paying $1.8 million to a woman who suffered brain damage in a semi-frontal collision. The epidemiology of motor vehicle injuries comprised part of the evidence to be used against the manufacturer to prove the scope and foreseeability of these injuries.

Thus, in the area of air bag protection, the epidemiology of injuries has been used in the arenas of legislation, regulation, and litigation to promote injury control.

Protecting children as motor vehicle occupants

In 1979, national data on motor vehicle occupant deaths in young children were analyzed for the first time by specific year of age, and by month of age for infants less than one year old (Baker 1979). The analysis revealed very high death rates in the youngest children (*Figure 6.8*). Previously the phenomenon had not been recognized because data were presented for larger age groups or included pedestrian deaths, which in young children increase with age and mask the high occupant death rates among infants.

The results of this analysis were widely and rapidly publicized

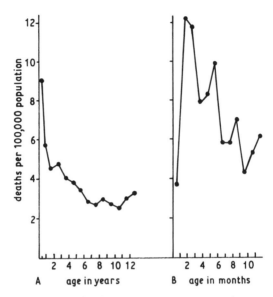

Figure 6.8 Occupant deaths per 100,000 population per year, 1976–77. A. Death rates for ages 0–12 years, with separate points for the first and second six months of life. B. Death rates for ages 0–11 months

Source: Reprinted with permission of the publisher, from S. P. Baker, Motor Vehicle Occupant Deaths in Young Children, *Pediatrics* 64(6): 860–61, 1979

in the scientific and lay press. The fact that death rates in infants are about three times the rates for children age 5–9 was used to make a strong case against what was then a widespread practice – namely, allowing infants to travel in cars on the laps or in the arms of parents and other passengers.

The first state law requiring that young children in cars be properly restrained in car seats was passed in 1978 in Tennessee, primarily because of the efforts of Dr Robert Sanders, a health officer who knew that motor vehicle crashes claimed the lives of more children than any other type of injury. The law was approved by the legislature only after the addition of an amendment excluding children traveling on the laps of older people! It was soon dubbed "the child-crusher amendment," because in a crash a lap-held child strikes the instrument panel and is then struck by the body of the person who had been holding the child. Although the amendment was eventually removed, an initial effect of the law was to *increase* on-lap travel of two- and three-year-old children (Williams and Wells 1981).

The data on high death rates in young children were emphasized by lobbyists and in information packets for legislators (IIHS 1985) when bills were subsequently introduced in other states. Combined with data on the relative importance of occupant deaths as a cause of child mortality and on the effectiveness of restraint systems in preventing such deaths and injuries, this formed the epidemiologic basis for sound public policy. Between 1978 and 1985, in an unusually swift adoption of a public health measure, all fifty states passed laws requiring child passengers to be restrained in private cars.

Recent epidemiologic analysis of the coverage of such laws reveals that there are unacceptable gaps in coverage (Teret *et al.* 1986). These gaps involve statutory language exempting children driven in out-of-state cars, by out-of-state drivers, by someone not their parent or legal guardian, or in particular vehicle body types. The data demonstrate the need to amend child restraint laws to provide greater and more uniform coverage throughout the states.

Rear lights on cars

On occasion, epidemiologic evidence has clearly influenced car design. Rear end collisions, although they represent only 2 per cent of fatal crashes, comprise about 15 per cent of all reported crashes. They are important not only for their numbers but because they cause injuries, especially neck injuries. They are particularly prominent among urban crashes. Case control experiments using several different brake light systems proved that a 50 per cent reduction in urban rearend crashes can be achieved by adding a single, centrally mounted brake light just below the rear window. Initial trials, in which different types of lights were randomly assigned to Washington, DC taxicabs, were subsequently verified by a case control experiment involving passenger cars in eighteen states (Rausch, Wong, and Kirkpatrick 1982; Reilly, Kurke, and Bukenmaier 1980). Consistently, the high, centrally mounted brake light evoked a quicker braking response from the drivers in the following cars. There was no significant change in other types of crashes. Thus, occupants of vehicles equipped with the modified brake lights were protected because of an automatic signalling device that allowed other drivers to perform better.

On the basis of several studies showing the same effect, the Department of Transportation promulgated a regulation requiring that new cars be manufactured with similar brake lights. The regulation is of particular interest because of the experimental design used to test the effectiveness of the new system under real-world conditions, the speed with which a regulation was promulgated, and the lack of strong industry opposition to the regulation.

Fire-safe cigarettes

House fires cause 5,000 deaths each year in the United States, or more than 80 per cent of all deaths related to fires and burns. Death rates are especially high in young children and the elderly. Rates in low income areas are twice the rates in high income areas (Baker, O'Neill, and Karpf 1984). Studies of fatal house fires show that more than 40 per cent are ignited by cigarettes. Typically, a cigarette falls onto upholstered furniture or a bed and smolders long enough to ignite the material. Fire often does not erupt until several hours after the cigarette was dropped, when everyone in the dwelling may be asleep. The peak time for fatal house fires is from about 2:00 a.m. to 6:00 a.m.

Alcohol, a prominent factor in almost all types of fatal injuries, is especially important in cigarette-ignited fires: about 50 per cent of adult victims have blood alcohol concentrations of 0.10 per cent or more (Mierley and Baker 1983). The involvement of alcohol makes it particularly unlikely that educational approaches to "safe smoking behaviors" will be effective.

Cigarettes vary widely in their fire igniting potential, which is related to the temperature at which they smolder and the length of time they continue to smolder without being puffed on. Several brands of cigarettes tend to automatically self-extinguish within a few minutes, and in controlled tests do not ignite upholstery (DeFrancesco and McGuire 1985; McLoughlin 1982).

Characteristics of the tobacco, paper, and design of cigarettes determine their ability to start fires. Congressional efforts to have the ignition potential of cigarettes placed under the regulatory authority of the Consumer Product Safety Commission were initiated in 1974, but were successfully blocked by the tobacco lobby. Federal legislation has created a study panel to explore the issue of fire safe cigarettes. In addition, bills have been introduced in several states prohibiting the sale of cigarettes that do not meet fire safe standards.

Product liability litigation is likely to have a major influence on cigarette design as regards fire ignition potential. In one study, 39 per cent of the people killed in cigarette-ignited house fires were children or adults other than the smokers of the cigarettes (Mierley and Baker 1983). Product liability suits on behalf of such innocent victims of cigarette-ignited fires in homes and hotels are considered to have an excellent chance of success. The fact that epidemiologic data have consistently and for many years pointed to the importance of cigarettes as an ignition factor contributes substantially to the likelihood of successful suits.

Firearms

Firearms cause some 34,000 deaths each year. Of these, about 2,000 are unintentional, 14,000 homicidal, 17,000 suicidal, and 1,000 of undetermined intent or caused by police intervention. Teenaged males have especially high death rates from unintentional shootings; at age fourteen, this is a major cause of injury death in males (Baker, O'Neill, and Karpf 1984). From age fifteen to thirty-four, firearm injuries (unintentional and intentional, combined) are the second leading cause of death in the United States. (Motor vehicles are in first place and cancer a distant third.) For black males firearms are the leading cause of death for ages 15–34. Among some occupational groups, including police officers, taxicab drivers, and gas station operators, shooting is an important cause of work-related death.

Four factors are of special pertinence to prevention policy. The first is the correlation between rates of private ownership of guns and firearm death rates. In many other countries private ownership of guns is illegal and firearm deaths are rare. In the United States, the ratio of firearm to non-firearm homicides is highest in regions where firearm ownership is most common (the south and west) (Baker, O'Neill, and Karpf 1984). Even among counties within a state the correlation holds: in South Carolina, counties with high gun ownership rates have significantly higher death rates than other counties (Alexander *et al* 1985).

The second factor is that in two-thirds of family homicides, the weapon used to kill is a gun (Rosenberg, Stark, and Zahn 1986). In such cases, many deaths result from arguments and fights, unplanned events where the outcome is largely dependent upon the lethality of the available weapons.

Given the spontaneous nature of many assaultive injuries and suicides, the lethality of available weapons is a major determinant of the outcome. Thus, the third factor is the high ratio of firearm deaths to non-fatal injuries. In Denmark, the case fatality rate for firearm injuries was found to be fifteen times the rate for knives (Hedeboe *et al.* 1985). Of special note is the fact that while the assaultive injury rate in Denmark was similar to that found in Northern Ohio, the homicide rate was four times as high in Ohio as in Denmark, where private ownership of guns is permitted only for hunting (Baker 1985).

Fourth, small, easily concealed handguns comprise the majority of the guns used in homicides, as well as a substantial proportion of the guns in suicides and unintentional death. The concealability of handguns is often crucial to their use in assaults but is not essential for other purposes. Self-protection, the reason given for handgun ownership by 43 per cent of owners, does not require that a weapon be concealable (Teret and Wintemute 1983). Because of their prominence among weapons used in homicides and the fact that their small size and concealability serve little purpose for legitimate use, handguns are often singled out by laws and ordinances limiting the purchase or ownership of guns.

Together, these facets of the epidemiology of firearm-related deaths and injuries have important implications. Combined with their lethality, the widespread *availability* of easily concealed handguns for impetuous use by people who are angry, drunk, or frightened appears to be a major determinant of the high firearm death rate in the United States. Each contributing factor has implications for prevention. Unfortunately, issues related to gun control have evoked such strong sentiments that epidemiologic data are rarely employed to good advantage.

Federal regulatory jurisdiction over firearms is within the Bureau of Alcohol, Tobacco, and Firearms of the Treasury Department. Regulatory agencies which are charged with the protection of the public's health and safety have either chosen not to deal with guns as a health problem or have been expressly forbidden to do so by their legislative authorization. Research on firearms as a public health problem has not been funded by the federal government.

As is the case with air bags and cigarettes, in the face of legislation and regulatory inaction, litigation is now being used to address the gun problem. Product liability suits that transfer the economic costs of gun injuries back to the gun's manufacturer have been initiated across the country. The epidemiologic evidence to support the risk:benefit analysis for these lawsuits has been compiled (Teret and Wintemute 1983). Recently, the highest court of Maryland ruled that the distributor of a Saturday Night Special, a cheap handgun of little legitimate value, could be held liable to a store owner wounded by the gun during a robbery (Maryland Court of Appeals 1985).

Conclusion

Injury prevention research has suffered from lack of both funding and properly trained scientists. The most perplexing problem, however, is the failure to apply known solutions and technology to present-day injury producing events. This may be largely due to the public's improper perception that injuries are unforeseeable, random events. Another major factor is that injury producing designs, products, and policies are strongly defended by those who profit by them. If the interests and health of the public are to be defended, our knowledge of the epidemiology of injuries must be applied. Health professionals have opportunities to enlighten and influence the regulators, legislators, manufacturers, designers, planners, and other decision-makers who influence the likelihood of injury from many sources.

204 *Epidemiology and health policy*

References

Alexander, G.R., Massey, R.M., Gibbs, T., and Altekruse, J. (1985) Firearm-Related Fatalities: An Epidemiologic Assessment of Violent Death. *American Journal of Public Health* 75(2): 165–68.
Baker, S.P. (1979) Motor Vehicle Occupant Deaths in Young Children. *Pediatrics* 64(6): 860–61.
—— (1980) Prevention of Childhood Injuries. *The Medical Journal of Australia* 1: 466–70.
—— (1981) Childhood Injuries: The Community Approach to Prevention. *Journal of Public Health Policy* 2(3): 235–46.
—— (1983) Medical Data and Injuries. *American Journal of Public Health* 73(7): 733–34.
—— (1985) Without Guns, Do People Kill People? *American Journal of Public Health* 75(6): 587–88.
Baker, S.P. and Harvey, A.H. (1985) Fall Injuries in the Elderly. *Clinics in Geriatric Medicine* 1(3): 501–12.
Baker, S.P., O'Neill, B., and Karpf, R.S. (1984) *The Injury Fact Book.* Lexington, Massachusetts: Lexington Books.
Barry, P.Z. (1975) Individual Versus Community Orientation in the Prevention of Injuries. *Preventive Medicine* 4(1): 47–56.
Committee on Trauma Research (1985) Injury in America: A Continuing Public Health Problem. Washington, DC: National Academy Press.
DeFrancesco, S. and McGuire, A. (1985) The Fire-Safe Cigarette Campaign. *Journal of Public Health Policy* 6(3): 342–48.
Department of Transportation, Washington, DC (1980) *A Report to the Congress on the Effect of Motorcycle Helmet Use Law Repeal – A Case for Helmet Use.*
Haddon, W., Jr. (1980) Advances in the Epidemiology of Injuries as a Basis for Public Policy. *Public Health Reports* 95(5): 411–21.
Haddon, W., Jr. and Baker, S.P. (1981) Injury Control. In Duncan Clark and Brian MacMahon (eds) *Preventive and Community Medicine.* Boston: Little, Brown and Company, pp. 109–40.
Haupt, B.J. and Graves, E. (1982) Detailed Diagnoses and Procedures for Patients Discharged from Short-Stay Hospitals: United States, 1979. DHHS Publication No. (PHS) 82-1274-1. Washington, DC: US Department of Health and Human Services.
Hedeboe, J., Charles, A.V., Nielson, J., Grymer, F., Moller, B.N., Moller-Madsden, B., and Jensen, S.E.T. (1985) Violence – Patterns in a Danish Community. *American Journal of Public Health* 75: 651–53.
Insurance Institute for Highway Safety (1980) Unhelmeted Motor-

cyclists are Taxpayers' Burden. *Status Report* 15(7): 7.

—— (1985) *Children in Crashes.* Washington, DC: Insurance Institute for Highway Safety.

Kemmerer, R.M., Chute, R., and Hass, D.P. (1968) Automatic Inflatable Occupant Restraint System. SAE Paper 680033.

Kraus, J.F., Franti, C.E., Riggins, R.S., Richards, D., and Borhani, N.O. (1975) Incidence of Traumatic Spinal Cord Lesions. *Journal of Chronic Diseases* 28: 471–92.

McLoughlin, E. (1982) The Cigarette Safety Act. *Journal of Public Health Policy* 3(2): 226–28.

Maryland Court of Appeals: Kelly vs. R.G. Industries, Decided 3 October, 1985.

Mierley, M.C. and Baker, S.P. (1983) Fatal Housefires in an Urban Population. *Journal of the American Medical Association* 249(11): 1466–468.

Motor Vehicle Manufacturers Association vs. State Farm Mutual, 103 S. Ct. 2856 (1983).

National Transportation Safety Board (1980) *Safety-Report – The Status of General Aviation Aircraft Crashworthiness.* Washington, DC: National Transportation Safety Board.

Rausch, A.R., Wong, J., and Kirkpatrick, M. (1982) A Field Test of Two Single Center, High Mounted Brake Light Systems. *Accident Analysis and Prevention* 14: 287–91.

Reilly, R.E., Kurke, D.S., and Bukenmaier, C.C. Jr. (1980) Validation of the Reduction of Rear-end Collisions by a High Mounted Auxiliary Stoplamp. Report No. DOT-HS-805-360. Washington, DC: US Department of Transportation, National Highway Traffic Safety Administration.

Robertson, L.S. (1983) *Injuries: Causes, Control Strategies, and Public Policy.* Lexington, Massachusetts: Lexington Books.

Rosenberg, M.L., Stark, E., and Zahn, M.A. (1986) Interpersonal Violence: Homicide and Spouse Abuse. In Maxcy-Rosenau, *Public Health and Preventive Medicine.* Norwalk, Conn.: Appleton Century Crofts.

Senate Report No. 1301, 89th Congress, 2nd Session, 1966; 1966 US Code, Congress and Administration News.

Smith, G.S. (1985) Measuring the Gap for Unintentional Injuries: The Carter Center Health Policy Project. *Public Health Reports* 100(6): 565–68.

Teret, S.P. (1985) Air Bags *and* Seat Belts – Untangling Standard 208. *Journal of Public Health Policy* 6: 5–6.

Teret, S.P. and Downey, E. (1982) Air Bag Litigation. *Trial* 18(7): 93–9.

Teret, S.P. and Wintemute, G.J. (1983) Handgun Injuries: The

Epidemiologic Evidence for Assessing Legal Responsibility. *Hamline Law Review* 6(2): 341–50.

Teret, S.P., Jones, A.S., Williams, A.F., and Wells, J.K. (1986) Child Restraint Laws: An Analysis of Gaps in Coverage. *American Journal of Public Health* 76(1): 31–4.

Transcript of Meeting on Inflatable Occupant Restraint Systems, Washington, DC, 27 August, 1969.

Waldron, H.A. (1976) *Lecture Notes on Occupational Medicine*. Philadelphia: J.B. Lippincott.

Waller, J.A. (1985) *Injury Control: A Guide to the Causes and Prevention of Trauma*. Lexington, Massachusetts: D.C. Heath.

Watson, G.S., Zador, P.L., and Wilks, A. (1980) The Repeal of Helmet Use Laws and Increased Motorcycle Mortality in the United States, 1975–1978. *American Journal of Public Health* 70(6): 579–86.

Williams, A.F. (1979) Restraint Use Legislation: Its Prospects for Increasing the Protection of Children in Cars. *Accident Analysis and Prevention* 11(4): 255–260.

Williams, A.F. and Wells, J.K. (1981) The Tennessee Child Restraint Law in Its Third Year. *American Journal of Public Health* 71(2): 163–65.

Williams, A.F., Wells, J.K., and Lund, A.K. (1983) Voluntary Seat Belt Use Among High School Students. *Accident Analysis and Prevention* 15(2): 161–65.

121 Congressional Record 40261 (1975).

34 Federal Register 11148, July 2, 1969.

15 U.S.C. 1381.

Seven

Infectious diseases

Abram S. Benenson

Epidemiology is defined as the study of the distribution and determinants of disease frequency in man (MacMahon and Pugh 1970: 1); one of its important purposes is "to provide the basis for developing and evaluating preventive procedures and public health practices" (Lilienfeld and Lilienfeld 1980: 4). It originated, as its name implies, because of the concern of man over the repeated emergence of disease epidemics. Long before the development of the science of epidemiology, wise men recognized cause and effect, perhaps with divine inspiration, and translated their findings into public policy by incorporating appropriate measures into religious doctrine. Deuteronomy 23 verses 12–13 states "And a place shalt thou have without the camp, whither thou shalt go forth abroad; And a spade shalt thou have with thy weapons; and it shall be, when thou sittest abroad, that thou shalt dig therewith, and shalt afterward cover that which cometh from thee"; a better method for preventing fecal-oral disease among military forces in the field has not been devised. Now we call the spades entrenching tools!

Someone in authority recognized that the epidemic of plague

which devastated Europe in the fourteenth century had entered
Europe from the East. This led to a thirty day restriction placed
on vessels entering Venice from the Levant; this was then
extended to forty days' quarantine because this was a number
related to the period that Moses and Christ had spent in the
desert! Again, a public health practice was promulgated as a
religious policy, evolving from astute observations by wise
men of the distribution of cases in the ongoing epidemic.

Who these wise men were, how their observations were
implemented into action, and the interval between observation
and establishment of the indicated health policy will remain
unknown. In both examples, it would appear that religion was
involved in establishing policy. It behooves us clearly to define
policy. The *Oxford Dictionary* (Onions 1955: 153) defines
policy as "5. A course of action adopted and pursued by a
government party, statesman, etc.; any course of action
adopted as advantageous or expedient." This definition indicates
the possibility that within a society there may, and probably
would be, differing health policies, such as that which is
promulgated by the government, and, at the other end of the
spectrum, that which is in practice among the people.

In the arena of infectious diseases, establishment of policy
has usually been motivated by fear. In earlier times epidemic
disease was not uncommon, and people lived in dread of the
next epidemic. When it did appear, a policy for some sort of
action was demanded. Sometimes the action was appropriate,
but often not. Discharging a cannon from Philadelphia City
Hall to stop an epidemic of yellow fever was inappropriate,
even though recommended by an eminent clinician, Benjamin
Church. Only a few years later, the report by Edward Jenner of
the protective effect of cowpox virus against the dread
smallpox disease became governmental as well as societal
policy. In the United States, this may well have been largely
due to the personal involvement of the President himself, Thomas
Jefferson, in promulgating its use and later in supporting an
act of Congress in 1813 "that required the federal government
to guarantee the efficacy of cowpox vaccine and to distribute it
free of charge to anyone requesting it." Many opposed any such
measures, and we have all seen the pictures showing cows'
heads emerging from various parts of the bodies of those who
might submit to vaccination; the anti-vaccination forces never

did cease their activities! To review some of the forces involved in the establishment and implementation of policy, several examples will be explored.

Cholera

Scientific disagreement is an essential part of scientific progress; it is the leaven which stimulates the further studies which are essential to establish the true facts. Unfortunately, old masters occupy dominant positions; they take a long time to fade away, and their disciples usually perpetuate their myths. In the cholera field, the miasma theory of von Pettenkofer held sway for many years and the dispute between the "contagionists" and the "anti-contagionists" lasted for more years.

Wade Hampton Frost, writing the introduction to *Snow on Cholera*, a reprinting of two papers by John Snow published in 1936, stated:

"Epidemiology at any given time is something more than the total of its established facts. It includes their orderly arrangement into chains of inference which extend more or less beyond the bounds of direct observation. Such of these chains as are well and truly laid guide investigation to the facts of the future; those that are ill made fetter progress. But it is not easy, when divergent theories are presented, to distinguish immediately between those which are sound and those which are merely plausible. Therefore it is instructive to turn back to arguments which have been tested by the subsequent course of events; to cultivate discrimination by the study of those which the advance of definite knowledge has confirmed."

John Snow published his pamphlet *On the Mode of Communication of Cholera* in the summer of 1849 in which he clearly presented his belief that cholera was due to a specific micro-organism, an obligate parasite, propagating only in the human intestinal tract and disseminated by ingestion of excreta. The cholera epidemic of 1854 provided Snow the opportunity to carry out his classic comparison of the incidence of cholera among the users of two different water supplies, one (provided by the Southwark and Vauxhall Company) which was so contaminated with excreta that the addition of a drop of silver nitrate produced a visible precipitate of silver chloride, and the other (from the Lambeth Company) which drew its water from the Thames River above the introduction of London sewage. By "shoe-leather epidemiology," visiting each house, Snow developed the well-known table showing that there were 315 cholera deaths in each 10,000 houses using the "bad" water in comparison to only 37 deaths among those using "good" water. The work of John Snow is today considered to have been an ideal epidemiological study, clearly defining the mode of transmission of the disease and pointing to the obvious method of prevention. While he did not demonstrate the specific etiological organism, he postulated that there was a specific agent involved (Snow 1855). Interestingly, the specific organism which causes cholera was identified, named *Vibrio cholerae*, and reported in an Italian journal in the same year, 1854, by Filippo Pacini. (However, today everyone believes that it was Robert Koch who discovered the etiological organism in 1883!)

With these facts available to the public, what was the effect on policy? The British authorities insisted at the International Sanitary Conferences of 1874, 1881, and 1885 that cholera was not transmissible from man to man. This was the official British policy; it was clearly motivated because British commerce with her important colony would be seriously interfered with if the epidemiologic observation made by scientists from other European countries that the homeland of cholera was in India was generally accepted. In 1888, Sir Joseph Frayer, an internationally honored physician (a fellow of the Philadelphia Academy of Sciences) declared at the annual oration of the Medical Society of London, that cholera "may depend on certain states of the atmosphere, deficiency or excess of electrical or magnetic tension, different degrees of moisture, of ozone, or other modifications of its physical properties." He dismissed "theories of contagion and diffusion by human intercourse" (Howard-Jones 1974: 416). This attitude was not that of an individual, but was shared by Frayer's fellow delegate to the conference held in 1885, Surgeon-General Sir William Hunter "whose 'unqualified opinion' was that cholera was non-communicable, non-specific, and endemic in Egypt"

(Howard-Jones 1974: 380). At last, at the International Sanitary Conference of 1892, thirty-nine years after Snow had published his work, the British representative, Dr Richard Thorne, stated that "the public health service of the United Kingdom is in perfect harmony with the scientific opinion of the great nations represented at this conference" (Howard-Jones 1974: 425). At the working level, when cholera reappeared in continental Europe in 1873, John Simon, the medical officer of the Privy Council and Local Government Board of London, stressed the vital importance of an uncontaminated supply of drinking water. He still was not prepared to accept Snow's findings completely; while he admits that "all matters which the patient discharges from his stomach and bowels are infective," he hedges by stating that there are "two main dangers: first, the contamination of water-supplies by 'house-refuse or other like kinds of filth'; second, 'breathing air which is foul from the same sorts of impurity' " (Howard-Jones 1974: 242).

These experiences demonstrate a few salient truths about the making of health policy: first, that men in authoritative positions tend to dominate policy, and those who have achieved these positions often are reluctant to change the convictions they have derived from earlier training and experience; and second, these convictions can be strongly influenced by economic or other factors of national interest. This may represent one of the definitions of policy given in *Webster's Seventh New Collegiate Dictionary*, 1970: "management or procedure based primarily on material interest" (Webster 1970: 656)!

These events took place 100 years ago. It is worth reviewing some events in the present era. Since 1960, extensive epidemiological work has been carried out in Asia and in research laboratories in the western world. These have conclusively shown that currently available cholera vaccines afford protection against infection for a short period of time (3–4 months), and that the disease can be simply and effectively treated by oral rehydration and appropriate antibiotics. For many years, vaccination against cholera was required for travel to or between many countries. Epidemiologic studies demonstrated and confirmed that cholera vaccine gave protection against manifest disease not only for a short period of time, but it also did not prevent asymptomatic intestinal infection (Benenson 1977). Thus, it constituted no barrier to importation, and the United States Public Health Service (PHS) eliminated any requirement for cholera vaccine for entry into the United States. Shortly thereafter, the World Health Organization (WHO) recommended to all members that cholera vaccine no longer be a requirement for international travel. Thus, national and international health policy with respect to vaccination requirements, an action at the governmental level, was established rapidly and effectively.

Ironically, the response of the practitioners to improvement in treatment has not been so prompt. Oral rehydration was shown to be effective not only in the treatment of cholera but of all patients with dehydration and was recommended in 1970 by WHO for use. Fifteen years later, physicians of the developed countries still resist its use, feeling that its effectiveness had been shown in the treatment of patients in underdeveloped populations and that its salt content would be dangerous for well-fed children. Appropriate studies have demonstrated the fallacy in this assumption (Santosham *et al.* 1982). One wonders whether here again economic factors enter the picture, since rehydration by intravenous infusion provides a much greater financial return than simply prescribing a liquid to be drunk.

Reye syndrome

This is another instance in which implementation of epidemiological findings is being delayed for economic reasons. In 1963, Reye in Australia described a clinical syndrome which occurred one day to a few weeks after a child was sick with influenza (predominantly influenza B) or chickenpox. During the previous year, 1962, Mortimer and Lepow had reported on two infants with chickenpox who developed a clinical and pathological picture similar to that later described by Reye; they had questioned whether these were cases of aspirin poisoning. Over the years, the association of this serious syndrome, fatal in about one-third of the cases, with the use of aspirin or other salicylates used to treat the fever of the initial illness has been reported by several physicians. In 1976, the

Neurological Drug Advisory Committee of the Food and Drug Administration recommended against the use of antiemetics, aspirin and acetaminophen in children with signs and symptoms suggesting Reye Syndrome (RS).

In 1980, case control studies comparing various factors in cases and in matched controls were published. In Arizona, all of seven RS cases had received salicylates before the onset of their symptoms, in comparison with eight of sixteen controls; in Ohio, the comparisons were 95 of 97 (97 per cent) versus 114 of 160 controls (71 per cent). In Michigan there were two studies; in the first, 24/25 (96 per cent) with RS had received aspirin in comparison to 34/46 (74 per cent) among controls. When the cases and controls were matched for height of fever, the comparisons were 14/14 versus 14/19. The second study was conducted with greater care and the cases and controls were matched for race, school grade, nature of antecedent viral illness and peak temperature; all of 12 children with RS had received aspirin in comparison to 13 of 29 controls (45%). These results are all statistically significant, that is they are unlikely to occur by chance more than five times in a hundred. The Ohio study was sufficiently large to estimate the relative risk from taking aspirin; this was 11.3 with 95 per cent confidence limits between 2.7 and 47.5; that is if aspirin is given to a child with fever from influenza or chickenpox, that child is between 2.7 and 47.5 times more likely to develop RS than if no salicylates had been given.

One definition of an epidemiologist is that he is an individual qualified to point out the flaws in the design or execution of any epidemiologic study. In March, 1981, a Consensus Conference was held at the National Institutes of Health which considered the data and potential errors in design; the group recommended caution in the use of salicylates in children with influenza or chickenpox. In October, the Center for Disease Control (CDC) convened a group of experts who felt, after reviewing the data and the arguments, that there was "sufficient evidence to support the cautionary statements on salicylate usage that had been published previously by the Center for Disease Control and the NIH Consensus Development Conference." On 11 June, 1982, the Surgeon General's Advisory on the Use of Salicylates and Reye Syndrome was published, with the statement that "the Surgeon General advises against use of salicylate and salicylate-containing medications for children with these diseases [influenza and chickenpox]. The association of salicylates with Reye Syndrome is based upon evidence from epidemiologic studies that are sufficiently strong to justify this warning to parents and health care personnel" (Center for Disease Control 1982). In a footnote to the Advisory, "The Surgeon General notes that the FDA will notify health professionals through its *Drug Bulletin*, will develop lay-language information for widespread distribution and will take the steps necessary to establish new labeling requirements for drugs containing salicylates." Thus was the policy of the PHS enunciated; what was the implementation?

This report predictably resulted in aspirin industry pressure, including threats of lawsuits. The "lay-language information" which was prepared and distributed essentially stated that earlier studies did not necessarily mean that aspirin products should not be used with children during influenza epidemics, but that caution should be used – the caption on the picture of a febrile child reads "A Word of Caution About Treating Flu or Chickenpox." In November, the directive for labeling was withdrawn, and the Secretary of Health and Human Services appointed a PHS Task Force comprised of members of the NIH, the FDA, and CDC to design and implement a new epidemiologic study concerning the nature of the possible relationship between RS and medications. The Institute of Medicine (IOM), National Academy of Sciences, was to advise and critique the protocol, monitor the study progress, and review study analysis and results. Between February and May, 1984 a pilot study was conducted to determine the study feasibility and establish a methodology. This included 29 RS cases and 143 controls drawn from four sources:

1 the same hospital;
2 the same emergency room;
3 the same school; and
4 a group identified by random-digit dialing.

Ninety-seven per cent of the RS cases had received salicylates during a preceding respiratory or chickenpox illness, compared with 28, 23, 59 and 55 per cent of the different control groups during their matched illnesses. The risk indicated in this study equals or is greater than that observed in other studies.

After the IOM reviewed these data in December 1984, they considered them so significant that they stated:

"2 Results of the pilot study should be released promptly to the public and to scientists for review and analysis.

3 Analysis of the pilot study data reveals a strong association between the Reye syndrome and the use of aspirin; considering data from previous studies also show an association of use of aspirin and Reye syndrome, the Committee recommends that steps should be taken to protect the public health before the full study is completed."

(Center for Disease Control, 1985)

We see here the operation of the different levels for health policy. The most important policy in protecting the health of the public is that which the public follows, and effective implementation of the declared policy depends on assuring that the potential user of aspirin is advised of its danger when used in cases of influenza or chickenpox. This is why labeling becomes important. Despite this announcement from the IOM, labeling still has not become national health policy. The aspirin industry has stated that their members will voluntarily carry out the indicated labeling. By June, 1985, aspirin with warning labeling had not appeared in the market.

This example demonstrates the power of industry to influence the development of health policy. The American Public Health Association, working with the Health Research Group, brought a suit against the FDA in 1982 to force the government to require warning labels on all products containing aspirin. In March, 1983, the US District Court issued a summary judgment for FDA, ruling that the delay in labeling was not unreasonable and that the court was reluctant to interfere with FDA decision-making. The court decision was appealed to the US Court of Appeals and in July, 1984, this court affirmed the decision of the lower court but returned the case for the lower court to decide if FDA's final ruling on the need for labeling was being unreasonably delayed, and stated, "The record of evidence indicating that industry pressure precipitated this reversal . . . is particularly troubling in that the pace of agency decisionmaking may jeopardize the lives of children" (American Public Health Association 1985).

Swine flu

In a litigious society, the development of health policy is heavily influenced by concern over any potential law suits. Our experience with the swine flu vaccination program is an excellent example.

In January, 1976, a nineteen-year-old military recruit at Fort Dix died of influenza. From him and from four other recruits hospitalized with influenza, five viruses were isolated which had the properties of the swine influenza virus. Six other individuals hospitalized at Fort Dix developed an increase in anti-swine flu antibodies, indicative that they had been infected by this virus. In addition, several hundred "healthy" recruits at Fort Dix were found to have swine flu antibodies. This outbreak had occurred during January, and the last case had appeared during early February.

While localized outbreaks of influenza among military recruits had not been unusual, there were here two elements of great concern. The first was the isolation of swine flu virus from a fatal case of influenza and from four other cases of clinical influenza. The swine flu virus, which causes epidemic disease among swine, had never been isolated in earlier outbreaks among military recruits; previous isolations of this virus had been only from individuals with swine contact. Man-to-man spread of the swine flu virus was most unusual, but serological studies at Fort Dix revealed that 34 per cent of the men in a platoon from which one of the confirmed cases had come had antibodies against this virus (Center for Disease Control 1976). Second, the death from influenza of a nineteen-year-old physically fit individual was unexpected, since influenza is normally lethal for those over sixty-five years of age and those with chronic disease. To complicate the situation further, during December, 1975 two patients admitted to a hospital in Charlottesville, Virginia, with pneumonia developed rises in titer of anti-swine flu antibodies; one had had contact with hogs but the other had not (Thompson 1976). These events immediately brought to mind the influenza pandemic of 1918–19, which has been attributed to epidemic swine flu virus, based on antibody studies carried out when influenza viruses became available for study fifteen years later. Specific antibodies against this virus were found in those who lived through the pandemic; antibody prevalence was markedly lower in those born after 1924 and essentially disappeared in those born after 1930.

The pandemic of 1918–19 first appeared as a mild wave of influenza, followed by a lethal second wave. This was truly catastrophic; it first appeared in Boston in September, 1918 and spread throughout the country to reach its peak by November. It hit the crowded military camps, with 24,000 troops dying. From 25 to 40 per cent of the people in affected communities were hit almost simultaneously; the highest mortality was among those between ages fifteen and fifty. The death rates ranged from 60 per thousand in New York to 158 per thousand population in Philadelphia. The estimated number of cases globally ranged from 200 to 700 million, with 20 million deaths; at least 500,000 of these occurred in the United States. Deaths often occurred within a day or two of onset; many were from bacterial pneumonia but many were caused by true viral pneumonias (Rogers 1968).

This was the setting in February, 1976; the same or a closely related virus had caused the death of a young healthy soldier, the population was devoid of antibodies against this virus, and man-to-man transmission of the infection had been demonstrated. The 1918 situation might be repeating itself but there was one significant difference; now we knew how to make influenza vaccines which could protect against infection. Urgent conferences concluded that action was imperative. While there might be no further spread and the preparation and administration of a vaccine would be a waste of money, if vaccine was withheld and a pandemic like that of 1918 developed, inaction would be utterly inexcusable. It became an issue of saving money or saving lives.

To have vaccine ready for the next influenza season, expected to be from September to March, would require that the manufacturers initiate work without delay. On 20 February, Fort Dix isolates were provided to all vaccine manufacturers; on 10 March, the HEW Advisory Committee on Immunization Practices (ACIP) met and the decision was made that vaccine production should proceed. On 24 March, President Ford endorsed a program for producing 200 million doses of vaccine for a mass immunization program. The plan was to immunize high risk individuals during July and August, and the general population during September through November, 1976. On 12 April, Congress passed a joint resolution which provided about $135 million for a comprehensive, nationwide immunization program. While this should have allowed adequate time for vaccine production, the question arose of liability insurance for the manufacturers who refused to accept the jeopardy of lawsuits based on any adverse reactions the vaccine recipients might experience. In July, they threatened to halt production and withhold vaccine already produced if their liability concerns were not resolved. Finally, on 10 August, Congress authorized the National Swine Flu Immunization Program of 1976 by which the federal government accepted liability for personal injury or death arising out of the program. With this issue resolved, production continued but time had been lost and the first vaccine was not available until 1 October, when about 25 million doses were distributed. By 1 December, fewer than 112 million doses had been shipped to the states, so that if an epidemic had occurrred, vaccine was available to only immunize 12 per cent of the population by 1 October and 53 per cent by 1 December against a disease which could hit as early as September.

The immunization program began on 1 October. It was terminated on 16 December because of the reporting of a large number of cases of Guillain-Barre syndrome (GBS) among those receiving the vaccine. This syndrome was occurring in those who had not been vaccinated as well as in those who had; cases were reported to the CDC based on reports to state health departments by local physicians. Diagnostic guidelines for GBS were not established and virtually every case reported to the state health officers as GBS was accepted. More than 4,000 claims for over $3 billion have been filed against the US government claiming that a variety of illnesses including GBS, multiple sclerosis (MS), transverse myelitis, polymyositis, and rheumatoid arthritis have resulted from the vaccine shot.

Studies carried out by Kurland and his group (1984) cast doubts on the validity of these claims, even though many have been awarded by court action. In Olmstead County, Minnesota, whose population is served by the Mayo Clinic, there was no increase in cases of GBS or of MS in the quarter of the year in which the flu shots were given, nor in the succeeding quarters. Extending these studies to another situation where each case would be carefully documented by qualified neurologists, there were no peaks in incidence of either disease noted among armed forces personnel.

In this instance, a public policy was established at the highest level of the government; this was to immunize the total population against what might become a catastrophic pandemic. Concern over possible litigation delayed the production of the vaccine so that the program would have failed; had an epidemic of 1918–19 proportion developed, there would have been a large and unnecessary loss of life. Actual litigation, much of which is apparently unjustified, has amounted to billions of dollars although the complications for which suits are filed and awards made remain questionable.

Pertussis vaccination

The final problem related to establishment and implementation of a public health policy is that presented by the enthusiasm of the communications media in supporting provocative causes without benefit of epidemiological restraints. Pertussis or whooping cough has been a serious disease worldwide, causing deaths, in the pre-antibiotic days, of 50 per cent of infected infants under three months old and 25 per cent of those under one year of age (Holt and McIntosh 1936); among those who survived, mental retardation, behavioral disorders, or chronic pulmonary disease were not uncommon. In the United States, the largest number of cases (265,269) reported since the disease became reportable in 1922 occurred in 1934; there were more than 7,000 deaths. Vaccination against the disease was introduced in the 1940s and markedly intensified in the 1950s; forty-one states now require immunization for school admission and national policy recommends vaccination against pertussis of all infants, starting at two months of age because of the great danger to such young children. It is given in a combination with diphtheria and tetanus toxoids, in the formulation known as DPT.

The effect of this policy has been very satisfactory. In 1981, only 1,248 cases were reported to the CDC and in recent years the number of deaths from pertussis have ranged from five to twenty annually (antibiotics have reduced the number of deaths due to bacterial complications). However, the vaccine elicts minor adverse reactions of local tenderness and redness, low level fever and malaise in a large proportion of the vaccines; vaccination is rarely followed by serious neurological disease with permanent residue such as may occur with clinical pertussis. In a study in the United States, no serious reactions occurred in over 15,000 children; in a British study persistent neurological damage one year after pertussis vaccination was found in 1:310,000 immunizations (95 per cent confidence limits 1:5,310,000 to 1:54,000 immunizations).

This situation led to two anti-vaccination activities. Legal suits were filed against the vaccine manufacturers under the doctrine of implied warranty; Melvin Belli advertised on television promising parents of any children who had adverse reactions that he would get money for them. The quality of many of these suits was absurd; one suit was brought against the vaccine producer by the parents of a club-footed child on the basis that this congenital defect had not appeared until after the child had received DPT!

Some children were indeed seriously affected. In Britain, dramatic television portrayals in 1974 of children with brain damage attributed to pertussis vaccine were shown, leading to a major decline in the acceptance of vaccine. Two major epidemics followed; one in 1977–79 with more than 100,000 cases and 36 deaths and a second in 1982 with 65,000 cases and 14 deaths (Hinman 1984). In the United States, there arose a militant anti-vaccination (or anti-government) group calling themselves "Dissatisfied Parents Together" which then could use the acronym DPT. Their activities resulted in three nationwide television programs, the first in April, 1982 on the NBC Today Show, in February 1985 a special 20/20 show was aired by ABC, followed in a few weeks by a program on ABC Nightline. While these programs admitted the value of vaccination, they charged that the government had held up the use of an acellular vaccine which caused fewer adverse reactions. Here propaganda came into direct conflict with sound epidemiologic principles; the new vaccine had never been shown in controlled studies to be protective against disease, and the fact that fewer minor reactions occurred did not preclude the possibility of serious reactions since these have occurred in children who had not had evidence of the minor reactions.

With extended use in Japan of an acellular vaccine, a few of the severe side reactions have been observed (Fulginiti 1985). What has been the outcome of these adversarial activities? In 1982, 1,895 cases of pertussis were reported; in 1983, 2,463 cases, an increase of about 600 each year since 1981. While these increases may not be the direct result of this adverse publicity, these lawsuits, often with awards over $1 million, have caused vaccine producers to cease production because of the increasingly high cost of insurance and the price of the vaccine has increased ten-fold.

The American Public Health Association has played an important part in the development of policy concerned with the control of communicable diseases by the publication every five years of the book entitled *The Control of Communicable Diseases in Man*, now in its fourteenth edition. This is prepared by experts in the various diseases, reviewed by governmental and non-governmental health agencies in the United States, and by the World Health Organisation and health authorities of the major English-speaking countries. It is essentially a consensus of these health experts and is the official policy in many political jurisdictions. In the United States, control of vaccine-preventable diseases is carefully established, with advisory committees composed of the outstanding specialists in the country providing input to the Bureau of Biologics of the FDA concerned with what goes into the bottle, and the Surgeon General's Advisory Committee on Immunization Practices (ACIP) working with the CDC personnel (for some decisions, such as stopping routine smallpox vaccination, foreign consultants were also involved). Based on epidemiologic surveillance activities, it became evident that measles outbreaks were occurring frequently among military recruits. These data were presented to the Armed Forces Epidemiological Board, which recommended to the Department of Defense a policy of immunization of all military recruits. No further cases occurred in this segment of the population.

Surveillance data indicate that the focus of measles lies on the university campuses, with outbreaks recently in at least twelve colleges and universities, including the outbreak in a Christian Science college with three deaths. National policy dictates that there should be a requirement for immunization of incoming university students against measles and rubella. A survey was carried out by the Infectious Disease Section of the California State Department of Health Services in the Fall of 1984, and they recommended that colleges and universities in the state adopt policies requiring documentation of measles, rubella and tetanus immunization of entrants. Only 12.5 per cent of the responding schools required measles and/or rubella vaccine for at least some students; only eighteen (32 per cent) of the fifty-six institutions without immunization requirements were interested in adopting these policies, at least for entering freshmen; thirty-three (59 per cent) were willing to officially recommend immunizations. Here a sound health policy is not being implemented on the grounds of increased costs required for enforcement.

Rational health policies are based on sound epidemiological data; their implementation to the level of the individual citizen too frequently fails for a variety of conflicting societal needs or concerns. Sometimes because there are inadequate resources, in money or in men, to implement a policy; sometimes it is fear of litigation; sometimes because undue stress placed by well-intentioned but misguided souls on the possibility of adverse reactions generates fear of the practice; sometimes because there are personal financial considerations; sometimes because national commercial interests are involved. It is thus that "The best laid schemes o' mice an' men gang aft a-gley."

Emphasis has been placed on the problems involved in the implementation of well-conceived policies. We have been concentrating on the empty half of the proverbial cup. Lest the impression be gained that there has been little or no progress, it behooves us to review some of what has been gained.

Smallpox: In 1938, 14,939 cases of smallpox were reported in the United States; no cases have occurred since 1959 in the United States and since October, 1977 no case has occurred on this globe. This was achieved by establishing and then effectively implementing a global program under the aegis of the WHO.

Measles: During World War I, there were 96,817 hospital admissions and 2,367 deaths from measles among US Army personnel. Among the US population, there were about 500,000 cases reported annually until 1965 when the vaccine which had been licensed in 1963 came into use. Over the period 1973–76, the annual average number of cases was 28,186. With increasingly more vaccine use, achieved by legislative requirements of immunization for school entry in the various states (a requirement if federal funds were to be received for immunization), only about 2,700 cases were reported in 1985 and hopes are high that endogenous measles can be eliminated.

Diphtheria: Between 1934 and 1945, 16,000 to 40,000 cases of diphtheria were reported each year. In 1984, only one case was diagnosed in the United States.

Pertussis: Over the period 1934 to 1948, annual case reports ranged from 100,000 to 200,000. By 1960, the annual count fell to less than 20,000; since 1965 it has been below 10,000. A low count of 1,248 was achieved in 1981; we are distressed by the subsequent increase in the number of cases, with 2,200 reported during 1984.

Poliomyelitis: In the five years before the inactivated polio vaccine became available (in 1955), the annual average number of cases was 37,857. By 1961, when the attenuated live vaccine became available, the annual incidence had fallen to 1,312. By 1967, after the American Medical Association had given belated approval to mass immunization programs, the count fell to and has remained under 100 per year. Over the period 1977–83, sixty-nine cases were reported as acquired within the United States; sixty of these were among vaccinees or contacts of recipients of the attenuated live vaccine. Only four cases of polio were reported in 1984, presumably vaccine associated.

Similar data can be presented for the other diseases for which there are effective vaccines. Among the diseases for which there is no vaccine or one is not in general use (such as typhoid fever), remarkable gains can also be presented.

Tuberculosis: The White Plague is no longer the formidable societal problem it once was. Over 100,000 cases were reported each year until 1952; since 1977 there have been under 30,000 cases annually and in 1984 fewer than 22,000 were reported. These results were achieved by an aggressive program of case finding, coupled with the availability of an effective treatment regimen.

Typhoid fever: During the period 1934 to 1941, 8,000–20,000 cases of typhoid and paratyphoid fevers were reported per year. Between 1942 and 1958, typhoid fever cases ranged from 1,000 to 5,000 per year. Since 1958, 300–800 cases were reported annually; in 1984, about 370 cases occurred. These results were achieved by the cooperation of epidemiologists, sanitarians, health workers, city planners, and elected officials in providing communities with chlorinated drinking water and proper sewage disposal.

Malaria: During the 1930s, over 100,000 cases of malaria occurred in the United States every year. Intensive mosquito control measures carried out during the World War II period (and maintained since) essentially eliminated malaria as a US disease. During 1983, 813 cases were reported; only eight were acquired within the United States. Five of these were associated with blood transfusions, two were congenital infections and the cause of the other case could not be determined. During the 1980–82 period, over 1,000 cases a year were diagnosed among immigrants, mostly from Southeast Asia, but there has been no spread within the country.

We are justly proud of the "full" half of the cup; it is replete with goodies. However, we continue to strive to achieve what can and should be achieved and to meet the WHO goal of "health for all by the year 2000." How can we best do this? Trite as it may sound, we need people who will work for the common good and not be motivated by personal gain; our national professional and service organizations should realize that they serve their own objectives best when they do the greatest good for the public. The media must learn that they too have a function in serving the common good and that this is not by accentuating every unusual event or incidental laboratory finding. The present hysteria over the transmissibility of the AIDS virus is an example; the finding of virus in tears and saliva, with no evidence of involvement in disease transmission, has been played up by the press so that people are afraid to live in the same apartment building or have their children in the same school as anyone infected with the viruses.

It is essential that there be appropriate legislative or social action to check the excessive number of unjustified lawsuits. The concept of implied warranty inhibits the development of new vaccines or drugs; experience has taught us that any drug or vaccine, given to enough people, will evoke adverse reactions in some. There should be appropriate, not excessive, compensation for those who are truly injured by an adverse reaction. This could be provided by the Social Security or similar agency. The public should appreciate that the exorbitant awards given by them when they sit on juries are not levied against the insurance companies only but that ultimately the money comes from their own pockets. And limiting the amount of fees chargeable by the attorney as his contingency fee will reduce the frequency of the prevalent multimillion dollar suits. We, as a society, have made great progress; by concerted action. With adequate available resources and access to data for indicated scientific studies, we can expect to further reduce the toll of infectious diseases.

References

American Public Health Association (1985) APHA/HRG Suit for Label Rule Continues. *The Nation's Health*, February, 1985.

Benenson, A.S. (1977) Review of Experience with Whole-Cell and Somatic Antigen Vaccines. In H. Fukumi and Y. Zinnaka (eds) *Symposium on Cholera. Sapporo, 1976.* Tokyo, Japan: US-Japan Cooperative Medical Science Program, National Institutes of Health.

Benenson, A.S. (ed.) (1985) *The Control of Communicable Diseases in Man.* 14th edition. Washington: American Public Health Association.

Center for Disease Control (1976) Swine Influenza. *Morbidity and Mortality Weekly Report* 25(8): 55.

—— (1982) National Surveillance for Reye Syndrome, 1981: Update, Reye Syndrome and Salicylate Use. *Morbidity and Mortality Weekly Report* 31(5): 53–6.

—— (1985) Reye Syndrome – United States, 1984. *Morbidity and Mortality Weekly Report* 34(1): 13–16.

Fulginiti, V.A. (1985) Some Current Developments in Immunization. *Infectious Diseases Newsletter* 4(1): 3–4.

Hinman, A.R. (1984) The Pertussis Vaccine Controversy. *Public Health Reports* 99(3): 255–59.

Holt, L.E. and McIntosh, R. (1936) *Holt's Diseases of Infancy and Childhood.* 10th edition revised. New York: Appleton-Century, p. 950.

Howard-Jones, N. (1974) The Scientific Background of the International

226 *Epidemiology and health policy*

Sanitary Conferences, 1851–1938. *WHO Chronicle* 28: 159–71, 229–47, 369–84, 414–26, 455–70, 495–508.

Kurland, L.T., Molgaard, C.A., Kurland, E.M., Wiederholt, W.C. and Kirkpatrick, J.W. (1984) Swine Flu Vaccine and Multiple Sclerosis. *Journal of the American Medical Association* 251(2): 2672–675.

Lilienfeld, A.M. and Lilienfeld, D.E. (1980) *Foundations of Epidemiology.* 2nd edition. New York: Oxford University Press, p. 4.

MacMahon, B. and Pugh, T.F. (1970) *Epidemiology: Principles and Methods.* Boston: Little, Brown, p. 1.

Onions, C.T. (1955) *The Oxford Universal Dictionary.* 3rd edition. Oxford: Clarendon Press.

Rogers, F.B. (1968) The Influenza Pandemic of 1918–1919 in the Perspective of a Half Century. *American Journal of Public Health* 58(12): 2192–194.

Santosham, M., *et al.* (1982) Oral Rehydration Therapy of Infantile Diarrhea – A Controlled Study of Well-Nourished Children Hospitalized in the United States and Panama. *New England Journal of Medicine* 306: 1070–076.

Snow, J. (1855) *On the Mode of Communication of Cholera.* 2nd edition. London: John Churchill. (Reprinted in 1936 as *Snow on Cholera.* New York: Hafner Publishing.)

Thompson, R.L., Sande, M.A., Wenzel, R.P., Hoke, C.H., and Gwaltney, J.M. (1976) Swine-Influenza Infection in Civilians: Report of Two Cases. *New England Journal of Medicine* 295: 714–15.

Webster's Seventh New Collegiate Dictionary (1970) Springfield, MA: G. and C. Merriam, p. 656.

Eight

Psychiatric epidemiology and mental health policy[1]

Gerald L. Klerman

Introduction

The relationship of epidemiologic knowledge to public policy

In the Introduction to this volume the editors delineate one model for the ideal formation of health policy (depicted in *Figure 8.1*). In their view, there is often a gap between the available epidemiologic knowledge and the application of this knowledge to the design and implementation of health policy.

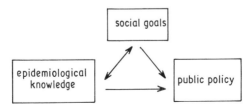

Figure 8.1 Ideal model for public policy

They indicate that the closing of this gap represents an ideal that is yet to be realized.

A broader model of policy formation, depicted in *Figure 8.2*, takes into account that in the "real world" formulation of public policy there is an interaction of a number of other influential groups and forces. Until recently, mental health policy decisions have been influenced only in small part by available epidemiologic data. They have also been influenced by three other factors:

1 The public perception of epidemiologic trends – incidence, prevalence, mortality, morbidity, and risk factors.
2 Traditions of psychiatric thinking and practice.
3 The overarching influence of political and economic conditions.

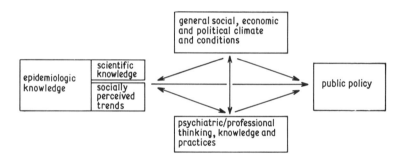

Figure 8.2 Determinants of public policy in mental health

Public perception of social trends plays a huge role in the design and implementation of mental health policy. In this country, in each historical epoch, there has been public discussion of epidemiologic issues. For example, in the nineteenth century, there was concern about the apparent increase in insanity and, in the mid-twentieth century, there has been a public concern about the increase in drug use among young people. Out of these perceptions public opinion has emerged, and it has played a significant role in the implementation of policy.

There are also areas in which professionals disagree among themselves. One such area was the diagnostic status of homosexuality, which was characterized as a psychiatric illness in the Diagnostic and Statistical Manual (DSM-II) of the American Psychiatric Association. Another area involves the health consequences of heroin. Psychiatrists like Zinberg have remarked on the large number of people who are able to use heroin and cocaine without becoming chronic dependent users, while the conventional wisdom teaches that heroin, and to a lesser extent cocaine, are addictive and have necessarily destructive effects. Finally, there are spheres in which conventional societal wisdom and professional opinion diverge.

The development of epidemiologic knowledge is also heavily governed by the general social, political, economic, and intellectual climate of the larger society. There has never been a fixed body of knowledge as to the epidemiology of psychiatric disorders; rather, the definition of the scope of psychiatry and the criteria for relevant knowledge have changed as new research is carried out and as the tide of public opinion shifts.

Given the complex interaction of these forces, what roles can the epidemiologic researcher play in bringing about improvement of policy? One answer was given by Nelson W. Polsby (Polsby 1984). Discussing political science in particular, he suggests that one purpose served by social science is to help us think rationally and dispassionately about policy issues. Formal scientific knowledge should be called upon to corroborate or falsify publicly held beliefs which have supported implementation of a given policy. The role of an epidemiologist should be to generate information – be it unpopular, unexpected or heretofore unsubstantiated – with the hope of ultimately influencing policy-makers.

What are the policy issues in mental health?

In assessing the contribution which epidemiology can make to the formulation of policy, it is important to articulate the policy questions in mental health. They include the following:

1 What is the role of governmental bodies in mental health, and how does this role relate to the role of other public agencies; that is the courts and law enforcement system, citizen groups, and religious and church groups? How does governmental responsibility relate to the role of private agencies, such as professional groups, general hospitals, the

insurance industry, universities, and the collective action of individuals and families?

2 Within government, what is the appropriate division of responsibility among federal, state, and local levels? And at each level, what are the respective roles of legislative, judicial, and executive branches of government? (See *Figure 8.3*).

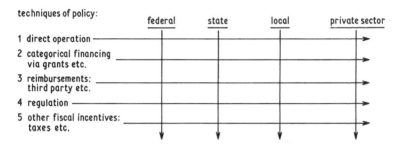

Figure 8.3 Levels of policy implementation

3 Decisions concerning the responsibility and the role of government also involve agreements or disagreements as to the nature of mental health concerns and their scope, particularly in terms of estimates of incidence, prevalence, mortality, morbidity, distress, and disability. This is a scientific question, which relies heavily on evidence from psychiatry, psychology, demography, and epidemiology, but it is also a social and political question, in that a society's definition of normality and abnormality contribute to its definition of appropriate mental health concerns. Important considerations here include: which individuals merit the sick role, with its attendant rights, responsibilities, and – in modern times – who is entitled to eligibility for benefits? And which direction should public initiatives take, and what should be the basis for decision?

4 What is the role of govenment and other public bodies in the regulation of mental health activities? These include certification of facilities, licensing of professional and other personnel, support and regulation of research activities, and promotion of preventive activities through regulation of environmental conditions, occupational health, and housing standards.

5 In addition to the role of government in the direct delivery of service, what financing mechanisms should be used at the federal, state, and local level with respect to grants-in-aid, categorical block awards, tax exemptions, and third party insurance reimbursements?

The policy issues listed above have implications for four domains of mental health policy:

1 Service delivery for care and treatment and rehabilitation.
2 Manpower and human resources.
3 Research and scientific investigation.
4 Prevention.

While all four domains are important areas for policy, it is significant that the history of mental health policy has involved service delivery almost exclusively. Issues of manpower, research, and prevention were not seriously considered by policy-makers until the founding of the National Institute of Mental Health (NIMH) in 1949. Accordingly, this paper will stress psychiatric epidemiology and policy as they relate to services, and will deal more briefly with manpower, research, and prevention.

Historical background

The evaluation of US mental health policy

Before turning to the current scene with respect to the domains of policy, it is valuable to look at the historical events which have contributed to both public mental health policy and the emergence of psychiatric epidemiology.

The late eighteenth century The establishment of public policy with regard to mental health concerns began in the late eighteenth century in North America and western Europe. During that period emerged the concept that insanity was a medical phenomenon and a legitimate object of governmental responsibility. Prior to the Enlightenment in the late eighteenth century, mental illnesses – that is psychosis, depression, phobias, dementia, and alcoholism – were not defined and legitimized as health problems. Rather, mental aberrations

were interpreted for the most part in religious terms, particularly
as demonic possession or as retribution for presumed sin.

Out of the Enlightenment a new definition of mental
illness emerged. The philosophers of this era argued that if
man was a rational animal and everywhere born free, then
mental illness represented a loss of his natural reason, and
could be explained on purely natural rather than supernatural
grounds. Due to this changing perception, the needs of the
mentally ill became differentiated from those of criminals and
paupers in North America, England, France, and other western
European countries. This era was ushered in by the appointment
of Phillippe Pinel as the first medical superintendent of the
Salpêtrière in Paris. The Salpêtrière and the Bicetre in Paris,
and "Bedlam" in London, had been established as public
institutions for paupers and socially disruptive and deranged
individuals, largely out of a concern by public authorities with
the increasing number of individuals and the threat they posed
to law and order. Pinel's appointment in 1793 officially
recognized for the first time the importance of bringing
medical authority to bear on the condition and care of the
mentally ill.

The nineteenth century   The policy that institutions for the
insane should be under medical leadership spread slowly in
western Europe and in the United States. It was not until 1844
that the American Association of Medical Superintendents for
the Asylums for the Insane (later to become the American
Psychiatric Association) was established as the first professional
society in the United States. The term "psychiatry" was not
even coined until 1846, and it did not become widely used
until the turn of the century. The small number of medical
physicians involved in institutional care at that time were
known as "superintendents," and were often called "alienists."
In the United States, a turning point in policy occurred during
and soon after the Jacksonian era. During the years 1810–60,
almost every state legislature mandated the creation of a state
hospital, and responsibility for the mentally ill was thus
partially transferred to state government. The leading figure
in this legislative program was Dorothea Dix. The policy
implications were to be momentous: first, the state government
began to assume responsibility for the care of the mentally ill

rather than private charity or local towns and cities; and second, these populations were separated into two types of facilities, the schools for the retarded and the hospitals for the insane. This established the basic mental health policy in the United States for at least a century.

The early hopes for the therapeutic and social success for institutions both for the retarded and the mentally ill were not fulfilled. After the Civil War, these institutions became increasingly crowded, and reported recovery rates dropped. The growth of the population, particularly with immigration from Europe, resulted in the need for new facilities. With the increasing urbanization and ethnic mixture of the population, the rate of mental illness increased, particularly observable in the newly freed slaves and the immigrant groups from Ireland, Italy, and eastern Europe. Various theories, such as Social Darwinism, were put forth to implicate hereditary stock and "racial taint" as causes of these changes.

The combination of criticisms of the asylum, plus the increasing attention given to "nervous disorders" in medical practice were to lay the groundwork for an important policy shift, namely the shift of locus of attention from institutional to community care. This policy shift was not to reach fruition until the second half of the twentieth century.

The beginning of the twentieth century Important trends emerged at the turn of the century, particularly in the decades known as the Progressive Era. There was increasing dissatisfaction with the state of practice and professional care in the institutions, and a growing awareness of the existence of nervous disorders, soon to be renamed "neuroses." Reports of hysteria, neurasthenia, melancholy, appeared with mounting frequency, and patients suffering from these disorders – often women from middle and upper social classes – became the focus of concern for general physicians, neurologists, and the small but growing band of neuropsychiatrists. Before 1870, private practice of psychiatry as we know it today was virtually non-existent, and until World War I, psychiatry was practiced almost exclusively within mental institutions. Up to that time, the diagnostic and classification systems were concerned almost exclusively with conditions we would consider today as psychoses, either organic or functional. The apparent increase in patients with non-psychotic conditions – variously called neuroses, hysteria, and hypochondriasis – soon led to a reappraisal of professional responsibilities. While the generation of neurologists of 1890–10 came to define the scope of their professional activities to include only those individuals with problems of sensory organs and motor function, a new medical specialty, psychiatry, emerged to respond to the growing number of patients whose distress was manifested by problems in emotion and behavior, but who were not so seriously impaired in cognitive functioning as to require institutionalization.

Psychoanalysis was introduced in Vienna, arriving in the United States, when Freud, Jung, and their associates visited in 1908. The highly innovative ideas, largely developed by Freud, became the dominant psychiatric theory used to explain the causality and development of non-psychotic conditions. They provided a rational basis for psychotherapeutic intervention which differed from the somatic-empirical practices of neurology and the rest of medicine.

Psychology emerged as a distinct academic discipline in the United States following the activities of William James, and the creation of the Psychological Laboratory at Harvard. Adolf Meyer was appointed the first professor of psychiatry at Johns Hopkins Medical School, the leader of academic medicine, and his influence through the first half of the twentieth century was to create the template for the academic specialty of psychiatry. The first professional activities in psychiatric epidemiology emerged under the influence of Adolf Meyer, particularly in the pioneering work of Lemkau, the first professor of mental hygiene at Johns Hopkins.

Among the other innovations in psychiatry and mental health policy during the Progressive Era was the psychopathic hospital movement, which advocated community-based, predominantly outpatient hospitals as an alternative to the state hospitals. This movement arose under the leadership of Adolf Meyer, as an attempt of a group of leaders to create an alternative locus of care to the state hospitals. A number of these institutions grew up in Boston, New York, Iowa City, and Ann Arbor, and became teaching hospitals for university medical schools.

The period before World War I was one of innovation, and many of the innovations developed in this period, both in mental health and in public health and child care were to sow the seeds of the Great Society movement. During that time, the Children's Bureau was formed, child labor laws were passed, the first district health centers were founded in the cities, and urban problems such as crowding and sanitation were dealt with for the first time.

World War I The military experience in World War I provided a major impetus for the growth of psychiatry. High rates of psychiatric casualties, particularly involving the syndrome of "shell shock" in American forces and "soldier's heart" in England, helped lead to the development of the mental hygiene movement. In addition, the child guidance clinics emerged soon after World War I, supported by the Commonwealth Foundation Fund, and with them, the sub-specialty of child psychiatry. Community-based clinics also arose as an alternative to mental hospitals.

In the United States throughout this period, the major locus of public responsibility continued to be state government. Instances of federal support were rare; they included the assistance provided for the pioneering research on the dietary basis of pellagra by Goldberger in the Public Health Service, and the development of the addiction hospital in Lexington, Kentucky in the 1920s. On the whole, however, federal responsibility remained minuscule.

World War II Large-scale federal responsibility for mental health care did not emerge until after World War II. A major impetus for this was the exorbitant rejection rate of young men from military service in the Selective Service for neuropsychiatric reasons. This was coupled with military reports of high rates of psychiatric casualties, particularly combat neuroses, fatigue, and anxiety states. A small band of social scientists, organized by the military under the leadership of Samuel Stouffer, undertook to apply social science research methods to document the role of stress and particularly the combat and life-threatening situations upon anxiety, morale, and performance. Social scientists also devised methods for screening personnel for specialized training, in intelligence services and the air force. Many of these social scientists, upon return to academic life, used their experience in searching for civilian sources of stress. Extending the military research on combat stress, "social stress" became a dominant concept in psychiatric epidemiology after World War II.

Historical trends in psychiatric epidemiology

Before discussing the policy developments of the post-World War II era, it is useful to turn the clock back to survey the history of psychiatric epidemiology. Its development parallels the development of public policy.

Psychiatric epidemiology originated in Europe in the late 1800s, when an interest arose in the societal and hereditary bases of mental disorders. In England, Scandinavia, and elsewhere on the continent, these concerns were the basis for reform in the education of mentally retarded children and for the planning of institutions for the mentally ill.

The first US attempt to investigate systematically the true prevalence of mental disorders, that is both treated and non-treated, was conducted by Edward Jarvis in 1855. At the behest of the Massachusetts legislature, Jarvis surveyed community leaders, as well as hospital and other official records, to determine the number of people suffering from "insanity" and "idiocy." The US census of 1880 also incorporated this distinction and provided the first national estimates of mental disorder.

The classifications "lunacy" and "idiocy" comprised the major nosological distinction of the time. This distinction had psychopathologic, epidemiologic, and policy components. In psychopathologic terms, it was based on age and developmental history. Idiocy was usually discernible by mid-childhood, often at the time a child entered the fledgling public school system, and proved unable to respond to the learning and educational demands of the public schools. Before the advent of public schools, people with mental retardation could function in a non-literate rural society where a large percentage of the work-force was engaged in menial activities. Yet as children were required to go to school, it became apparent that some had a great deal more trouble learning than others. Thus, by virtue of the social structure, retardation became more noticeable, which in turn initiated the perception of a need for public care. On the other hand, lunacy – or insanity as it was called later in the nineteenth century – usually occurred in adults who had passed through a period of apparent normality, and who had an ability to learn in school and to enter into some form of occupational activity. This was followed in their developmental histories by a "loss of reason" and irrational behavior.

Psychiatric epidemiology emerged as a scientific field at the beginning of the twentieth century, when several studies on psychiatric illness were conducted which made use of the epidemiologic approach. The classic work of Goldberger in 1914, which used a case control method and careful observation, demonstrated that pellagra psychosis was due to nutritional deficiency (for a detailed review, see Shepherd *et al.* (1966)). Indirect procedures of ascertaining information from medical records and key informants characterized most studies conducted prior to World War II, as reported by Lemkau, Tietze, and Cooper (1942) in the Eastern Health District of Baltimore in 1933 and 1936, and by Roth and Luton (1943) in Williamson County, Tennessee, in 1935. Lemkau, Tietze, and Cooper supplemented these procedures with data obtained from direct interviews determining frequency of "nervousness" that had been conducted coincidentally by the National Health Survey in the same district. Taking a different approach from community surveys, Farris and Dunham (1967) examined the ecological distribution of first admissions to mental hospitals in Chicago in the 1930s. Diagnoses from hospital records were related to the area of residence of the patients. The highest rates of hospitalization for mental illness occurred in residents from areas with the highest social disorganization. This careful study demonstrated the importance of social variables in mental illness. While these studies shared some basic methodological limitations, they were the first steps in the creation of a psychiatric epidemiology.

Despite a moratorium on community surveys in the United States during World War II, the mental health experiences of the Selective Service and the armed forces were to have an important impact. In the rejection of large numbers of young men from the Selective Service, psychiatric reasons accounted for the largest proportion of non-acceptances. It is of note that these psychiatric rejections included a large group who were mentally retarded and also many who were mentally ill or emotionally troubled. The scientific and military justifications for the rejections were criticized and the accuracy of the diagnostic procedures was questioned; nevertheless, the publicity given to the high rates of psychoneurosis, personality disorders, psychosomatic problems, focused public attention on mental health problems and supported efforts to obtain more information on rates of psychiatric disability.

Neuropsychiatric specialists were widely dispersed in the military medical services and contributed clinical descriptions and statistical documentation of mental disorders, such as combat fatigue, transient functional psychoses, dissociative states, and stress reactions. Whereas the rates of psychoses in the military remained relatively stable, the rates of psychoneuroses and personality reactions fluctuated and were related to combat and other situational stresses.

The observation that rates of psychiatric reactions varied in relation to combat stress was of practical utility and theoretical importance. Using the best available sampling methods, survey techniques, and statistical analyses, social scientists conducted a wide range of studies and developed neuropsychiatric screening questionnaires to relate neurotic symptoms to combat stress and morale problems.

From today's vantage point, the methods of screening were far from ideal. However, their implications for studies in the post-World War II phase were very important. The planners of epidemiologic research in the post-World War II period were impressed by the Selective Service and military experience and concluded that predisposing vulnerability and concurrent mental and physical illness had been adequately screened. Therefore, it seemed reasonable at that time to conclude that precipitant stress, rather than predisposition or vulnerability, was a major risk factor for psychiatric illness. The role of stress as an immediate precipitant of mental illness was supported powerfully by these observations and "stress" was to be a major unifying concept in the post-World War II studies in civilian settings. Poverty, urban anomie, rapid social change, and social class were to become the civilian stress equivalents of combat and threat of death experienced in the military duty.

Trends since World War II

Psychiatric epidemiology   After World War II, the experience gained by the military and the growing public awareness of the high prevalence of mental illness prompted epidemiologic studies in the general population. Moreover, there was financial and policy support for community surveys, when the NIMH was created legislatively in 1947 and became operational in 1949. The creation of the Institute prompted a vast increase in the amount of epidemiologic research conducted.

Studies representative of the community surveys of this period were the Midtown-Manhattan survey by Rennie, Srole, Langner, and the Cornell group (Srole *et al.* 1962), which assessed the impact of urban life on mental health by interviewing more than 1,000 adult residents selected by probability sampling in midtown Manhattan; the nationwide survey of mental health by Gurin, Veroff, and Feld (1960) of the University of Michigan survey research center in which more than 2,000 adult Americans were interviewed; and the well-known study by Leighton *et al.* (1963) that assessed the impact of social and economic change on the mental health of a previously stable community in Stirling County, Nova Scotia. All of these studies reported high rates of mental impairment. For example, the Midtown-Manhattan study found that only 19 per cent of the subjects were free of significant symptoms and that 23 per cent were substantially impaired.

Mention should be made of the Hollingshead and Redlich (1958) study of treated prevalence in New Haven, Connecticut. This study established social class as an important factor in determining whether an individual is treated for mental illness. The results of this study were replicated when Myers and Bean (1968) followed up the sample ten years later.

Progress in American psychiatric social epidemiology drew to a halt in the late 1960s. There were few new findings, although controversy continued over previously generated ones. For example, a continuing debate ensued as to whether the relationship between social class and schizophrenia was a direct social cause or a reflection of social drift. Meanwhile, in other areas of psychiatric research, psychopharmacology, genetics, psychopathology, and neurobiology, considerable progress was under way. The developments in these fields led to advances in validity and reliability of diagnoses and to a strengthening of the evidence for biological factors in the etiology of mental illness.

Advances in genetics and neurobiology   Research in genetics strengthened evidence for the biological as well as the psychosocial factors in the causation of mental illness. The studies of Heston (1966) and those done in Scandinavia by Mednick *et al.* (1974) and Rosenthal *et al.* (1968) using the cross-rearing adoptive technique established the high likelihood that genetic factors were involved in schizophrenia. In the 1960s, independent research groups in the United States, Europe, and Scandinavia studied primary affective disorders and found that by dividing their population into unipolar and bipolar groups based on the presence of a history of manic episode, strong familial association could be found that supported a genetic transmission hypothesis for the primary affective disorders, especially the bipolar forms.

Evidence for biological factors in psychiatric disorders also emanated from studies in mental retardation where the classical medical strategy led to discovery of new nosological subclasses. Using laboratory methods, the large group of mental retardation could be divided on the basis of origin, particularly subclasses due to aminoacidurias and to chromosomal abnormalities. However, in the other mental disorders, particularly schizophrenia, affective states, and anxiety states, evidence for biological factors has been slower to emerge and what evidence there is derives indirectly from psychopharmacology.

Advances in psychopharmacology   The introduction of psychotropic drugs in the mid-1950s led to changes in both the scientific investigation and the treatment of psychiatric disorders. The initial contribution of modern psychopharmacology was to stimulate the development of methodology for systematic assessment of patients' symptoms, social function, and diagnosis. Case reports and clinical experience could no longer be relied on to evaluate the flood of new agents that followed the introduction of chlorpromazine. The need to establish efficacy led to controlled clinical trials. Randomized designs, double-blind techniques, and placebo controls became the standards for therapeutic evaluation. These studies demonstrated that the new drugs, which had been shown to have varying neuropharmacologic modes of action, had different patterns of clinical efficacy. These were explainable partially by diagnostic type, for example schizophrenic patients responded to pheno-thiazines whereas depressed patients responded to tricyclic antidepressants, and the bipolar subtype of affected patients showed response to lithium carbonate. These findings supported the concept that psychiatric disorders were discrete and heterogeneous and prompted reevaluation of diagnosis.

Advances in psychopathology By the mid-1960s, there was a growing awareness among clinicians and researchers that the absence of an objective and reliable system for description of psychopathology and for psychiatric diagnosis was limiting research. In 1965, the NIMH, Psychopharmacology Research Branch, sponsored a conference on classification in psychiatry taking note of the problems created by inadequate diagnosis and classification. In the decade since that conference, there have been major achievements in three areas: understanding sources of cross-national differences in diagnostic practices, improving their precision and reliability, and developing methods for their validation.

Mental health services and public policy The war, as well as other factors, contributed to the passage by Congress in 1947 of legislation creating the NIMH. The responsibilities of the NIMH were at first restricted by statutory authority to the promotion of research and training of professional manpower. There was an explicit exclusion of federal responsibility from support of service functions. With the American commitment to the welfare state in the mid-1960s, this policy was changed dramatically. During the Kennedy–Johnson administrations, the federal government assumed increasing responsibility for mental health services, particularly through Medicare and Medicaid. In addition, categorical programs for child health, neighborhood health centers, and the community mental health center programs were created, as well as programs for alcoholism treatment and drug abuse.

The period since World War II has witnessed an unprecedented expansion in utilization of mental health services, and a corresponding expansion of the mental health sector of health services. Many of these trends were directly or indirectly influenced by federal activity, particularly since the creation of the NIMH. From the end of World War II through the election of President Reagan in 1980, there was a significant shift in the locus of public responsibility, with the federal government becoming increasingly the source of public finances and the source of leadership and initiative.

This expansion was reflected in a number of important trends, which include:

1 Overall utilization has expanded. In 1955, 1 per cent of the adult population saw a mental health professional, while in 1980, 10 per cent of the population saw a mental health professional.
2 This tenfold expansion of utilization does not represent a dramatic increase in incidence or prevalence. Rather, the epidemiologic evidence indicates that although there have been some increases in the incidence of certain disorders, such as depression and alcoholism, there have been concomitant decreases in other disorders, for instance involutional melancholia and postpartum psychoses. Thus, the net change in incidence and prevalence has probably been minimal.
3 The expansion in utilization therefore represents a change in the attitude of the public and an increasing willingness to bring to the attention of mental health professionals symptoms and disorders which heretofore would have been considered suitable for treatment by other health professionals or, more likely, by other types of providers.
4 There has been a corresponding expansion in the number of mental health professionals. In 1955, there were about 10,000 psychiatrists, the majority of whom worked in institutional settings, plus perhaps 1,000 clinical psychologists and social workers in clinical practice. In 1980, there are probably over 120,000 mental health professionals, including 30,000 psychiatrists, 30,000 psychologists who identify themselves as mental health providers, and about 30,000 MSW social workers, as well as an increasing number of psychiatric nurse practitioners, pastoral counselors, marriage and family therapists.
5 Almost all this expansion has been in outpatient services. Hospitalization rates remain very constant. Yet hospitalization patterns have changed dramatically. In 1955, almost all hospitalization was in public institutions – state, county,

and Veterans Administration (VA). Currently public institutions represent the minority of hospitalization settings, with a marked growth of psychiatric units in general hospitals, community mental health centers, and the more recent growth of private-for-profit hospitals, many of which are becoming amalgamated into corporations.

Many forces have contributed to this expansion of the mental health sector. These include the rapid increase in population associated with the "baby boom" after World War II; the rising economic prosperity of the United States and most industrialized countries, and the corresponding increase in expectations for personal satisfaction and material well-being; the decline of the power of religion, the church, and the influence of the counseling role it traditionally provided; the growing acceptance of the concept of the welfare state wherein it is expected that government will contribute to health services and personal well-being; and the growth of reimbursement for mental health services including ambulatory psychotherapy under health insurance. All these forces have converged to produce a thirty year period of unprecedented growth in all aspects of mental health: utilization, professional manpower, types and numbers of facilities, and funds allocated and spent.

It is not clear whether this growth will continue. There are a number of powerful forces, mainly economic, which are operating in the 1980s and which will probably inhibit further growth, and perhaps even reduce the level of expenditures and utilization. These forces are part of a general conservative shift, not only in the United States but throughout western Europe. One aspect of this shift is a reappraisal of the continual expansion of social services, including medical and psychotherapeutic services. In accordance with a conservative view of welfare state activities, the Reagan administration repealed the Mental Health Services Act inaugurated by the Carter administration. It also ended the program of direct grants-in-aid to community health agencies, and consolidated the community grants for mental health, drugs, and alcoholism services to the states. It is not yet clear what the impact of the Reagan policy changes has been. Within a few years there should be some data on patterns of utilization and funding. At the present time, it is too soon to tell.

One policy issue concerns the desirability of further increases in patterns of utilization. The expansion of utilization does not reflect any increase in the prevalence of serious mental disorders, but rather a significant redefinition of the scope of mental health. Increasingly, problems of living, which previously were regarded as a personal responsibility, have now been redefined as worthy of therapeutic intervention. This is not so much an outcome of new scientific findings; rather, it is attributable to the influence of social values and the dynamics of public policy.

Earlier in this chapter, decisions as to public policy involved implicit areas of agreement or disagreement as to the nature of mental illness and mental health. In this respect, the creation of the NIMH represented a profound statement of US public policy. The new institute created in Congress in 1947 was named the National Institute of Mental Health, rather than a National Institute of Mental Illness, thus inviting a major public policy concern for a broad definition of the scope of mental health. The historical trend in mental health policy in the United States over the past 250 years has involved a gradual but systematic shift in responsibility. During the colonial era, there was a shift from private charity to local governmental responsibility. In the nineteenth century, the states took over the responsibilities for public mental health services previously provided by the local towns and cities. By the mid-twentieth century, beginning with the Roosevelt New Deal and continuing through the democratic administrations of Truman, Kennedy, and Johnson, the federal government became increasingly involved in all aspects of health including mental health, alcoholism, and drug abuse. In this historical context, the actions of the Reagan administration represent an attempt to change the direction of public policy by decreasing the commitment of the national government to mental health services, and shifting the locus of responsibility to state government.

The scope of mental health

Defining normal and abnormal

The resurgence of interest in nosology and diagnosis after World War II, particularly based upon the advances in psychopathology, genetics, and psychopharmacology described in the previous section, contributed to more reliable and at times valid criteria for mental illness, as codified in the DSM-III. Based upon such criteria, it has been estimated that 15 per cent of the population, or about 32,000,000 individuals, have a diagnosable mental illness by DMS-III criteria (Murphy 1980; Regier, Goldberg, and Taube 1978; Weissman and Myers 1978). What about the other 85 per cent of the population? Are they to be considered "mentally healthy?"

From one point of view, normality or mental health is defined as the "absence of a diagnosable disorder"; from this vantage point, the remaining 85 per cent can be regarded as "normal" or "mentally healthy." However, very few mental health professionals or social scientists would accept this conclusion. Rather, it is widely accepted that health is not just the absence of disorder. The mental health field, and increasingly, the general health field, are not satisfied with the goals of reduced mortality or morbidity, or even the elimination of illness, but have attempted to achieve a more positive goal: the enhancement of health.

In the realm of mental health, this goal has generated considerable discussion, and at times, controversy. How is mental health to be defined? By what criteria? Are there criteria which are "objective," free of social values or cultural bias?

Among those interested in probing the meaning and character of mental illness, discussion usually proceeds from abstract, intellectualized questions about the nature of the human psyche. The approach of the epidemiologist is different; psychiatric epidemiology focuses first and foremost on demonstrating the relevance of psycho-social and cultural factors to mental illness and health. In this effort, it is hoped that the application of the approach and techniques from medical epidemiology to mental health will not only help answer questions as to the nature of mental illness and its causation, but will lead, first and foremost, to preventive interventions.

If one attempts a definition of normality and health other than "the absence of disease," there is no consensus as to how best to approach the problem, either on a theoretical or empirical basis. One prominent approach has been to derive listings of attributes and characteristics of hypothesized ideally "healthy" persons. This approach was summarized in a volume by Marie Jahoda, prepared for the Joint Commission on Mental Health and Mental Illness in the late 1950s (Jahoda 1959). However, when attributes such as competence, rationality, flexibility, capacity to cope, and levels of psycho-social fixation serve as criteria for the definition of "health," it is clear that value judgments and philosophical bias are inherent in the categories themselves.

An alternative approach has been to relate the criterion of normality to the life cycle and build upon developmental psychology. This approach is embodied in the writings of Erikson (1950), Levinson (1978), Neugarten (1975), and Vaillant (1981), who define normality and mental health as the capacity to adapt successfully and to master the developmental tasks of life cycle stages.

The epidemiologist approaches mental illness and mental health by looking at the prevalence and incidence of certain symptoms within a population, and examining the distribution of people who suffer from mental disorders. He begins in that way to define the boundaries between mental illness and mental health. The link of this approach to policy becomes clear when we use these definitions to determine which populations merit what kind of service. What follows is an epidemiological profile of various populations.

The "inner core": the chronically disabled mentally ill

Fifteen per cent of the population annually suffers from a definable and diagnosable mental disorder, and within this group, there is an "inner core," comprised of individuals with chronically disabling mental illness, particularly schizophrenia, other psychoses, and severe alcoholism.

The image of the "inner core" derives from two ideas. First, it illustrates the historical sequence with which mental conditions have been labelled and categorized as mental illness. Psychiatry began with the treating of psychotic patients. In a study prepared for the United States Department of Health and Human Services Task Force on the Chronically Ill, chaired by Richmond and Klerman (1980), it was estimated that there are about 1.5 million mentally ill. People in this category have historically been the main concern of psychiatry. Second, this "inner core" not only comprises the group of traditional concern for the field of psychiatry, but represents those patients of greatest social cost due to their high level of disability, demand for residential and financial supports, economic and vocational maladjustments, and frequent use of public institutional settings.

The "outer core:" those with diagnosable mental disorders

Since the turn of the century, the scope of mental illness has increased to include, in addition to the psychoses, new categories of neuroses, depressions, and personality disorders.

As cited above, current prevalence is estimated at fifteen per cent annually. Besides prevalence, epidemiologists are also interested in lifetime expectancy. Although full data are not available, it appears that about 40 per cent of the population will experience some diagnosable mental illness during their lifetime. For example, 25 per cent of women and 12–15 per cent of men can expect to suffer from depression in the course of a lifetime (Weissman and Myers 1978). When the 10 per cent alcoholism rate for men and various types of activities and phobia are included, the figure of 40 per cent is conservative.

We do not have comparable estimates of familial prevalence. It is likely that at least 50 per cent of families will have at least one family member with a mental illness at some time during the "life of the family." The impact upon family functioning and social and economic status remains to be investigated.

Those coping with stress and distress related to life events and social adversity

In addition to the two populations of individuals with diagnosed illness, there are two other populations of interest for an epidemiologic approach to mental illness. One of these populations includes the large number of individuals coping with stressful life events, and the other consists of individuals attempting to enhance their personal happiness, fulfillment, and satisfaction.

A major achievement in psychiatric research since World War II has been the clarification of the concept of stress and the development of quantitative measures for the assessment of the stressful impact of life events. A key advance in this research was the development by Holmes and Rahe of a scale for quantitative rating of life events. Their scale has been employed in a large number of clinical studies, social surveys, and epidemiologic research. Based upon this approach, it is now possible to estimate that between 30 and 50 million persons in the United States each year experience a stressful life event which calls upon their capacity to cope.

It should be emphasized that experiencing a stressful life event does not necessarily result in an episode of diagnosable mental illness. However, there is increasingly persuasive evidence that individuals coping with these life events and experiencing distress are at greater risk of illness. Of greater significance for public policy, they are likely to increase their utilization of the health care system during the period of coping. Moreover, a significant fraction will fail to cope adequately and this will be reflected in a subsequently higher chance of medical illness in general, and mental illness in particular.

For example, about 2 million persons die in this country annually. Assuming that each person who dies has one to three close relatives and friends who experience a period of loss and mourning, about 5 million people are coping with bereavement and mourning over the death of a loved one each year. As bereaved individuals go through the period of mourning there is an increase in distress, reflected by poor sleep, loss of appetite, bodily complaints, feelings of sadness. During this period, they may make greater use of the health care system and increase their use of various drugs, particularly sedatives. Furthermore, there is epidemiologic evidence to suggest that men are at greater risk for cardiovascular diseases and other manifestations of increased mortality at this time.

The growing epidemiologic and social survey research on stress has been paralleled by sophisticated endocrine and physiologic research which has elucidated mechanisms by which adverse environmental events can influence physiologic functioning. The three main mechanisms are: the hypothalmic-pituitary-adrenal systems, the autonomic nervous system, particularly its sympathetic components, and the immune system.

Studies are needed to extend the epidemiologic approach to life events and to determine more precisely the incidence of these adverse life events. If we view these "pathogens" as similar to an infectious organism or chemical toxic agent, one could then apply epidemiologic measures such as exposure rate and other quantitive techniques. By these methods, one could estimate not only the frequency of these events in various population groups, but also the extent to which they affect health. The epidemiologic hypothesis would be that exposure to these life events would result in: increased morbidity, as measured by symptoms both emotional and physical; increased utilization of the health care system including outpatient visits, hospitalization, laboratory tests, and drug ingestion, both with and without prescription; and increased risk for subsequent illness, such as cardiovascular disease, depression, and alcoholism.

Enhancement of individual potential: personal mental health as a utopian ideal of normality

In addition to the large groups of individuals who are suffering from definable mental disorder or coping with stressful life events, there is a group of individuals who are not overtly ill, nor necessarily attempting to cope with stressful life events, but who seek to realize their personal potential and enhance their satisfaction and happiness. These individuals most often come from the better-educated, middle and upper-middle class segments of the community, and their lifestyles often involve frequent geographic relocation for educational and professional advancement. They generally have strong values connected with individuality, achievement, and mastery.

In the United States, there have been a growing number of organized efforts to meet the need of these people, through groups such as EST and other human potential groups. Many of these efforts operate outside the health care system and use various kinds of seminars or quasi-educational methods, usually charging fees for service. The origins of this help-seeking are multiple and have been portrayed in the sociologic and popular literature as deriving from the "me generation" and narcissism (Lasch 1979).

Increasing numbers of individuals seek professional assistance from mental health professionals to enhance their state of well-being, to actualize their potential and to increase their competence in interpersonal relations. It is estimated that about 6–10 per cent of the population saw some mental health professional in 1980, and that a significant proportion of these individuals would not meet the DSM-III Axis I criteria for definable disorder.

Numerous attempts at comprehensive mental health benefits have been unsuccessful because of the apparently unlimited demand for such services, particularly in health programs serving professionals, managers, and better-educated segments of the population. These individuals often seek individual long-term psychotherapy, services which are highly expensive. The legitimacy of these services under the health insurance umbrella has been frequently challenged. The failure to resolve this issue is manifested in frequent changes in mental health benefit packages, varying proposals for national health insurance, and a continuing debate as to the efficacy of psychotherapy and its appropriateness as a health procedure. Government plays two major roles with regard to third party payments. First, it is the underwriter of about a quarter of all third party payments through Medicare and Medicaid. Second, many states have mandated mental health benefits as part of their insurance statutes. For example, Massachusetts requires that any insurance program offered in that state provides $500 per year of ambulatory mental health benefits. When national health insurance was being discussed in 1977 and 1978, there was a range of policies as to whether mental health benefits should be included at all, and if so, whether it should be inpatient only or outpatient, etc. Third, the government is involved in determining which type of mental health professional is eligible for reimbursement. There have been numerous legislative and court battles brought by psychologists and social workers to win the right for direct payment, rather than only via medical supervision and authorization.

Applications of mental health policy: mental health services

Having identified trends in utilization and those populations potentially suitable for mental health services, we now will consider specific areas of mental health policy: mental health services, manpower and human resources, research, and prevention. Reference to *Figure 8.3* may prove useful in describing the relation of these domains with locus of governmental responsibility.

The dominant policy in most modern and urbanized western societies over the last thirty years has been to identify barriers to utilization – lack of facilities, financial impediments, social prejudices and attitudes – and to use public resources to reduce these barriers. For the most part, this policy has been highly successful since World War II in the United States and most countries, as the increase in utilization has shown. While there are still severe maldistributions, due particularly to geography, social class, and racial-ethnic factors, major advances have been made since World War II.

In the current, more conservative view of government, however, primary emphasis is given to those individuals who require public attention, either because of the degree of their disability, or because the manifestations of their mental illness are socially disruptive and even violate the legal and criminal code. Fewer resources are available for people with less severe disability. The conservative view is reflected in attacks on the insanity defense, proposals for reversal of the policy of deinstitutionalization and increased use of mental hospital beds, and the emergence of proposals for a policy of "reinstitutionalization."

Direct governmental operation of services

One major issue concerns the extent to which government should actually run mental health facilities. The policy in the United States throughout the nineteenth and twentieth centuries has been for government not to run health programs, except as the agency of last resort. In the case of mental illness, the last-resort population has been those individuals who are very disturbed or disturbing, and have exhibited a severe chronicity. The states have differed in the extent to which they have maintained direct services for these classes of individuals, particularly those where chronic illness has exhausted one's financial resources and/or resulted in disability.

At the federal level, the government runs extensive programs of direct mental health services, particularly through the VA. Patients with psychiatric diagnoses occupy half of all VA beds. Half of all the recipients of VA services have neuropsychiatric diagnoses (including alcoholism, senile dementia, schizophrenia, and personality disorders). The federal government also operates an extensive program of mental health services through the military. A small amount of service is also provided through the Public Health Service. In addition, the federal government operates its own mental hospital, St Elizabeth's, which services the District of Columbia; this is the only case in which a federal agency meets the needs of one particular local community, an obvious exception to what has been a long-standing policy.

Regulation of mental health services

A second policy issue of public psychiatry is the role of government, whether local, state, or federal, in regulating mental health care. There are a variety of regulatory devices the government can use to control and direct aspects of health care. In the United States, decisions regarding the licensing and certification of health facilities, such as nursing homes and state hospitals, are primarily – but not exclusively – a state responsibility. The state is also responsible for professional certification and licensure of medical doctors, psychologists, social workers and other health providers.

In addition to the state governmental system, there is a large national professional system. Specialty certification is provided by intraprofessional groups rather than government agencies. Thus the American Board of Psychiatry and Neurology, the National Association of Social Workers, and other professional groups, provide for the certification of specialists within their professions. Through this system, a professional organization such as the American Psychiatric Association through the

American Board of Psychiatry and Neurology, provides a professional non-governmental mechanism for regulating the number, composition, and quality of personnel. The Joint Commission on Accreditation of Hospitals, again a non-governmental intraprofessional body, plays an important role in accrediting hospitals. These professional bodies serve to supplement and complement the legal responsibility vested in the state government. However, the legal basis for the power that these professional regulatory bodies hold is being challenged and their status may be resolved by legislation or litigation.

Slowly, the federal government has become involved in this regulatory process, since considerable funds flow to hospitals and nursing homes through Medicare and Medicaid. The federal government, through the Health Care Financing Administration (HCFA), has become involved in the creation of standards for institutions which receive federal funding.

Governmental role in financing mental health services

A final major area of policy involves the financing of mental health services. In the 1960s, during the Johnson era, the federal government became involved in the financing of health through Medicare and Medicaid. Mental health in particular was financed through grants-in-aid for community mental health centers and alcoholism and drug abuse programs. Until now, except during the Carter administration, there has never been serious discussion of any form of national health service or of a national mental health service wherein the federal government directly operates mental health facilities. The US policy is in contrast to that of the United Kingdom, where the decision was taken at the end of World War II to create a national health service directly operated by the government. In the United States, the federal government opted to improve and extend mental health services through financing mechanisms.

Currently the major governmental financing mechanism is the reimbursement system, primarily direct reimbursement to providers for services rendered through Medicare and Medicaid. The federal dollars in Medicare and Medicaid comprise about one-fourth of all the health expenditures in the United States, whether from private or public sources. Medicare and Medicaid expenditures are currently at about $80 billion, of which an estimated 10 per cent goes for mental health care, mostly in nursing homes and hospitals. Most federal money does not go to the support of community services, although Medicare has begun somewhat hesitantly to support home care services. The amount of federal money channeled into programs such as day centers or after-care is minimal. Among the chronically mentally ill it is more substantial, since meeting the criteria of Medicaid helps states to acquire federal subsidization of health services.

Federal support for services was almost undertaken in the categorical programs of grants-in-aid for discreet categories of disability and illness. During the 1960s, there was a wide range of such programs, including the community health centers program, the grants-in-aid to local communities for alcoholism and drug abuse, methadone clinics, and grants-in-aid for categorical programs in general health (neighborhood health centers, child health programs, and elderly home care programs).

Nevertheless, federal dollars are predominantly allocated to direct reimbursement services. While categorical programs capture the attention of professionals identified with one particular constituency, they have relatively small disbursement levels. During the Carter administration, expenditures for the categorical programs never exceeded $2 billion, whereas, in contrast, Medicare and Medicaid consumed about $40 billion. As for the community mental health centers program, which during the previous era were considered the crowning achievement in the NIMH's provision of direct service, their budgets never exceeded $600 million.

During the Carter administration the HCFA could not accurately determine what proportion of Medicare and Medicaid spending went for patients with diagnoses of a psychiatric nature, but they estimated it at roughly 10 per cent. About 50 per cent of patients in nursing homes (mainly supported by Medicare and Medicaid) were diagnosed as having senile dementia. Yet even those diagnoses were suspect, since any nursing home whose population with the diagnosis of senile dementia exceeded 50 per cent had its reimbursement formula changed resulting in a consistent pattern of misdiagnosis and underdiagnosis.

Manpower and human resources

In general, public policy regarding manpower and human resources in mental health has followed policy concerning services, since manpower and other human resources are the means by which to achieve service policy goals. Only since World War II has public policy concerned itself with the supply and quality of mental health manpower. The initial policy decision was made in the late 1940s when Congress authorized the NIMH. Among the NIMH mandates was the use of federal funds for expansion in the types and number of mental health personnel.

Basic to NIMH policy concerning manpower was the decision as to which professional groups should be included. The NIMH early identified four mental health professional categories: psychiatry, psychology, social work, and occupational therapy. Later psychiatric nursing was added. It is to be noted that at that time a number of other professional groups, such as pastoral counselors and marriage and family counselors, were not given federal priority. Efforts to augment the supply of para-professionals did not arise until the 1960s, when there was interest in developing programs which incorporated ex-addict drug counselors, former alcoholic counselors, and indigenous para-professionals for community mental health centers.

Policy decisions also had to be made regarding the extent of government participation in training these classes of professional personnel. The VA, the Department of Defense, and the Public Health Service have all operated training programs. While the training and education activities of the Department of Defense and the Public Health Service have been relatively small, the VA has had extensive activities, which have contributed greatly to the expansion of psychiatry and clinical psychology in the decades immediately after World War II.

Since the advent of government funding for mental health manpower, governmental assistance for training has been mainly provided through grants-in-aid to academic institutions and stipends and fellowships to individual trainees for pre- and post-doctoral programs and for internships and residencies. Extensive federal dollars have been made available for training grants to departments of psychiatry in medical schools, programs in clinical psychology in academic institutions, schools of social work, and schools of nursing. While grants-in-aid go to faculty support as well as institutional costs, the majority of funds go to direct stipends to trainees in psychiatry, clinical psychology, social work, nursing, and occupational therapy. This funding has contributed to a marked expansion of mental health personnel, so much so that in the 1970s, beginning in the Nixon administration, efforts were made to decrease and then eliminate federal support for clinical training. This has been one of the most hotly contested areas of mental health policy, with continuing changes in congressional action and disagreements between executive, congressional, and professional groups.

One source of concern in the area of mental health manpower has been whether or not there exists a shortage of psychiatrists. The recent Gemanic report identified general psychiatry, and child psychiatry in particular, as suffering from shortages in personnel. These findings are being seriously disputed, in view of the evidence that the total number of physicians has increased, to the point where a surplus of physicians is being projected for the late 1980s and early 1990s.

As discussed above, the government, usually state government, also plays a role in regulating the number and quality of mental health professionals through licensing and certification. In recent years, there has been increasing movement for licensing and certification of social workers and psychologists. The goal is not so much to regulate the quality of these professionals, but rather to legitimize reimbursement through third party insurance mechanisms. The majority of states have passed legislation which allows "right to choice," whereby beneficiaries of health insurance with mental health benefits can choose psychologists and social workers without the prerequisite of medical authorization or medical screening. This has been an area of heated interprofessional rivalry and controversy, with the psychiatric societies almost universally contesting these legislative dicta. In almost all states, the trend of legislation has been to broaden the categories of mental health professionals eligible for independent vendorship under third party insurance.

Research policy

As with manpower and human resources, a public policy with regard to mental health research did not emerge until after World War II.

In the first half of the century, a number of states created research institutes as part of their mental health programs. The impetus was provided by the pioneering efforts of Adolf Meyer in Illinois, and in New York by the creation of the New York Psychiatric Institute. During the Progressive Era, some states, notably Massachusetts, New York, Illinois, and California, had developed small research activities, usually as part of existing state hospitals. A number of these achieved great scientific prominence, particularly the program in schizophrenia at Worcester State Hospital in Massachusetts and the broad range of activities in the New York State Psychiatric Institute.

With the creation of the NIMH after World War II, the locus of public responsibility for research shifted to the federal level. The federal government now maintains direct research activities, notably through the intramural program of the NIMH, located on the campus of NIH in Bethesda, Maryland. In addition, small amounts of research are conducted in the VA hospitals, and to a lesser extent in Department of Defense military establishments, notably the Walter Reed Army Institute of Psychiatry, and the National Naval Medical Center at Bethesda.

The most significant development in policy regarding research has been the grants-in-aid program initiated through the NIH and the ADAMHA Institute (NIMH, NIDAN, NIAAA). These provide the major sources for public funding for research.

While there is controversy within the profession as to the role of government in providing mental health services and in directing manpower and human resources policy, there is a strong consensus as to the necessity of maintaining federal support of extramural research. Government policy is currently at odds with professional consensus on this front, with the Reagan administration proposing reduction in support, and at times even closure of federal intramural laboratories, in mental health, as well as in other fields. Other significant areas of policy controversy revolve around the question of which areas of research should be supported. One of the early acts of the Reagan administration's Office of Management and Budget was to discontinue the NIMH support of social and behavioral research. This was paralleled by a dramatic reduction in NSF support of social and behavioral research. As evidence of the strong professional opinion on this matter, many but not all of these cuts have been restored, largely through the vigorous lobbying by the research and scholarly associations.

Epidemiology has played two roles in these developments. The epidemiologic evidence made available by the World War II experience indicated high prevalence of mental illness and related problems, and these data were used as justification of the necessity of federal action, not only to support the expansion of services and manpower, but to develop better knowledge as to the etiology, development, treatment, and prevention of mental illness.

Through the expansion of federal support, epidemiologic research flourished. Training programs in psychiatric epidemiology were established in a number of major medical centers and schools of public health. Most recently, the NIMH has developed the extensive Epidemiologic Catchment Area Program, which will involve the largest sample of patients directly investigated.

Prevention

Following the conquest of infectious disorders and the successful curbing of nutritional deficiency disorders, public and governmental concern has recently begun to focus on prevention in the area of mental health.

Prevention emerged as a public policy concern during the Carter administration, with the President's Commission on Mental Health, established in 1977. Although previous federal legislation had mentioned prevention, particularly following the Kennedy Message to Congress in 1961, it was only after the Report of President Carter's commission that specific congressional appropriations were earmarked for prevention activities. At that time, the NIMH was directed to develop a branch whose express function would be to administer programs for research and prevention.

In general, mental health policy has emphasized the expansion of direct services over prevention. There are serious limitations, however, as to how much direct services can ultimately affect morbidity and mortality. As with other forms of health, the main determinants of the mental health of the population are not primarily the quality of direct services to those already ill, but psycho-social factors (such as family history) and general conditions in the society (such as quality of housing, nutrition, sanitation, and the economy). Solving problems in these areas probably limits the incidence and prevalence of mental illness more effectively than does the continued expansion of direct mental health services.

The state of mental health knowledge and research indicates that we are not yet ready for a truly preventive program. However, a number of biological, psycho-social, and socio-cultural risk factors can be identified, which might in the future be investigated by a preventive mental health program. Biological risk factors include the quality of nutrition and control of environmental hazards. Our knowledge of environmental toxins in the sphere of mental health is far below our knowledge of carcinogens. Yet we do know, for instance, that lead in the air will affect mental functioning, as will mercury (as proven by the so-called "Mad Hatter" syndrome in the nineteenth-century hat industry). Among the socio-cultural factors are migration, racial and ethnic discrimination, the changing role of women, unemployment, and financial insecurity.

There is evidence that recent social policies have helped improve the mental health of a number of groups. For example, Srole and Fischer (1978) have demonstrated that the mental health of older women appears to have improved in recent years, and they attribute this to the changing status of women. The mental health of the elderly also appears to have improved, not only because of better physical health, but also as a function of the effect of social security on their general economic well-being.

On the other hand, adverse social conditions not dealt with by social policy are observed to produce mental health problems. For instance, the continuing high unemployment rate among young black males is related to suicide and also to the continued disruption of the black family. Also, recent epidemiological research has indicated the adverse consequences for children raised in single parent households.

The dilemma for mental health policy is that there is no clear mandate for the mental health professionals as to how and under what circumstances to influence policies with regard to nutrition, housing, and employment. Most mental health professionals traditionally share a liberal view of government and have supported an expansion of welfare and health services. The danger here, however, lies in the possibility that they will be identified with one political point of view, meaning that with shifts in the direction of a more conservative political climate, their claims on behalf of the mentally ill will receive less attention. One further aspect of prevention involves early detection and early intervention. There have been many efforts at mental health education, and it is not clear that these have had beneficial effects.

There remains considerable disagreement as to the nature of preventive activities in mental health, and the appropriate types of research and service programs to be developed for mental illness prevention.

Conclusions: future policy directions

As discussed above, the history of governmental involvement in providing mental health services has followed the same path as general public policy. Over the last forty years, federal expenditure and involvement in public health has increased, and has expanded to include a broader population than just the chronically mentally ill. Now, a reversion to a more conservative political philosophy has brought about a reduction in federal expenditures.

Ironically, the public today expects more in the way of mental health services than ever before. At a minimum, 10 per cent of the population now looks to mental health services for assistance in the problems of living, diagnoses of depression, and anxiety, as well as for the treatment of severer forms of mental illness. Although the growth curve in the expansion of mental health services may be leveling off, there is still a much greater degree of public acceptance, and the expectation of receiving mental health services is considerably higher than previously.

In the 1980s, there also seems to be a greater willingness of communities to assume responsibility for mental health services. When the Reagan administration repealed the Mental Health Systems Act and created block grants, transferring funding responsibility for mental health, alcoholism, and drug abuse centers to the states, many professionals were concerned that this would mean an end to or a marked diminution of community responsibility. This has not happened. At many mental health centers, the loss of federal funds and the creation of state block grants has provided a stimulus for citizen groups to improve their ability to negotiate for contracts with local agencies, such as the courts and school systems, as well as to improve their billing systems. Local initiative is increasingly evident throughout many communities. This may be due both to the recent stabilization and diminution in programs, as well as an attitude shift on the part of local community leaders. Federal efforts made during the 1950s, 1960s, and 1970s have formed the expectations of local community leaders, who now may be working hard to maintain services in the face of diminishing resources. In the United States, the trend of public policy since the 1930s has reflected the belief that the federal government is more responsive to the needs of ethnic, racial, and religious minorities and the poor than is the state government. Historically, state government has been far less responsive to the needs of minority groups, the poor, and disadvantaged groups such as the mentally ill, the mentally retarded, and the elderly. The efforts during the liberal period of government policy (1933–80), may have created important constituencies at the local level, particularly among the mentally ill and their families, and among the elderly, who will now take up the responsibility of ensuring adequate services. It is possible that the expectations created in the past twenty-five years and the impressive expansion of utilization of services will be sustained at the grass-roots and community level without dependence on the same sort of federal largesse that was necessary to initiate these programs.

Notes

1 Preparation of this manuscript was supported in part by funds from the George Harrington Trust, Boston University, and from a MacArthur foundation program in health policy and education.

References

Angst, J. (1973) The Etiology and Nosology of Endogenous Depressive Psychoses. *Foreign Psychiatry*, Spring. International Arts and Science Press.

Easterlin, R.A. (1973) Does Money Buy Interest? *The Public Interest* 30: 3–10.

Erikson, E.H. (1950) *Childhood and Society*. New York: Norton.

—— (1968) *Identity: Youth in Crisis*. New York: Norton.

Farris, R.E.L. and Dunham, H.W. (1967) *Mental Disorders in Urban Areas: An Ecological Study of Schizophrenia and Other Psychoses*. Chicago: University of Chicago Press.

Goldberger, J. (1914a) The Cause and Prevention of Pellagra. *Public Health Report* xxix: 2354–357.

—— (1914b) The Etiology of Pellagra: The Significance of Certain Epidemiological Observations with Respect Thereto. *Public Health Report* xxix: 1683–686.

Grob, G.N. (1973) *Mental Institutions in America: Social Policy to 1875*. New York: Free Press.

Gurin, G.J., Veroff, J. and Feld, S. (1960) *Americans View Their Mental Health: A Nationwide Interview Study*. New York: Basic Books.

Heston, L.L. (1966) Psychiatric Disorders in Foster Home Reared Children of Schizophrenic Mothers. *British Journal of Psychiatry* 112: 819–25.

Hollingshead, A. and Redlich, F. (1958) *Social Class and Mental Illness*. New York: John Wiley.

Illich, I. (1976) *Medical Nemesis: The Expropriation of Health*. New York: Pantheon.

Jahoda, M. (1959) *Current Concepts in Mental Health*. New York Basic Books.

Jarvis, E. (1971) *Insanity and Idiocy in Massachusetts: Report of the Commission on Lunacy*. Cambridge: Harvard University Press.

Kety, S., Rosenthal, D., Wender, P.H., and Schulsinger, F. (1968) The Types and Prevalence of Mental Illness in the Biological and Adoptive Families of Adopted Schizophrenics. In D. Rosenthal and S. Kety (eds), *The Transmission of Schizophrenia*. New York: Pergamon Press.

Lasch, C. (1979) *The Culture of Narcissism*. New York: Norton.

Leighton, D., Harding, J. *et al.* (1963) Psychiatric Findings of the Stirling County Study. *American Journal of Psychiatry* 119: 1021–026.

Lemkau, P. Tietze, C., and Cooper, H. (1942) Complaint of Nervousness and the Psychoneuroses. *American Journal of Orthopsychiatry* 12: 214–23.

Levinson, D. (1978) *The Seasons of a Man's Life*. New York: Alfred Knopf.

Maslow, A. (1954) *Motivation and Personality*. New York: Harper and Row.

Mednick, S.A., Schulsinger, F., Higgins, J. *et al.* (eds) (1974) *Genetics, Environment, and Psychopathology*. New York: North Holland Publishing.

Murphy, J.M. (1980) Continuities in Community-Based Psychiatric Epidemiology. *Archives of General Psychiatry* 37.

Myers, J.K. and Bean, L.L. (1968) *A Decade Later: A Follow-Up of Social Class and Mental Illness*. New York: John Wiley.

Neugarten, B.L. (1975) Adult Personality: Toward a Psychology of the Life Cycle. In B.L. Neugarten, *The Human Life Cycle*. New York: Jason Aronson.

Perris, C. (1966) A Study of Bipolar (Manic-Depressive) and Unipolar Recurrent Psychoses. *Acta Psychiatry Scandinavia* 42(supplement 194): 7–189.

Polsby, N.W. (1984) America's Hidden Success: A Reassessment of Twenty Years of Public Policy. A book review by John E. Schwartz. *Commentary*, April.

Regier, D.A., Goldberg, I., and Taube, C.A. (1978) The De Facto US Mental Health Services System: A Public Health Perspective. *Archives of General Psychiatry* 35(June).

Richmond, J.B. and Klerman, G.L. (1980) *National Plan for the Chronically Mentally Ill*. Washington: DHHS.

Rosenthal, D., Wedner, P.H., Kety, S.S., Schulsinger, F., Welner, J., and Ostergaard, L. (1968) Schizophrenics' Offspring Reared in Adoptive Homes. In D. Rosenthal and S. Kety (eds) *The Transmission of Schizophrenia*. New York: Pergamon Press.

Roth, W.F., Jr. and Luton, F.H. (1943) The Mental Health Program in Tennessee. *American Journal of Psychiatry* 99: 662–75.

Shepherd, M., Cooper, B., Brown, A.C., and Kalton, G.W. (1966) *Psychiatric Illness in General Practice*. London: Oxford University Press.

Srole, L. and Fischer, A.K. (1978) Generations, Aging, Genders, and Well-Being. The Midtown Manhattan Follow-Up Study. Presented at the Eastern Sociological Society Annual Meeting, Philadelphia.

—— (1980) The Midtown Manhattan Longitudinal Study vs. "The Mental Paradise Lost" Doctrine. *Archives of General Psychiatry* 37: 209–21.

Srole, L., Langner, T.A., Michael, S.T., Opler, M.K., and Rennie, T.A.C. (1962) *Mental Health in the Metropolis.* New York: McGraw Hill.

Stouffer, S.A. (1950) *Measurement and Prediction.* New York: John Wiley.

Stouffer, S.A. and Lumsdaine, M.H. *et al.* (1949) *The American Soldier: Combat and Its Aftermath.* Princeton: Princeton University Press.

Vaillant, G.E. (1981) *Adaptations to Life.* Boston: Little, Brown.

Weiss, R.S. (1976a) Transition States and Other Stressful Situations: Their Nature and Programs for Their Management. In G. Caplan and M. Killilea (eds) *Support Systems and Mutual Help: Multidisciplinary Explorations.* New York: Grune and Stratton.

Weiss, R.S. (1976b) The Emotional Impact of Marital Separation. *Journal of Social Issues* 32(1): 135–45.

Weissman, M.M. and Klerman, G.L. (1978) Epidemiology of Mental Disorders: Emerging Trends in the United States. *Archives of General Psychiatry* 35: 705–12.

Weissman, M.M. and Myers, J.K. (1978) Affective Disorders in a US Urban Community: The Use of Diagnostic Criteria in an Epidemiological Survey. *Archives of General Psychiatry* 35: 1304–311.

Winokur, C. and Reich. (1969) *Manic Depressive Insanity.* St Louis: C.V. Mosby.

Zinburg, N.E. and Jacobson, R.C. (1976) The Natural History of "Chipping" *American Journal of Psychiatry* 133: 37–40.

Nine

Epidemiology and alcohol policy[1]

Diana Chapman Walsh and

Ralph W. Hingson

Unlike most other public health problems, those associated with alcohol use were at one time the object of a comprehensive and straightforward national control program, albeit one that came widely to be viewed as the apotheosis of benighted and failed public policy. The program, of course, was Prohibition, and the decades since its repeal in 1933 have been spent scrambling back from and disavowing so draconian a policy and then testing alternative and much more modest approaches to mitigating the disruptions associated with alcohol use.

Epidemiology and alcohol policy

The wellsprings for Prohibition, according to most accounts, were moral, cultural, and political, not scientific; if an epidemiological appreciation of problems associated with alcohol abuse played a role at all, it was a negligible and crudely intuitive one. Epidemiology is concerned with the patterns of disease and health in populations and with unraveling etiologic factors (Lilienfeld and Lilienfeld 1980: 3; Stallones 1980: 71). In the case of alcohol, this means exploring the distribution of drinking practices over space, time, and social groupings, as well as problems those practices may entail. In the byzantine evolution of alcoholism policy, epidemiology has seemed until quite recently to function less as guide than as handmaiden, providing post-hoc justifications and philosophical support for public postures toward alcohol that reflect political, cultural, and economic currents more than they represent "science."

Having made that assertion, one must hasten to acknowledge that sorting out the various influences behind anything so diffuse and complex as the nation's alcohol policy is difficult at best. The historical framework and current policy options have been developed in several different ways: through analyses by social scientists, usually sociologists (Beauchamp 1976, 1980a, b; Conrad and Schneider 1984; Gusfield 1963; Hingson, Matthews, and Scotch 1979; Reigier 1979; Room 1984; Vaillant 1983; Wiseman 1970), and through collections of essays in the same vein (Filstead, Rossi, and Keller 1976; Pittman and Snyder 1962), through the work of consensus groups and expert panels, in the private sector (Hamburg, Elliot, and Parron 1982; Institute of Medicine 1980; Moore and Gerstein 1981; West 1984), or acting on behalf of government (United States Department of Health, Education, and Welfare, 1971, 1974, 1978; US Department of Health and Human Services (hereafter, DHHS), 1981, 1983). A number of specific empirical studies are also highly germane; some we cite below.

Focus of the chapter

Drawing on that scholarship, this chapter pursues the particular question for the alcohol field of the interplay (or its absence) between developments in epidemiology and those in policy. In that pursuit, we first outline major insights from the epidemiology of alcoholism, alcohol abuse, and related problems; second canvass the pre-eminent trends and shifts in policies aimed at cushioning the effects of these problems, especially as those trends may relate to changes in the epidemiological knowledge base; and, finally, in a tentative way, sketch the lineaments of what might constitute a comprehensive policy, grounded in epidemiology.

The epidemiology of alcoholism and related problems

Major strides have been taken in recent decades in the measurement of alcohol use and abuse, but vexing difficulties persist. Until the late 1950s, with Jellinek's seminal work (1959), the prevalence of alcohol problems was estimated from observations of highly biased clinical populations: hospitalized or jailed alcoholics or those appearing at welfare offices, at Alcoholics Anonymous (AA) meetings or in physicians' practices (Nace 1984). Jellinek's well-known formula sought generality beyond these alcoholics in treatment by extrapolating presumed alcohol abuse rates from overall records of liver cirrhosis mortality (Jellinek 1959, 1960; Keller 1975).

During the 1960s these indirect epidemiologic approaches began to yield to studies of drinking practices among general populations, using survey research techniques. Survey technology had been refined during the post-war period, but drinking remained under enough of a taboo that direct questions concerning the use or misuse of alcohol were evaded by respondents (Keller 1975). This stigma has waned sufficiently in the past two decades that the method of choice for estimating the incidence and prevalence of alcohol use and abuse has become the large-scale sample survey, marred though it continues to be by chronic underreporting. For example, Room (1971) observed that his group's "best survey questions uncover about two-thirds of the total expected consumption," based on known production and/or sales figures. (Tobacco use surveys, in contrast, now pick up about 75 per cent of cigarette sales, compared to about 90 per cent only a decade ago, before smoking became stigmatized after the health effects became clear (Warner 1979).)

Frequency and quantity of alcohol use

In periodic reports to Congress, the National Institute on Alcohol Abuse and Alcoholism (NIAAA) summarizes current research on alcohol and health. The fifth special report, released in December, 1983, indicates that overall per capita consumption of alcoholic beverages (from sales and excise tax data) has increased steadily since the Second World War; an acceleration in the rate of increase, since the early 1960s, is now leveling off although consumption continues to rise. The 1981 estimated per capita consumption rate of 2.77 gallons of absolute alcohol a year, or 1 ounce a day (averaged across the total US population aged fourteen and above) is 37 per cent higher than the 1961 figure, but only 7 per cent above the 1971 rate (DHHS 1983). Beer accounts for nearly half of this consumption, distilled spirits just over a third and wine the balance.

Rates extrapolated from sales records suggest marked regional variations in alcohol use, but these are subject to the vagaries and distortions of idiosyncrasies in state laws and policies. The task of discerning variations (by beverage, region, demographic group, type of drinker, drinking context, and so on) has been carried by survey research, much of it funded by the NIAAA. The 1979 national survey, conducted by Clark and Midanik (1982), sought not only to establish a cross-sectional understanding of patterns of use and abuse at a given point in time but also to compare these findings to eight previous NIAAA-funded drinking practice surveys covering a thirteen-year span. Although this second objective was complicated by the definitional imprecision and diversity that has plagued epidemiological research in the field, the investigators found no evidence of trends (or changes) in alcohol use or associated problems.

What the exercise did reveal was an apparent consistency over the decade in general patterns of alcohol use and abuse. On quantity and frequency measures, the adult population consistently divides roughly into thirds:

– "abstainers" said they drank no alcoholic beverages in the year preceding the survey;
– "light drinkers" reported average daily use of no more than 0.21 ounces of absolute alcohol (at most three drinks a week);
– "moderate" drinkers (about 25 per cent of the population) and "heavy" drinkers (roughly 9 per cent of adults) reported, respectively, average daily consumption of 0.22–0.99 ounces (up to two drinks) and 1–5 or more ounces (2–10 or more drinks).

Distributions in these categories are summarized in *Table 9.1* (Moore and Gerstein 1981: 28), which shows that close to two-thirds of the adult population reports drinking no more than three drinks per week.

Table 9.1 *Distribution of alcohol consumption by adults in the United States*

estimated average quantity of pure alcohol consumed daily in ounces		mean percentage (standard deviation)	
		1971–76	1979
0	"abstainers"	35.0 (1.4)	33
0.01–0.21	"light drinkers" – up to three drinks weekly	32.0 (3.4)	34
0.22–0.99	"moderate drinkers" – up to two drinks daily	22.0 (3.0)	24
1.0 +	"heavy drinkers"	11.0 (1.5)	9
1.0–2.0	2–4 drinks daily	6.5 (1.1)	
2.01–5.0	4–10 drinks daily	3.4 (0.7)	b
5.01 +	10 + drinks daily	1.2 (0.5)	
Number		a	1,758

Source: Moore and Gerstein 1981: 28.

Notes:
[a] 7 national surveys, total number = 12,139, mean number = 1,734, range 1,071–2,510.
[b] Breakdown not available.

Among subgroups, men drink more than women (the "heavy drinking" category is weighted three-to-one for men and twice as many women as men claim to be abstainers), drinking declines with age (more precipitously for men than for women) and abstinence is slightly more common among lower than higher income and educational groups, among blacks, especially black women, and in the East, South, Central, and South Atlantic regions of the country. Extensive subgroup analyses are difficult to do in national surveys, owing to sample size limitations (Clark and Midanik 1982).

Patterns of problems or "abuse"

As challenging as it has been to determine how much, how and when various categories of people drink, the complexities multiply when the question turns to isolating important effects. Clark and Midanik (1982) examined the nine "problem areas" listed in *Table 9.2*, and compared their prevalence to earlier surveys.

Among both men and women, the comparison reveals an apparent increase in "symptomatic drinking." Thought perhaps to indicate physical dependence and loss of control, symptomatic drinking includes such self-reported behaviors as sneaking drinks, gulping drinks, difficulty stopping drinking, memory lapses (or "blackouts"), skipping meals while drinking and drinking to relieve a hangover. But the apparently contradictory decline in "psychological dependence" (defined as drinking in order to alter one's mood) stands as a reminder of the caution that must be exercised in interpreting comparisons across independent studies (Light and Pillemer 1984).

At a higher level of magnification, the major effects of alcohol use and abuse fall into four broad categories: physical or medical consequences, psychological impact, social disruptions, and economic costs. The first three are most relevant here because they constitute epidemiological questions, answers to which the economist converts into the common metric of money to arrive at estimated economic costs.

Medical consequences   Evidence is accumulating on the extent and severity of harmful physical effects of chronic alcohol abuse. Wolf (1984) catalogues the predominant ones: disturbances to tissues, disruption of regulatory mechanisms, and damage to various organs. In its fifth report to Congress, the NIAAA traces "the trail of adverse effects of alcohol throughout the body:" to the brain, the digestive system (the mouth, esophagus, stomach, intestine, and pancreas), the liver (to which it has recently been established, alcohol is directly toxic), the muscle systems (including the heart), the blood, the kidneys, the lungs, the endocrine system, sexual functioning, and reproductive outcome (DHHS 1983). Relative risks, dose-response relationships and biological mechanisms of action have yet to be fully established, but epidemiological studies of correlations between various levels of alcohol use and various physical sequelae are increasingly being refined.

In 1979, the recorded US mortality rate for "alcoholism" as a specific diagnostic entity was 1.8 per 100,000 population, or roughly 4,000 deaths. In addition, "alcoholic psychosis" resulted in 440 deaths (0.4/100,000) and cirrhosis of the liver, the eighth

Table 9.2 Prevalence of problems associated with drinking in the past 12 months and types of drinkers for males and females in the 1967 and 1979 national surveys (in percentages)[a]

problem area	National 1967			National 1979		
	Lighter	Moderate	Heavier	Lighter	Moderate	Heavier
Males						
Health problems	5	8	15	0	5	11
Belligerence associated with drinking	2	4	18	1	9	32
Problems with friends	—[c]	2	8	184	7	67
Symptomatic drinking	2	11	46	2	26	45
Psychological dependence	39	66	83	13	40	25
Job problems	—[c]	3	10	2	7	5
Problems with the law, police, accidents	—[c]	2	0	0	2	2
Binge drinking	0	1	2	0	1	
Problems with spouse[b]	—[c]	1	6	1	4	5
(N)	(153)	(312)	(111)	(140)	(323)	(92)
Females						
Health problems	6	9	11	2	4	9
Belligerence associated with drinking	1	7	29	1	12	27
Problems with friends	0	1	11	1	3	2
Symptomatic drinking	1	14	42	4	22	54
Psychological dependence	28	66	96	18	43	51
Job problems	0	5	20	1	4	13
Problems with the law, police, accidents	0	—[c]	0	0	2	8
Binge drinking	0	1	2	0	1	2
Problems with spouse[b]	0	0	0	0	0	4
(N)	(241)	(187)	(22)	(304)	(264)	(32)

Notes:
[a] The percentages are weighted figures. Totals shown are the actual number of cases. Slight variations in these totals occur because of nonresponse etc.
[b] Last 2½ years for National 1967; last 3 years for National 1979.
[c] Less than 0.5 per cent.
Source: Clark and Midanik 1982: 19.

leading cause of death in the United States, accounted for about 29,000 deaths in 1979 and a mortality rate of about 13.2/100,000, of which approximately 5 deaths/100,000 were specified as alcohol-related (DHHS 1982). It is believed, however, that most liver cirrhosis deaths – perhaps up to 90 per cent – are in fact alcohol-induced.

Some 200,000 hospital discharges in 1971 involved diagnoses of alcoholism, alcohol psychosis, and cirrhosis of the liver; these statistics are widely believed to seriously understate the true prevalence of alcohol abuse as a factor in medical care utilization (Walsh and Egdahl 1985). Also, figures such as these exclude deaths and disabilities resulting from accidents and other events in which alcohol may be implicated, even if no one involved can accurately be labeled an "alcoholic."

Overall, alcohol misuse is believed to be a factor in more than 10 per cent of all deaths in the United States, roughly 200,000 per year, including traffic accidents, liver cirrhosis, and cancers of the liver, esophagus and mouth (DHEW 1979: 125). It should be noted, however, that aggregate statistics like these are fairly crude extrapolations from smaller scale studies of varying quality.

Psychological dimensions   Acute alcoholism results in serious mental illness, including alcoholic dementia and hallucinosis, delerium tremens, Wernicke's encephalopathy, Korsakoff's syndrome, and other, less well-defined forms of psychosis, dementia, and cognitive impairment.

Depression is the psychological syndrome most closely linked with alcohol abuse, which is implicated in some 30 per cent of suicides. Neither the causal mechanisms nor even their directions are at all well understood. Reports that alcoholics have family histories of depression or themselves experienced depressive episodes before the onset of heavy drinking hint at a depressive tendency as a possible risk factor for problem drinking. However, the best longitudinal research fails to support this hypothesis (Vaillant 1983).

Efforts to piece together the biological mechanisms have resulted in several intriguing metabolic studies. They indicate that alcohol consumption produces abnormal levels of diols in the blood of diagnosed alcoholics with manic-depressive disorders. How to interpret these findings, and how they bear on the debate concerning a genetic predisposition toward alcoholism, is still a matter of controversy (Wolf 1984).

Much discussion over the years of "the alcoholic personality" has depicted a self-centered, insecure, vulnerable individual who is overly sensitive to social nuances to the point of paranoia. Combined with a stubborn streak and a capacity for self-deception, this profile is remarkably robust in the stories alcoholics tell of their own struggles (Wholey 1984). Whether it is a cause or an effect of problem drinking, or indeed, a post-hoc interpretation distorted through the lens of AA, has yet to be established (Bandura 1969; Vaillant 1983; Wolf 1984).

Social sequelae Like the physical and psychological toll of excess drinking, social consequences are difficult to isolate from a web of confounding factors. Drinkers are overrepresented as victims and participants in the whole spectrum of accidents, crimes, and family disruptions, but correlational studies often fail to control for the fact that many heavy drinkers are overexposed to other risks (for example, non-use of seat belts) which may be unrelated to their drinking. A great deal still remains to be learned about associations between amounts and kinds of drinking and varieties of harmful effects. Moreover, the direction of causal relationships is frequently less than clear, as in the case of family disruptions, where alcohol may antedate, arise out of, or interact in intricate ways with a disintegrating family fabric.

Nevertheless, there is strong and mounting evidence that alcohol plays an independent role in producing injuries and fatalities associated with accidents on the highways, in aviation, at work, in the home, and during recreational activities, as well as those associated with violent crime. Our recent review of these studies can be found in the NIAAA's fifth special report to Congress (DHHS 1983: 83–99).

Risk factors

On the other side of the causal equation from harmful effects lie equally perplexing questions of etiology. Risk factors for alcohol abuse include genetic predispositions, psychosocial factors (stress, social supports, and coping styles), as well as aspects of the biological, physical, and social environment.

These are thoroughly reviewed in the Moore and Gerstein volume, which includes a schematic model for organizing the range of factors that underlie alcohol problems (1981: 46).

A central theme of that report is its identification of moderate drinking as a risk factor for many of the social consequences of alcohol misuse. Moderate drinkers as a group greatly outnumber heavy drinkers, and therefore probably account, in absolute numbers, for more than half of all alcohol-related problems (Moore and Gerstein 1981: 44). For this reason and also in the hope of achieving early detection of problems that may worsen if undetected, considerable effort is being channeled into the development of screening strategies and instruments that may help detect low level or incipient alcohol problems.

A large international project, sponsored by the World Health Organisation (WHO), has been developing and field testing an instrument for use in primary care settings (Canavan 1985) and several specific sets of diagnostic criteria − most notably as part of the third Diagnostic and Statistical Manual (DSM-III) of the American Psychiatric Association − are being refined. While they facilitate clinical decision making, these diagnostic tools also lay essential groundwork for epidemiologic advances in estimating the prevalence of alcohol-related disorders and tracing their etiology.

The goal of early detection and early intervention rests on a linear model of alcoholism as a progressive disease. Although firmly entrenched in AA doctrine, this metaphor is challenged by the phenomenon of "spontaneous remission," observed in some cross-sectional studies and longitudinal research (Vaillant 1983). Consensus is nevertheless building that responsible clinicians should be alert to subtle signs of prodromal alcohol dependence (the "symptomatic drinking" behaviors documented in survey research) and should urge their patients who exhibit these symptoms to abstain from further drinking. Where alcohol is concerned, medicine has always tended to err on the side of omission.

Summing up

In sum, the partial picture of alcohol problems epidemiology has pieced together includes a small segment of the population with very acute or advanced alcoholism, accompanied, often, by a constellation of devastating physical, psychological, and social decrements. Who these people were before they became alcoholics, and what propelled them down that "slippery slope" (to the extent that it indeed is one) are mostly missing pieces. A much larger group has occasional or periodic bouts with alcohol. Sometimes these are disruptive or harmful to the drinkers or those around them; too often they are even fatal.

Epidemiologists interested in these problems are just beginning to define how various factors combine, with positive and negative results: the host (predisposing characteristics of individual drinkers), the agent (types, and amounts of beverage alcohol), and the environment (physical hazards and protections, social supports, cultural and economic pressures and the contexts of drinking episodes). Combinations of these variables produce a range of outcomes that also still await adequate conceptualization and measurement. Meanwhile, public policy – establishing social goals and allocating resources for their pursuit – must be fashioned one way or another, however primitive the information base.

Salient trends in policy

Understanding the driving currents in social policy toward alcoholism and alcohol abuse involves observing when, why, and how this problem traverses jurisdictional boundaries that separate broad systems of social control: moral, legal, and medical. These questions have inspired a lively scholarly tradition in which the alcohol problem has served as an object lesson in how deviant behavior becomes medicalized (Conrad and Schneider 1984), how definitions of a social problem evolve to justify transfers in its "ownership" (Gusfield 1963), and how these collective definitions can distort and paralyze (Beauchamp 1980a) or at least shape (Moore and Gerstein 1981) public debate and the formulation of rational policy. There seems little doubt that the "governing ideas" (Moore and Gerstein 1981) behind alcohol policy have until recently precluded epidemiology from playing a meaningful role because they have denied the feasibility and/or the relevance of locating problems in subpopulations, which is the very essence of the epidemiologist's task.

Principal periods and themes

The nation's posture toward alcohol use and its sequelae has undergone a historical evolution that lacks clear lines of demarcation except for the chasm surrounding the Prohibition years (1919–33). Otherwise, trends blend into each other, overlap and coexist for periods of time in complex combinations and weave an intricate mosaic of several discernible strands (Beauchamp 1980a; Conrad and Schneider 1984; Moore and Gerstein 1981). Three strands are centrally relevant to our purposes here:

1 a moral focus on alcohol and its abuse as categorical evils;
2 a medical orientation toward alcoholism, defined as a disease; and
3 the beginnings of a public health perspective, with two distinct parts.

A public health perspective　First, epidemiological knowledge of the diversity of drinkers, drinking contexts and problems encountered or precipitated by drinkers is laid as a foundation for an integrated structure of preventive interventions focusing not only on the host (the "alcoholic"), nor just the agent (the intoxicating drink), but also on the environments (physical and social) and the interactions that may result in harm where alcohol has played a part. Second, these interventions are implemented in an experimental way, and systematically evaluated using techniques that put them "in the camp" of "experimental epidemiology" because they look for health and disease status as ultimate outcome measures (Stallones 1980: 72).

Moral, legal, and medical strands in early alcohol policies
During the Colonial and Revolutionary periods in the United States heavy drinking was the accepted norm (estimates place the per capita consumption rate at over six gallons of absolute alcohol a year, compared to a current figure of roughly 2.7) (Beauchamp 1980a: 25) and became an object of opprobrium

only when it resulted in a "pattern of repeated and highly consequential drunkenness" (Conrad and Schneider 1984: 78). Drinking behavior that did violate community decorum was often addressed by the church, the period's dominant institution of social control, and the explanatory paradigm the church applied at the time was the Puritan doctrine of free will, which characterized intoxication as an exercise of choice. To over-indulge and encounter problems with alcohol was to reveal moral defects. Civil penalties were applied too, including fines, whipping, confinement in the stocks and other forms of public humiliation such as the enforced wearing of a "D" and even, on occasion, banishment (Aaron and Musto 1981: 132).

Toward the end of the 18th century, this punitive orientation was already beginning to yield to a first-generation view of habitual drunkenness as a disease. The physician-statesman, Benjamin Rush, was the chief originator in the United States of the disease concept. He wrote in a famous and widely circulated tract that those who "lost control" of their drinking suffered from the "disease of inebriety," the behavioral symptoms of which he catalogued in vivid detail (Conrad and Schneider 1984: 79). This progressively inspired effort to shield the drinker from the blame inherent in the "free will" doctrine adumbrated the post-Prohibition construct of alcohol*ism* as a disease and even laid the groundwork for the more comprehensive public health approach (Aaron and Musto 1981: 139). But its first application was as a cornerstone for the temperance move-ment, distinguished by its view of *liquor* as a categorical evil capable of destroying the life of anyone so unfortunate as to come under its thrall. It was not until after the repeal of Prohibition that the disease concept became a device to deflect attention from the agent ("demon rum") to the few unfortunate alcoholics infected by the disease.

Armed with Rush's indictment of liquor as a physical and moral toxin, the temperance movement grew prodigiously from the 1820s on (with a short hiatus during the Civil War), and reached a zenith in 1919 with the passage of the 18th Amendment (criminalizing the manufacture and sale of "intoxicating liquors" but not their purchase or use) and the Volstead Act specifying procedures for implementation. Gusfield (1963) and subsequent scholars have argued that the saloon and "traffic in liquor" symbolized for the temperance advocates all that was threatening and destabilizing (intemperate) in the rapid industrialization and cultural modernization taking place at the time. Dismantling the malign industry was seen as an appropriate and a sufficient step toward stopping the spread of addiction because "the appetite for drink would wither away without the artificial stimulation of an organized traffic" (Aaron and Musto 1981: 159). Rush's disease motif was influential here too; it was used to transfer all blame from consumers to purveyors and to characterize consumers as hapless and hopeless victims who could not be identified in advance, nor immunized, nor effectively treated when stricken. All logic (but no data) therefore pointed to "decontaminating" the environment as the control strategy of choice.

Prohibition effectively "chilled debate" for thirteen years on whether, and if so specifically how, alcoholism was a disease (Conrad and Schneider 1984: 85). Also any serious epidemiology was caught during that period in a polemical crossfire between the "wet and dry forces," each side producing volumes of "spurious" data to show that Prohibition was or was not dampening overall consumption of alcoholic beverages (Aaron and Musto 1981: 163). In retrospect, the balanced answer seems to be that it did reduce consumption by anywhere between one-third and one-half (Clark 1976: 164), but the "noble experiment" went out as it had come in, on a wave of empirically unexamined but ardently held ideological propositions. Conventional wisdom came to see the experiment as anything but noble; so strong and uncritical was this backlash that it became even less an "experiment" from which policy-makers might extrapolate any but the most globally negative lessons (Aaron and Musto 1981: 130).

A medical thread: repairing a defective "host"   Meanwhile, the repeal of Prohibition bespoke recognition of irreversible cultural and economic trends, including the opening of a new consumer era (Moore and Gerstein 1981). With the restoration of alcohol as a legal and popular product to be marketed to the sophisticated and convivial, drunken and disorderly conduct had to be explained in new terms shorn of the temperance hostility toward the alcohol beverages industry. Alcohol needed an "alibi," in Beauchamp's lexicon, and found a convenient one in a "kinds-of-people" explanation that revived and extended the disease model by drawing a sharp dichotomy between normal or "social" drinking on the one hand and, on the other, "alcoholic" or problem drinking that only certain kinds of people developed.

Simple epidemiological concepts lay at the heart of this ideological shift. The observation that serious difficulties with alcohol are found in a small slice of the total population was used to reject the temperance assertion that alcohol was a necessary and sufficient cause of all drinking problems. That substantial numbers of drinkers developed no manifest difficulties was self-evident; the focus of concern could thus be redirected from the producers and their product to a small minority of exquisitely "susceptible" consumers who would need to abstain entirely from drinking intoxicants. But the real epidemiological work – teasing out subtler correlations in a range of drinking behaviors and sequelae, then testing alternative explanations – remained for a long time undone because the central project was to isolate and characterize the alcoholic as the problem (Beauchamp 1980a: 39–40).

The disease concept was refined and buttressed in research conducted at the Yale Center for Alcohol Studies, founded in the late 1930s and for many years the intellectual hub of American alcohol-related research. The work of E.M. Jellinek and his colleagues set forth in painstaking detail the model of alcoholism that remains the dominant metaphor today. In a principally conceptual or clinical formulation (as opposed to an empirical one) Jellinek drew on case studies from members of AA to describe a degenerative disease of addiction progressing through four distinct stages ("prealcoholic", "prodromal," "crucial," and "chronic"), each involving symptoms of increasing severity (Jellinek 1960). Only those drinkers who actually become addicted, who lose control over their drinking, are diagnosable as alcoholics in Jellinek's view; he believed they have a predisposition of some kind (an "X factor") that differentiates them from the many heavy drinkers who are able by and large to maintain their drinking under control. He argued also for a sharp distinction between those with the disease (who should be exempted from blame and treated) and those who deserved society's moral censure for electing to drink irresponsibly (Beauchamp 1980a: 75).

Defining alcoholism as a disease not only buffered the

sufferer from blame but also opened the possibility of his or her treatment, strongly advocated by the Yale group. The treatment movement, like the disease concept, had pre-Prohibition roots; more than fifty specialized asylums for the treatment of chronic inebriates had been founded between 1830 and 1900 under public and private auspices, usually with physician leadership (Beauchamp 1980a: 7–8). The early asylums sought to provide "needed physical and, more important, moral care" (Conrad and Schneider 1984: 83). After Prohibition, the moral theme gave way to "the increasingly therapeutic and treatment-oriented [thrust] of the American criminal justice system" (Conrad and Schneider 1984: 87) and, in 1944, the Yale Center joined with the Connecticut state prison authority to establish the Yale Plan Clinics as prototypes for the medical treatment of alcoholism (Beauchamp 1980a) and emblems of the state's responsibility to treat this disease (Room 1984: 298).

Two other organizations, both strongly committed to the disease concept, were gaining adherents at this time: Alcoholics Anonymous (AA), the self-help group founded in 1935 by a New York stockbroker and a physician from Akron, Ohio, and the National Council on Alcoholism (NCA), founded in 1944 by three women (a former alcoholic, a journalist, and a psychiatrist) with close connections to the Yale Center and to AA. Both the NCA and AA had various incantations that declared alcoholism a treatable disease and the alcoholic a sick person worthy of help; the NCA's mission was to promote this cause as a public responsibility (Conrad and Schneider 1984: 88).

All these groups were in the public relations business because they needed members or financial support or both. Their spokespeople accordingly took great pains to distance themselves from the teetotaling, reactionary, and radically interventionist stigma coupled in the public mind with the temperance movement. The concept of alcoholism as a disease to which the great majority are immune was the distancing device, but it still left to be explained the etiology of the disease and Jellinek's mysterious "X factor" underlying the alcoholic's unique sensitivity.

Epidemiological data undermining the disease model   By the 1960s enough data had accumulated to sketch one beginning answer to this question. Known as the "integration hypothesis," it was articulated in a commission report published in 1968 (Beauchamp 1980a: 41) and called for research not only on alcoholism but also on other types of alcohol use and potential abuse: "problem drinking" and "social drinking." In this respect it seemed to break with the monolithic disease conception, but in other important respects it still fit squarely in the alcoholism tradition.

From a line of epidemiological research on ethnic and cultural differences in drinking, the integrationists argued that problems are more common in cultures where drinking is less well integrated into daily routines. This theory buttressed a laissez-faire position because it suggested that efforts to control alcohol might have unintended negative effects if they created "cultural ambivalence" about drinking and drove it underground, preventing it from being integrated into normal living (Room 1984). Beauchamp views this as merely an elaboration of the alibi for alcohol, a new and more sophisticated way of declaring drinking acceptable for the vast majority of people, who are better off if government spares them any hang-ups or conflicts about drinking so they can integrate it appropriately into family life (Beauchamp 1980a: 41). The theory provided fuel for an educational thrust, sponsored by the NIAAA in its early years, which sought to teach children and others how to be "responsible drinkers."

The empirical opposition to this integration theory was developed by econometricians and other investigators. They studied overall patterns of alcohol consumption, found no evidence of a bimodal distribution (challenging the basic notion of alcoholics as a separate group), and developed evidence for the case that controls on alcohol would have a salutary effect on drinking problems (contrary to the pessimistic view of regulation held by the "integration" theorists). The pessimism emanated largely from the disease model, which held that alcoholics have lost reason and control. From this it followed that their drinking habits, unlike those of the general population, should be relatively insensitive to market forces, relatively irrational or price inelastic. But the consumption studies established that drinking patterns are best fitted to a single (lognormal) curve, which is highly skewed. The skewness signifies that the heaviest drinkers consume a large proportion of all the alcohol consumed, and "that a sizeable reduction in total consumption will not occur unless some of the heavy drinkers reduce their consumption" (Bruun *et al.* 1975: 45). In short, the models were felt to support the contention that policies to reduce a general population's overall consumption of alcohol should affect those drinkers whose drinking is of greatest concern.

Bringing focus to the "problems" in problem-drinking   As epidemiological findings came more to the fore, they continued to chip away at alcoholism as a unitary explanatory model. The notion of a single, progressive, and debilitating disease failed to comport with growing evidence of a wide range of drinking problems distributed throughout the general population. Robin Room, a leading proponent of replacing the monolithic disease construct with a problem-oriented perspective, documents the strong resistance to empirical threats to the disease model: "unpalatable" research findings were ignored or even suppressed when the evidence they contained pointed to the need for a more aggressive and more widely applied alcohol control policy (Room 1984: 295).

The orthodox disease approach defined the control problem exclusively in terms of treatment. Prevention, to the extent that it fit at all, was conceived as a task of early detection, case finding, intervention, and breaking down a system of denial so that alcoholics could be coaxed earlier into treatment. By definition (supported intuitively by observations of clinical populations) the alcoholic's behavior, controlled as it was by alcohol, would be utterly impervious to attempts by the state to regulate the sale or use of alcohol.

When advances in epidemiology widened the framework by sampling and generalizing to whole populations, rather than just making inferences from clinical observations of patients in treatment, this unitary notion of alcoholism could be disaggregated, showing a range of different patterns and manifestations of problems which pointed clearly to the need for an equally diversified policy framework. Moreover, as was emphasized by a special panel commissioned by the NIAAA, attending to the problems associated with drinking instead of the "problem drinkers" (that is, applying epidemiological reasoning) reveals that although the heaviest drinkers are at the greatest risk of developing problems, their numbers are proportionately so few (relative to the general population), that the preponderance of the *problems* (in absolute terms) are encountered by the less heavy drinkers.

Working from population surveys and a special Air Force study (Clark and Midanik 1982), the panel estimated that the heaviest drinkers (those who drink five or more drinks a day) constitute only about 5 per cent of the total population (and drink about half of all alcohol consumed) but account for only about one-quarter of all the "drunk days" and less than half of reported problems: illness and accidents, belligerence, problems with friends, spouses, jobs, and the law (Moore and Gerstein 1981: 43–7). Grounded in epidemiology, this finding invited the policy inference that "treating alcoholics is not sufficient response to the problem . . . because it affects many more of us than we are accustomed to believing" (Moore and Gerstein 1981: 47). From this springboard, the remainder of the report reviewed the available options for framing a more adequate response.

Several scholars now argue that alcohol policy has been transported by these epidemiological findings to a major fork in the road. The disease concept, it is felt, is in a state of "crisis" because of wide fissures in the fundamental propositions at its core. Pittman and Snyder (1962), Mello (1972) and others have enumerated the scientific findings (many epidemiologic) with which it is increasingly difficult to reconcile the construct of alcoholism as a disease.

1 Investigators have tried and failed to identify predisposing characteristics that might constitute Jellinek's factor X. The search for an "alcoholic personality" has been bootless and all available evidence to date suggests that the one feature alcoholics have in common is their drinking (Mello, 1972).
2 The bedrock belief that alcoholism is inexorably progressive is shaken by longitudinal studies showing that people move in and out of heavy- and problem-drinking categories as they move through time (Cahalan and Room 1974; Cahalan, Cisin, and Crossley 1969; Vaillant 1983).
3 The notion that alcoholics lose control has been challenged on both its levels. On the level of personal control, many studies have shown that even skid row alcoholics can at

times control their drinking (Pattison, Sobell, and Sobell 1977). On the larger issue of social control, the disease proponents' *a priori* assumption that alcoholics would certainly not be affected by policies controlling the availability of alcohol had by the early 1970s been empirically invalidated (Room 1984: 302).

4 The conviction that abstinence is the only effective treatment goal has been challenged if not shaken by the highly controversial debate over controlled drinking. That debate is still unfolding and the findings are still mixed; the anger and emotion it continues to spark suggest the enormous threat it represents to the disease proposition.

5 As discussed above, the notion that drinkers divide decisively into two immutable classes – the normal and the alcoholic – has been undermined somewhat by research on the distribution of consumption.

6 As discussed above, the view that alcoholism is a unitary disorder has begun to give way to a much more sophisticated picture (reflected in clinical diagnostic instruments and in epidemiological research) of a wide variety of problems (physical, emotional, and social), some related to the development of an "alcohol dependence sydrome" and many others arising in the absence of actual physical and/or psychological dependence on alcohol.

As weaknesses in the disease concept have seemed to move alcohol out of the exclusive domain of the medical care system, attention refocuses on what has been the chief institutional alternative: the criminal justice system.

Picking up the legal strand   The summary legal approach to alcohol control was roundly discredited with the repeal of Prohibition, but laws against public drunkenness remained on the books for three decades until they were excised temporarily in a series of three Supreme Court cases. The court held in 1962 and 1966 that drug and alcohol addiction are illnesses and that penalizing their victims violates the 8th Amendment protection against "cruel and unusual punishment." In one case, however, the court went on to say that the protection extends only to public intoxication *per se*; alcoholic persons remain responsible for other deviant and unlawful behavior they may commit while under the influence (Conrad and Schneider 1984: 100–1). Then another case, in 1968, essentially reversed the first three, the impact of which had been to swamp the inadequate treatment system with skid row alcoholics who used to spend their nights in jail. Reacting to this situation the court found the fourth case against the alcoholic defendant and dealt a temporary blow to those advocating treating alcoholism as a disease. Finally, in 1971, Congress was persuaded to redress the situation and to pass the Uniform Alcoholism and Intoxication Treatment Act, abolishing the crime of public drunkenness, recommending the establishment of statewide detoxification centers to be housed administratively in state health departments, and requiring hospitals to treat alcoholics. For a variety of reasons, that law has had little impact (Reigier 1979).

A much more important law, the "Hughes" Act (named for its chief sponsor, Senator Howard Hughes, himself a recovered alcoholic and a member of AA), was enacted in the same year and established the NIAAA to promote and coordinate federal alcohol policy, initiatives and research. The NIAAA early aligned itself with the established alcoholism forces and adopted the disease perspective, placing a strong emphasis on treatment programs and on education for responsible drinking. But in more recent years, as evidenced in its periodic reports to Congress, the agency has begun to recast its thinking in public health terms. The 1981 report it commissioned (through the National Research Council) articulates a comprehensive, politically sensitive but scientifically founded blueprint for the prevention of alcohol problems. The NIAAA's most recent report to Congress ends with a chapter entitled "Prevention: A Broad Perspective," arguing that since the previous report "there appears to have developed a consensus that the public health approach can provide a useful conceptual framework for developing prevention strategies. This model derives from epidemiological studies of communicable disease indicating that proper planning requires knowledge not only of host, agent, and environment but also of their interaction" (DHHS 1983: 123).

Paradigm shift to epidemiologically based policy?   Increasingly, this public health model is being advanced as the new

Table 9.3 *A conceptual framework for comprehensive public health policy (*
examples for alcohol policy)

Mechanism (mobilizes)	Legal (Behavior)		
	Direct via sanctions	Indirect via market	Indirect via persuasion
Target: Host	Drinking age laws; public drunkenness laws	Mandatory financial penalties for alcohol abuse	Mandatory alcoh⬛ education progra⬛
Agent	Prohibition	Taxes on alcohol; product liability	Regulation of alcohol advertisin⬛ labeling requirements
Environment	Driving while intoxicated laws	Third party liability suits vs. purveyors of alcohol (dram shop)	Statutes requirin⬛ protection of drinkers (from themselves) and others (from the⬛

paradigm to replace the disease concept as the fountainhead of alcohol policy. To be comprehensive, such an approach should include interventions that mobilize the law (directly through sanctions and in less direct ways), market incentives (both negative and positive), and persuasive strategies (on clinical, organizational, and community levels). A conceptual framework for specifying the elements of such an approach appears as *Table 9.3*.

However strongly public health thinking seems to be taking hold, Conrad and Schneider reiterate Kuhn's caveat (1962) that dominant paradigms are extraordinarily resistant to change and tend not to crumble when confronted simply by difficult data requiring a new interpretative schema. Political impetus is necessary as well. It may be that the major transformations now taking palce in American medicine (Starr 1982), against a changing demographic background (a post-Prohibition generation and an aging population), will provide

Market (Incentives)				Education (Beliefs)		
Supply side		Demand side		Individual (e.g. parent to child; physician to patient)	Organiz- ational (e.g. schools, work-places, churches)	Community (e.g. mass media campaign)
+	−	+	−			
ds for ling to able tions	Penalties for marketing to vulnerable populations	Rewards for not abusing alcohol	Penalties for alcohol abuse	Messages:	"Responsible drinking;" resisting peer pressure to drink	
				Focus:	individual motives and choices	
ds for ative tion	Penalties for producing alcoholic beverages	Rewards for not purchasing alcohol	Penalties for purchases	Messages:	How much is too much; the health, psychological, and social consequences of alcohol abuse.	
				Focus:	the substance of alcohol and its effects	
ds for g the safer nkers ose l them	Penalties for absence of protections	Rewards for taking safety precautions (e.g. using seatbelts)	Penalties for failing to take safety precautions	Messages:	Don't drink and drive; don't ride with drunk drivers.	
				Focus:	the situations in which alcohol use combines with the environment to engender high risk	

the momentum for a public health approach to preventing problems associated with alcohol use.

Certainly the pressures on medicine are manifest in a new emphasis in national health policy on primary prevention of disease (DHEW 1979). This finds support in the corporate drive to contain health care costs, which is also altering the rules for alcoholism treatment facilities. Major revisions in the labor-management contracts of several of the nation's largest employers (the automobile manufacturers and General Electric Company are recent examples) have imposed tight administrative strictures on insurance coverage for in-patient alcoholism treatment. Companies hope to improve their ability to identify incipient drinking problems and either prevent them or refer them earlier for less intensive treatment. In essence, this implies a public health approach. The successful negotiation of what unions view as "take-aways" is probably influenced also by secular changes (toward a more punitive, moralistic mindset) that have been reshaping public attitudes toward problem drinkers, especially those who drive drunk and engage in other practices that endanger innocent people.

If these and other trends do propel a shift in alcohol policy toward a public health model that increasingly emphasizes prevention, then epidemiological reasoning should have an increasingly central role to play. Meanwhile, it is safe to say that epidemiological results have contributed to the policy shift, although to what extent, and precisely how, are difficult to know.

Note

1 The work on which this chapter is based was funded in part by grants (to both authors) from the Commonwealth Fund, the National Institute on Alcohol Abuse and Alcoholism, and (to Dr Walsh) from the Pew Memorial Trust.

References

Aaron, P. and Musto, D. (1981) Temperance and Prohibition in America: A Historical Overview. In M.H. Moore and D.R. Gerstein (eds) *Alcohol and Public Policy: Beyond the Shadow of Prohibition.* Washington, DC: National Academy Press.

Bandura, A. (1969) *Principles of Behavior Modification.* New York: Holt, Rinehart and Winston.

Beauchamp, D.E. (1976) Exploring New Ethics for Public Health: Developing a Fair Alcohol Policy. *Journal of Health Policy, Politics and Law 1*: 338–54.

—— (1980a) *Beyond Alcoholism: Alcohol and Public Health Policy.* Philadelphia, PA: Temple University Press.

—— (1980b) Public Health and Individual Liberty. *Annual Review of Public Health 1*: 121–36.

Bruun, K., Edwards, G., and Martti, L. (1975) *Alcohol Control Policies in Public Health Perspective.* New Brunswick, NJ: Rutgers Center of Alcohol Studies.

Cahalan, D., and Room, R. (1974) *Problem Drinking Among American Men.* New Brunswick, NJ: Rutgers Center of Alcohol Studies.

Cahalan, D., Cisin, I.H., and Crossley, H.M. (1969) *American Drinking Practices.* Monograph No. 8. New Brunswick, NJ: Rutgers Center of Alcohol Studies.

Canavan, K. (1975) The World Health Organization Project on Identification and Management of Persons with Harmful Alcohol Consumption. Washington, DC: American Public Health Association Annual Meeting, Tuesday November 19 (Session 2098, Forum on Alcohol and Drug Problems).

Clark, N.H. (1976) *Deliver Us from Evil: An Interpretation of American Prohibition*. New York: Norton.

Clark, W., and Midanik, L (1982) Alcohol Use and Alcohol Problems Among U.S. Adults. In National Institute on Alcohol Abuse and Alcoholism, *Alcohol Consumption and Related Problems* (Alcohol and Health Monograph No. 1). Washington, DC: US Government Printing Office, pp. 3–52.

Conrad, P. and Schneider, J. (1984) *Deviance and Medicalization: From Badness to Sickness*. St Louis, MO: C.V. Mosby, pp. 73–109.

Department of Health, Education, and Welfare (1971) *Alcohol and Health*. First Special Report to the US Congress. Washington, DC: US Government Printing Office, Superintendent of Documents.

—— (1974) *Alcohol and Health*. Second Special Report to the US Congress. Washington, DC: US Government Printing Office.

—— (1978) *Alcohol and Health*. Third Special Report to the US Congress. Washington, DC: US Government Printing Office.

—— (1979) *Healthy People: The Surgeon General's Report on Health Promotion and Disease Prevention*. DHEW (PHS) Pub. No. 79-55071. Washington, DC: US Government Printing Office.

Department of Health and Human Services, Public Health Service, Alcohol, Drug Abuse, and Mental Health Administration, National Institute of Alcohol Abuse and Alcoholism (1981) *Alcohol and Health*. Fourth Special Report to the US Congress. Washington, DC: US Government Printing Office.

—— (1983) *Alcohol and Health*. Fifth Special Report to the US Congress. Washington, DC: US Government Printing Office.

Edwards, G. (1973) Epidemiology Applied to Alcoholism: A Review and an Examination of Purpose. *Q. J. Stud. Alcohol* 34: 28–56.

Filstead, W.J., Rossi, J.J., and Keller, M. (eds) (1976) *Alcohol and Alcohol Problems: New Thinking and New Directions*. Cambridge, MA: Ballinger.

Gusfield, J. 1963. *Symbolic Crusade: Status Politics and the American Temperance Movement*. Urbana, Ill.: University of Illinois Press.

Hamburg, D.A., Elliot, G.R., and Parron, D.L. (eds) (1982) *Health and Behavior: Frontiers of Research in the Biobehavioral Sciences*. Washington, DC: National Academy Press, pp. 88–99.

Hingson, R.H., Matthews, D., and Scotch, N.A. (1979) The Use and Abuse of Psychoactive Substances. In H.E. Freeman, S. Levine, L.G. Reeder (eds) *Handbook of Medical Sociology*. Englewood Cliffs, NJ: Prentice-Hall.

Institute of Medicine (1980) *Alcoholism, Alcohol Abuse, and Related Problems: Opportunities for Research.* Washington, DC: National Academy Press.

Jellinek, E.M. (1959) Estimating the Prevalence of Alcoholism: Modified Values in the Jellinek Formula and an Alternate Approach. *Q. J. Stud. Alcohol 20*: 261–69.

—— (1960) *The Disease Concept of Alcoholism.* New Brunswick, NJ: Hillhouse Press.

Keller, M. (1975) Problems of Epidemiology in Alcohol Problems. *Q. J. Stud. Alcohol 36*: 1442–451.

Kuhn, T.S. (1962) *The Structure of Scientific Revolutions.* Chicago, Ill.: University of Chicago Press.

Light, R.J. and Pillemer, D.B. (1984) *Summing Up: The Science of Reviewing Research.* Cambridge, MA: Harvard University Press.

Lilienfeld, A.M. and Lilienfeld, D.E. (1980) *Foundations of Epidemiology.* New York: Oxford University Press.

Mello, N. (1972) Behavioral Studies of Alcoholism. In B. Kissin, H. Begleiter (eds) *The Biology of Alcoholism,* vol. 2. New York: Plenum, pp. 219–91.

Moore, M.H. and Gerstein, D.R. (eds) (1981) *Alcohol and Public Policy: Beyond the Shadow of Prohibition.* Washington, DC: National Academy Press.

Nace, E.P. (1984) Epidemiology of Alcoholism and Prospects for Treatment. *Annual Review of Medicine 35*: 293–309.

Pattison, E.M., Sobell, M.B., and Sobell, L.C. (1977) *Emerging Concepts of Alcohol Dependence.* New York: Springer-Verlag.

Pittman, D.J. and Snyder, C.R. (eds) (1962) *Society, Culture, and Drinking Patterns.* New York: John Wiley.

Reigier, M.C. (1979) *Social Policy in Action.* Lexington, MA: Lexington Books.

Robins, L.N. (1980) Alcoholism and Labelling Theory. In D. Mechanic (ed.) *Readings in Medical Sociology.* New York: Free Press, pp. 188–99.

Room, R. (1971) Survey vs. Sales Data for the U.S. *Drinking and Drug Practices Surveyor 3*: 15–16.

—— (1984) Alcohol Control and Public Health. *Annual Review of Public Health 5*: 293–317.

Stallones, R.A. (1980) To Advance Epidemiology. *Annual Review of Public Health 1*: 69–82.

Starr, P. (1982) *The Social Transformation of American Medicine.* New York: Basic Books.

Vaillant, G.E. (1983) *The Natural History of Alcoholism.* Cambridge, MA: Harvard University Press.

Walsh, D.C. and Egdahl, R.H. (1985) Treatment for Chemical

Dependency and Mental Illness: Can This Utilization Be Managed? *Health Affairs* 4(3): 128–37.

Warner, K.E. (1979) Clearing the Airwaves: The Cigarette Ad Ban Revisited, *Policy Analysis* 5(4): 435–50.

West, L.J. (ed.) (1984) *Alcoholism and Related Problems: Issues for the American Public*. Englewood Cliffs, NJ: Prentice-Hall.

Wholey, D. (1984) *The Courage to Change*. Boston, MA: Houghton-Mifflin.

Wiseman, J.P. (1970) *Stations of the Lost: The Treatment of Skid Row Alcoholics*. Chicago, Ill.: University of Chicago Press.

Wolf, S.G. (1984) Alcohol and Health: The Wages of Excessive Drinking. In L.J. West (ed.) *Alcoholism and Related Problems: Issues for the American Public*. Englewood Cliffs, NJ: Prentice-Hall, pp. 27–56.

Name index

Aaron, P. 277, 278
Agate, J.N. 158
Alcalay, R. 106
Alexander, G.R. 202
Anderson, A. 24

Baker, S.P. 181, 184, 185, 187, 188,
    189, 191, 192, 200, 201, 202
Baldwin, S. 41
Bandura, A. 273
Barry, P.Z. 191
Battista, R. 152
Bean, L.L. 239
Beauchamp, D.E. 266, 275, 276, 278,
    279, 280, 281
Behar, M. 60
Benenson, A.S. 212
Berkman, L.F. 94
Berry, G. 167
Blazer, D. 94
Brand, R.H. 95
Brown, R.F. 141
Brownie, C. 60
Buckell, M. 158
Budetti, P.P. 20
Bukenmaier, C.C. 199
Bulbrook 137

Butler, J. 20
Byre, K V. 90

Cahalan, D. 283
Cain, V.S. 41
Call, Dr D. 68, 70
Cassell, J. 35
Church, B. 208
Chute, R. 196
Cisin, I.H. 283
Clark, N.H. 268, 269, 278, 283
Cleary, P.D. 107
Conrad, P. 266, 275, 276, 277, 278,
    280, 285, 286
Cooper, H. 237
Crossley, H.M. 283

David, R.J. 39
Davis, K. 23–4
DeBakey, Dr M. 30
DeFrancesco, S. 200
Dekker, E. 107
Dix, D. 232
Doll, Sir R. 132, 136, 137, 143
Donabedian, A. 29, 34
Downey, E. 197
Dubos, R. 35

Subject index

AIDS 123, 140, 224
abortion 17, 42
accidents *see* injury
age factors, in cancer 124–25; in CHD 87–8
Agricultural Adjustment Act 66
Aid for Dependent Children (AFDC) 22
Alan Guttmacher Institute 41–2
alcohol and alcoholism: and accidents 47, 179, 185, 200, 273; the 'alcoholic personality' 273; alcoholic psychosis 270, 272; and cancer 133, 134–35, 141, 271, 272–73; cultural differences 281; disease model 277–78; in early US history 276–77; integration hypothesis 281; and mental health services 241, 242, 243, 244, 246, 247, 252, 253, 254, 261; National Council on Alcoholism 280; National Institute on Alcoholic Abuse and Alcoholism (NIAAA) 267–68, 270, 273, 281, 282, 285; and pregnancy 40; problem drinking 281, 282–84; problems of data collecting 267, 268;

psychological dependence 270; public health model 285–86; racial factors 269; related illnesses 133, 134–35, 141, 270, 271, 272–73; risk factors 273–75; sex differences 269; social consequences 273; symptomatic drinking 270, 274; temperance movement 277–78
alcohol policy 265–66, 275–88; and criminal law 284–85; 'Hughes Act' (1971) 285; Prohibition 265, 276, 277–78; public health model 285–86
Alcoholics Anonymous 267, 274, 279, 280
American Heart Association 72–4, 75, 96
American Medical Association 22, 74, 223
American Psychiatric Association 229, 232, 252, 274
American Public Health Association 215, 221
anemia, iron deficiency 19, 37, 41
angina pectoris 87
anthropometry 59
asbestos 133, 142, 152, 162–68, 169